CENTRAL & SOUTH AMERICA
BY ROAD

Pam Ascanio
with Robb Annable

Bradt Publications, UK
The Globe Pequot Press Inc, USA

First published in 1996 by Bradt Publications,
41 Nortoft Road, Chalfont St Peter, Bucks SL9 0LA, England
Published in the USA by The Globe Pequot Press Inc,
6 Business Park Road, PO Box 833, Old Saybrook, Connecticut 06475-0833

The author and publishers have made every effort to ensure the
accuracy of the information in this book at the time of going to press.
However, the publishers cannot accept any responsibility for any loss,
injury or inconvenience resulting from the use of information contained in this guide.

British Library Cataloguing in Publication Data
A catalogue record for this book is available from the British Library
ISBN 1 898323 24 0

Library of Congress Cataloging-in-Publication Data
Library of Congress Cataloging-in-Publication Data is available
US ISBN 1-56440-816-7

Cover photograph *Front:* Torres del Paine (Exodus, see page 50)
Back: Bicycling in Chile: Volcán Llaima (Hallam Murray)
Photographs: Pam Ascanio (PA), Mark Atkinson (MA),
Hilary Bradt (HB), Marc Gutmann (MG),
Steve Hyde, Exodus (SH), Edward Paine (EP)
Maps: Based on maps supplied by Robb Annable
and Rich Normyle

Typeset by Concise Artisans
Printed and bound in Great Britain by the Guernsey Press Co Ltd

THE AUTHOR

Pam Ascanio and Robb Annable embarked on nomadic lives as babies. During adolescence they became aware of personality abnormalities... they not only looked at pictures of 'naked, primitive people' in the *National Geographic* magazines, but read the text. Many years and trips later, they met and began sharing their maps. They were eventually married overlooking Machu Picchu, Peru. When not traveling, they live in a jungle in Rockledge, Florida with their mutt, Pachamama.

Pam's first book chronicles a year-long adventure through Africa, *White Men Don't Have Juju*, The Noble Press, Chicago, IL.

Contributors

Josef (José) Breitsameter comes from a pig farm in Gerolsbach, Germany. We first met Josef on the Congo River, in Zaire, Central Africa, after he'd been robbed of everything but a loin cloth. He has since changed his name to José and reports on cycling in Latin America. We thought him the best man for the job, from a minimalist's point of view.

Thanks also to Mo Fini for providing the information on motorbike preparation. Mo runs Tumi, shops which sell South American handicrafts.

This book is dedicated to Robb Annable, my husband, friend, co-author, chauffeur, cartographer and photographer.

"When you come to a fork in the road, take it."
Yogi Beara, a famous US baseball coach

CONTENTS

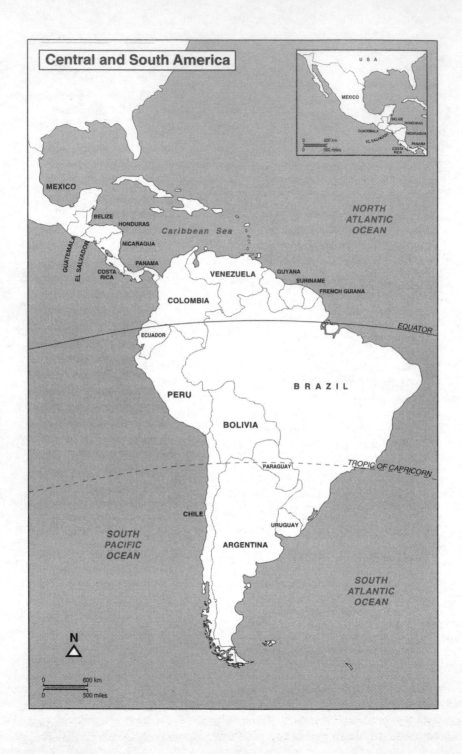

Introduction

HOW TO USE THIS BOOK

Many fine guidebooks are available to the South America traveler. It is not the intention of this book to repeat the same information, but rather to amplify and emphasize information needed by those with their own vehicle or cycle — the self-propelled traveler.

The word **vehicle** is used generically and includes cars, trucks, recreational vehicles, motorcycles and bicycles. A specific class of conveyance will be mentioned where exceptions are appropriate. **Driving styles** refers to unique traffic patterns within individual countries — who stops for red lights, who runs over pedestrians, etc.

Chapters are sequenced so that the first five detail preparation and outfitting. The remaining 11 chapters guide you through individual country highlights and their resources.

No-one travels in alphabetical order through countries, so we've created a separate map section to illustrate the best, proven road routes through regions. Camping, fuel, mountain passes and water crossings are indicated to aid trip planning and get you to cities with maps.

A *Glossary of Road Terms in Spanish and Portuguese* is included in the Appendix.

Special thanks go to Josef (José) Breitsameter of Germany who contributed the cycling information; Rich Normyle for navigating the treacherous roads on his computer; Dana Rae Pomeroy and U Nickles who lent commas and computer support.

Maps in this book

Maps featured in this book are not meant to replace individual country road maps but to assist when maps are not available (a common problem) and in trip planning. They are not drawn to scale.

Maps depicting routes through Mexico, Central America and the Western coast of South America along the Pan-American Highway indicate distances in kilometers and conservative driving times along the main route. Other maps are less detailed since there is no main route and numerous alternatives. The maps included in this book are listed below together with their page number.

Chapter One

First Steps

The Americas are open! A new ferry service between Panama and Colombia revolutionizes inter-American travel for the first time since the advent of air travel. Inaugurated in December 1994, an economical passenger/vehicle ferry skirts the impassable Darién Gap and unites the hemisphere. Drive on in one continent and, 14 hours later, drive off in another. At last, motorists and cyclists can transport themselves and their equipment *together*.

Panama's Darién Gap divides Latin America north from south. Until now, its swampy terrain effectively stopped overland travelers from traversing the narrow land bridge between the continents. For many, the end of the road was Yaviza, Panama and not Ushuaia, Argentina.

The ferry is long overdue, but timely. For now, it will stymie construction of a newly approved road. The ecologies and cultures of the Darién are temporarily preserved from devastation. Central and South America are like succulent, ripe mangoes, ready to be enjoyed.

Buy a bicycle, motorcycle, a car or truck, or join an overland tour group, and immerse yourself in the vibrancy of colorful Latin America. Obstacles have been eliminated, adventure and majestic beauty await your discovery. You are about to embark on one of the most rewarding travel experiences of your life.

OUR TOP TEN

Everyone will develop their list of favorite locales and sights. The following are our nominees.

Maya archeological sites

The grandeur of pre-Columbian civilizations is shown off in Palenque, Chichén-Itzá, Cobá and Tulum in Mexico, Tikal in Guatemala, Copán in Honduras.

Canaima
Towering mesas, thundering waterfalls, including one of the world's tallest, and nearly soundless mesa-top savannahs are found in southeastern Venezuela.

Brazil's beaches
The beaches in Brazil's northeast are among the most serene and least visited in the world. With time to explore and experience, inveterate sun worshippers will discover beach perfection.

Iguazú Falls
Argentina and Brazil share these absolutely majestic waterfalls. The combined force delivers more pounds per pressure (and ozone mist) than any other waterway in the world. It is an unforgettable *sense-a-rama* of experience.

Valdés Peninsula
Remote yet easily accessible, the Valdes is where right whales mate, penguins nest, sea elephants nurse their young, seals frolic and try to evade hungry killer whales.

The end of the world
Uncork a bottle of champagne in Ushuaia, Tierra del Fuego, Argentina and congratulate yourself. Only the fittest endure the overland challenge of arriving here.

Torres del Paine
This national park in southern Chile reverberates with color. Glaciers cast a menthol-blue sheen over rugged green valleys, lakes and snowy peaks.

Andean altiplano
Averaging 3,200m above sea-level, a rolling plain extends from Peru southward across western Bolivia to northern Chile. Startlingly sharp mountains thrust into a blue sky.

Machu Picchu, Peru
No visit to South America is complete until you peer down upon the Lost City of the Incas. Machu Picchu and environs is a spiritual high energy zone, but the founding Incas knew that. Near by was their capital Cuzco, which translates as "the navel of the earth".

Peruvian coastal desert
The barren coastal region is strewn with pre-Incan cities, giant

glyphs etched in stony ground and sweeping sand-dunes testifying to the power of human achievement through co-operation. Sophisticated arts flourished amidst early inter-continental trade.

The Amazon
Number 11 on the top ten list is the Amazon jungle. Rivers and tributaries feed veins and arteries to the world's lungs and nature's nursery for medicants. Don't miss this sprawling green world.

Bicyclists, motorcyclists, and motorists are still discovering unexploited niches and new routes through a diversity of cultures and terrains. Today's cities resist stereotypes of developing nations. Nothing is underdeveloped on Rio's Ipanema beach. The Caracas metro system is a marvel of order and efficiency. And, in Chile's lake region or Argentina's ski slopes near Bariloche, the similarity to Switzerland is inescapable.

Sand-dunes in Peru crest higher than in the Sahara; Angel Falls in Venezuela plunges deeper than Victoria in Zimbabwe; the Patagonia in Argentina is bleak and arid. For wildlife, Costa Rica is hard to beat. Howler monkeys are as numerous as tourists, and flocks of parrots seem as dense as the clouds in Monteverde Cloud Forest.

ROUTE PLANNING

Where you begin and end your trip will depend on your personal interests, budget and time. Bicyclists and people joining overland tours, can easily fly to any point in South America, whereas North America is the easiest place to purchase and oufit a vehicle, so motorists should consider starting from there. See *Chapter Two Your transport* for details.

For travelers coming from North America, the new Panama/ Colombia ferry makes the journey by road through Central America more economical than shipping from Texas, Miami or Europe.

Shipping deletes at least US$2,000 from your travel budget and consumes two or more weeks of travel time. The overnight *Crucero Express* charges US$98 per person and US$150 for a car and trailer or full-size truck.

It is possible to drive from Texas to Panama in less than a week. Cyclists and first-time visitors typically spend three to six months exploring Central America. The eight countries are beautiful and diverse as any in South America and shouldn't be missed. Border formalities for vehicle entry are fairly standard between all countries and much of the political turmoil has subsided, freeing visitors to enjoy the bountiful treasures of this region.

ROUTES FROM THE USA – JOURNEY TIMES AND DISTANCES

1. CROSSING BORDER – NOGALES, AZ

From Nogales	Time	Km
Guaymas	5:23	419
Mazatlan	9:12	803
Puerta Vallarta	6:45	462
La Mira	8:36	361
Acapulco	5:26	361
Pto. Escondido	5:50	339
Tapachula	9:49	692

5. CROSSING BORDER – BROWNSVILLE, TX

From Brownsville	Time	Km
San Luis Potosi	9:09	720
Mexico City	4:58	413
Oaxaca	7:41	450
Tapachula	9:05	674

2. CROSSING BORDER – NOGALES, AZ

From Nogales	Time	Km
Guaymas	5:23	415
Mazatlan	9:12	803
Guadelajara	7:57	521
Mexico City	9:19	563
Oaxaca	7:41	450
Tapachula	9:05	674

6. CROSSING BORDER – BROWNSVILLE, TX

From Brownsville	Time	Km
Tampico	7:06	504
Veracruz	8:05	502
Villahermosa	8:39	530
Cancun	4:32	319
Belize	8:10	583

3. CROSSING BORDER – EL PASO, TX

From El Paso	Time	Km
Ciudad Jimenez	7:54	600
Durango	6:51	488
San Luis Potosi	6:40	481
Mexico City+	4:58	413
Oaxaca	7:41	450
Tapachula	9:05	674

7. TAPACHULA TO PANAMA CITY

From Tapachula	Time	Km
Guatemala City	4:30	294
San Salvador	2:00	183
Choluteca	2:40	285
Managua	2:18	212
San Jose	5:15	423
Panama City	8:36	701

4. CROSSING BORDER – LAREDO, TX

From Laredo	Time	Km
Monterrey	3:20	236
San Luis Potosi	6:18	537
Mexico City	4:58	413
Oaxaca	7:41	450
Tapachula	9:05	674

South America

Ferry passengers disembark in Cartagena, Colombia where they must decide which fork in the road to follow: East to Venezuela or south on the Pan-American (Pan-Am) highway, toward Ecuador. Through Venezuela runs the only road to Brazil's Amazonia. Venezuela is also the only country that will sell, to foreigners, the desirable *libreta* (*see Insurance, page 10* and *Chapter 11, Colombia*).

A very popular circuit includes Colombia, Ecuador, the Peruvian highlands, Bolivia and sometimes Brazil. It can be traveled in three to six months and within one season, eg: spring and summer. Travelers have dubbed it "the gringo trail". Indeed, you'll never be lonely for the sound of your own language. Overland companies build their itineraries along this route.

Seasons

If you travel far and long enough, you'll cross every season several times. Luckily, seasonal timing isn't as crucial as it was before paved highways.

Seasons reverse below the equator. Fair months are between November and April. A wide band of 10° to either side of the equator is consistently hot and muggy, with heavy rainfall between April and July. Temperatures in the mountains are always more brisk than in the lowlands.

Southern Argentina and Chile comprise the coldest and windiest of regions. Winter sets in early June and doesn't truly let go of the land until mid-October. This is the perfect time for cross-country skiing and snow camping. A stiff, dry wind blows 80-100kph out of the south and peaks at 150kph in December.

Cyclists

A counterclockwise route is advantageous due to a southwest wind blowing over the eastern side of the southern Andes. Keep the wind to your back, descend on the Pacific side following the Pan-American highway, and ascend north on the Atlantic side.

Our route

September is the ideal time to depart North America to South America by road. The tourist season in Central America has waned, along with exaggerated prices, climatic conditions are temperate and the seasonal timing puts you on a leisurely trajectory through Latin America. Unavoidably delayed, we left Florida on a blustery, cold day in December. The important thing is to go when ready.

With our 19-year-old VW van, we crossed the US from Florida to California and there began the southward journey through the Baja Peninsula. A ferry took us to the Pacific coast mainland of Mexico, a region we didn't know. The impressive Baja was a well-chosen introduction to free camping Latin-style, but the mainland is agro-industrial and commercial. We regretted not taking a familiar route through the eastern, laid-back, side of Mexico into the Yucatan or through the scenic central mountain range (the cyclists' choice).

The Pan-American highway is mostly two-lane throughout Latin America, yet it by passes many places we wanted to visit, so we found adequate secondary roads.

El Salvador requires US$30 visas, and our adopted kitten created unforeseen border complications, so we skipped it. Since we had visited El Salvador before, we chose a dirt road from Guatemala into northern Honduras.

The fork in our road came in Panama. The ferry was announced, but not inaugurated in time to save us from the costly dilemma of where to ship to in South America. We chose Venezuela.

Having penetrated the Amazon by foot and canoe from adjacent countries, we were eager to try the only road route. The rainy season welcomed our April arrival in northern Brazil by washing out the dirt road between Boa Vista and Manaus. There was nothing to do but wait for the river to swell enough to float a barge for a 1,000km journey to Manaus. This voyage was one of the highlights of our trip.

We spent nearly five months criss-crossing Brazil from north to Uruguay in the south, and east to west into Bolivia and Paraguay. We moved quickly through Argentina. It is too expensive for our pockets, and in October (their spring), wind rocked us to sleep while snow piled around our camper. Lured by the natural beauty, we nevertheless found ourselves bouncing between borders as far as Ushuaia, the end of the road. Then, pointing our compass to the opposite pole, we started our return north.

Adventures and breakdowns shanghaied the northern leg. The Atacama desert is formidable, more arid and lonely than we had imagined. By whatever name, the same desert terrain extends along Peru's coast to Ecuador. The Andes mountains ascend sharply into Bolivia. Rugged roads crest at higher altitudes than maps indicate. (Towns and mountain passes are at lower levels.) The extremes of nature challenge anything that breathes oxygen, including motors.

Ecuador and vivacious Colombia enchanted us. We alternated between sultry coastal routes and the cooler highlands. But now it was time to return home. Fifteen months on the road had exhausted our savings. We'd met many new friends and camped in the midst of nature's most grandiose spectacles. Our country maps were worn and torn but our internal maps bore fresh impressions and imprints of new knowledge. We swore to return, soon.

LANGUAGE

Spanish is very helpful, indeed necessary, if traveling independently. You'll need to ask directions and understand the reply. The further you roam from cities and tourist centers, the less likely it is that you'll meet anyone who speaks your language. Only in Belize is English spoken.

Portuguese is spoken in Brazil. It looks similar to Spanish but sounds very different. Brazil is such a fun place that language acquisition comes naturally. The sixth most populous country in the world has more than 156 million people but, owing to its size, it is also one of the least densely populated countries in Latin America. With so many people to talk to, you'll soon be fluent in Portuguese. Start with the word for beach, *praia*, and you won't go wrong.

When we arrived in Brazil, I walked out of a restaurant because I couldn't read the menu or understand the waiter. Faced with learning the language or starvation, I chose to learn the language. Shop owners read labels aloud, strangers read newspapers and bank tellers counted each bill, so that I could repeat after them. I taped vocabulary lists to our dashboard.

Indigenous languages are spoken in several regions, such as Quiché in Guatemala, Guaraní in Paraguay, Quechua in Peru, and Aymara in the *altiplano* (high plain) of Chile and Bolivia. There you'll probably meet someone who'll offer to teach commonly used phrases and words.

Begin language studies before leaving home, then add new vocabulary each day. A decent dictionary with common verb conjugations is extremely helpful. We met two Canadians in a VW who had invested in 32 Spanish language tapes. They practiced while driving and mastered a grip on the lingo. Many other people find that language schools reinforce their studies. Language schools offering open enrolment can be found by the dozens in every major city and town frequented by tourists. Some schools offer home stays to reinforce classroom studies. When you get to Latin America, shop for the school best for you.

Latin American people are gregarious and love the sound of their languages. Songs croon of love, and conversation often pivots on jocular interchanges. If you make any effort to understand and to speak their languages, you'll find no end to Latin hospitality.

BUDGETING

Few countries are bargains, except Honduras and Bolivia. In Brazil, Uruguay and Argentina you'll find economies more akin to European price standards than to North America. A ski instructor from St Moritz, Switzerland described Argentina as "unimaginably more expensive than Europe".

Budget US$20-$30 per day, per person. Some days and some countries will cost less, but budget padding will allow you to take advantage of excursions along the way. For instance, Angel Falls in Venezuela is not reachable by road, but it shouldn't be missed. Nor is anyone completely immune to tempting bargains found in markets.

A fine quality alcapa sweater, *chompa*, might cost US$40 in Peru but at home the same sweater often runs to more than US$100.

The nasty word, **repairs**, deserves mention right up front. Nothing else will slow you down, divert your intentions, and use up your time and money. Only overland passengers escape the vagaries of leaking oil seals, clogged injectors and broken suspension systems. Two thirds of our budget went to vehicle maintenance and repair.

Camping yields the best savings, especially free camping. We camped for 87% of our trip and enjoyed every moment. Shopping for food and cooking are adventures which not only save money, but provide an entrée to conversations with locals.

Be aware that inflation and/or devaluations will, some time or another, cause your budget to fluctuate. Also expect deviations from prices quoted in guidebooks.

Easy to overlook are pre-trip expenses. They will siphon your precious savings at a startling rate. Costly items to consider are passports, visas, immunizations, insurances, transportation to and from Latin America, maps, guidebooks, film, and outfitting your vehicle.

Amassing funds sounds like an insurmountable task, but don't let it daunt you. Make saving a lifestyle priority. Unless you're financially set, you'll probably have to sacrifice luxuries at home or delay the start of your trip. It happens to all of us.

DOCUMENTATION

You will need a passport, visas (if you know your itinerary), and an international health card.

Passports

All South American countries require that six months remain before the expiration of your passport. Carry it at all times. Police routinely check identification of nationals and foreigners. A passport is also required for transactions such as cashing money and checking into hotels.

The US passport costs US$65 and is valid for ten years. Processing can take two days, but normally up to six weeks. Renewals cost US$55.

Latin American officials love to obliterate other country stamps with their own. This practice can be aggravating. We met travelers who were detained while smeared immigration stamps were verified (Colombia and Venezuela). If you find your passport crowded by stamps and short of pages, *don't* get a new one. Any US embassy abroad will insert supplemental pages at no charge to US citizens.

Report a lost or stolen passport to your embassy, *immediately*. A new one will be reissued, for a fee. You'll also have to go to an immigration office or a police station to receive a new immigration stamp for the country you're in. This can be a real hassle.

Visas

A visa is a stamp in a passport that gives permission to enter a country within a specified time frame. It indicates the maximum length of stay and your official status, eg: tourist, business, en transit, etc. Visas usually cost money and always require time, a photo or two, and a simple application form. They are issued by consulates *in advance* of the border you'll be crossing. Capital cities and border towns always have consulates. Immigration officials also stamp the passport upon entry and exit. Most Latin American countries routinely grant 90-day tourist cards.

American citizens need visas for only five Latin American countries: El Salvador, Brazil (free and same-day service), Suriname, Guyana, French Guyana and Venezuela.

Visa extensions

Extensions are purportedly easy to obtain once inside the country. In reality, the internal appeal process is usually more expensive and time-consuming than to leave the country and re-enter. This is certainly true if you have a vehicle. Ecuador is the only country that limits tourist visits to 90 days within any 12-month period.

International health certificates

These booklets, usually yellow, are required as proof that you've been immunized against certain contagious diseases, specifically yellow fever. They are issued free by public health departments and travel clinics and provide ample space to record pertinent health information, such as eye-glass prescriptions, tetanus shots, etc. You're rarely asked to produce this document, unless there is an epidemic, eg: cholera.

Driving licenses

A valid driver's license, issued from your home country, will be required in order to operate a motorized vehicle and to obtain an international driving permit. If traveling with companions, you can share-drive, as long as each driver is properly licensed.

Most South American countries require international driving permits, and all accept them in lieu of your home license. The multi-page document razzle-dazzles petty officials. Keep the original, more valuable license, hidden away.

International driving permits

Obtain a permit in your home country from the automobile club. In the US, contact the **American Automobile Association**. (Note: AAA will not issue to holders of foreign drivers' licenses.) Members and non-members must be at least 18 years of age, hold a valid US driver's license and produce two passport photos. The cost of the permit is US$10 and is valid for one year.

AAA also issues the Interamerican Driving Permit, which is printed in Spanish, but not required anywhere in Latin America.

Proof of ownership

You must own the title to your vehicle and carry the document with you. The registration for your license plate is also required. With these two documents, your vehicle can cross borders.

In Central America, the vehicle might be stamped into your passport. In South America, customs officials at each border will issue a permit for temporary import of a vehicle, or request a *libreta* (*see page 11*). Show your import permit or *libreta* to the police when asked. Do not hand them the title.

A bill of sale for your vehicle is not needed, although you may be asked for it. Hold firm. Bicyclists, though, have mentioned that a sales receipt is helpful to establish proof of ownership. Some have created their own official-looking document, complete with photo and fake stamps.

INSURANCE

At least four kinds of insurances need to be weighed against your ability to assume risk. These are health insurance, property insurance, vehicle insurance and the *libreta*.

Health insurance

Independent travelers from the US will find their health insurance nearly useless in situations where it is most needed. Many companies require prior permission for hospital admissions or a minimum qualifying stay in an approved facility, and that is hardly workable. More flexible policies can cost up to US$500 per person per month. We left home without it, but budgeted for emergencies.

Canadians and most European nationals have available many fine insurance companies that tailor to travelers' emergencies. Overland tour companies offer optional health insurance to their participants. Check it out and read the fine print.

The best health insurance is to practice preventive care. Just in case, check these other resources: **CIEE**, Insurance Department, 205

E. 42nd Street, New York, NY 10017-5706, offers reasonable coverage for eligible international students or teachers. Non-eligible persons may inquire about the Trip-Safe plan. Also try **Assit-card International**, 15 Rue du Cendrier, Ginebra, Switzerland; tel: 41 220 7320 320.

Property insurance

Homeowner or renter insurances offset the loss of personal belongings due to theft, loss or destruction, even when abroad. The real trick is getting a police report, which you'll need in order to collect from your insurance company. The report is called a *denuncia*. Police are unwilling to write one, even when you've been clearly wronged. Their reluctance stems from travelers who use this as a scam to make money, or so they say. They also say that robbery reports are intentional subversive acts, by foreigners, to make their country look bad. Don't be put off by excuses (such as a broken typewriter) or discouraging comments ('this could take weeks…'). Tactful persistence helps.

Vehicle insurances

Vehicle insurance should be carried at all times although, in reality, it is not always possible to obtain. Unfortunately, there is no such thing as universal coverage. US and European insurance is not valid in Central and South America. Each country sells their own and rarely will you find a convenient border location or company willing to write short-term policies for non-residents. You may have to go into a major city. Motorcyclists will have a terrible time finding insurance and, when you do, it will be very expensive. Theft and damage protection are nearly impossible to get.

Only two countries strictly enforce mandatory liability insurance laws — Mexico and Colombia (*see country chapters*). We drove uninsured most of the time and prayed that we didn't have an accident.

If taking your vehicle from the US, don't simply drop your domestic insurance because you won't be able to use it. Carefully check laws in your state pertaining to the export of your vehicle. More than one Floridian has had his/her driver's license revoked for failure to maintain insurance on a vehicle taken out of the country.

Libreta de Paso por Aduana

The *libreta* is known in Europe as a *Carnet de passage*. It is a type of insurance that, like a bond, guarantees payment of import duties on the value of the vehicle or motorcycle if sold, stolen or abandoned.

The *libreta* is a ten-page booklet with two detachable sections on each page for use by customs officials. Each section contains a description of your vehicle. When you enter and exit a country with your vehicle, the stub will be stamped, signed and a section torn off. Additional pages cannot be added.

Is it really necessary? Not if you have a bicycle, and not in Central America. Ecuador requires it (there called a *triptico*) and several other countries are insistent. Required or not, a *libreta* definitely facilitates border crossings.

Where to buy it

Whereas *carnets* are common in Europe, not one US insurance company sells them and, in South America, only Venezuela will issue to non-residents. One traveler deposited US$9,000 for one year, interest-free, with the Canadian Automobile Association in order to get a *carnet* for his 1971 VW van.

The **Touring y Automovil Club de Venezuela** currently requires the physical presence of both the vehicle and the driver and three days' processing time. Offices are at borders and in Caracas. (See *Chapter Sixteen, Venezuela* for specific addresses.)

Members of automobile clubs pay US$170 for the *libreta*, a refundable deposit of US$58 and a non-refundable US$88 for document preparation (non-members pay US$176 for preparation). Fees are the same for motorcycles. At year's end, return the *libreta* with proper customs stamps, and you will be reimbursed the deposit plus half the cost of the *libreta*, US$85. The refund will be paid in the same currency as your original payment. (Use dollars because Venezuelan bolivars are occasionally devalued.)

Credit cards are not accepted at the touring club offices. Spanish only is spoken. You will need to allow three days for the processing of paperwork. In order to obtain a *libreta*, you will have to produce a photocopy of your title, license plate registration (if applicable), copies of your international driver's license, and whatever document(s) authorizes entry of your vehicle to Venezuela.

Touring and automobile clubs throughout South America grant full recognition to members of foreign automobile clubs, eg: the American Automobile Association. Foreign card holders are entitled to emergency road service, trip planning and discounts.

HEALTH

Sorry to disappoint people who imagine South America to be a caldron of disease. We met no-one who had experienced anything worse than mild diarrhea or a simple cold. Routine inoculations, good common sense, regular exercise and a healthy diet help protect your body against exotic diseases. Preparing your own food will eliminate many sources of infection.

Routine inoculations
Begin inoculations well before you leave home as some require boosters to be effective. Everyone should get shots for typhoid, tetanus and hepatitis.

Common hepatitis A is spread through unsanitary conditions, as easily as sharing a glass with an infected person. Hepatitis B is caught much the same way as AIDS — dirty needles, blood transfusions or sex. The shot for B is expensive but lasts for 10 years. Less effective but cheaper is *gamma globulin* which gives some protection against the infectious hepatitis A and lasts for five to six months, so get it at the last minute.

Cholera vaccines have proven ineffective. Like hepatitis A, it is spread by unsanitary conditions and by contaminated shellfish.

Long-term travelers to rural areas should take boosters against polio and spinal meningitis. Bicyclists should definitely undergo the pre-exposure rabies vaccination.

No malaria prophylactics protect 100% against the mutations of this mosquito-borne illness. Likely malarial breeding grounds are jungles and low-lying coastal areas (mosquitos rarely survive above 2,500m). Pill regimens must begin one week before entering an infected area and continued for another month afterward. There are many choloroquine-resistant strains of malaria. Many prophylactics (and treatments) have not passed USDA approval so US travelers should seek advice from a specialized travel clinic or from an embassy doctor abroad. Common sense precautions include mosquito-proofing your tent or vehicle, wearing long-sleeved shirts and pants at sunset and sunrise when mosquitos are most active, and using a strong repellent.

It's also a good idea to go to the dentist before you leave. High altitudes can exacerbate pre-exisiting problems. Ask your dentist about preventive care and an emergency dental kit.

Fitness
Preventive health maintenance is the single most undervalued asset of travelers. Too many assume they'll get in shape along the way, and don't. Bicyclists who don't train at home tend to quit early. And sedentary passengers can't expect to climb a mountain after sitting for weeks. Plan your day to include walking or swimming, jogging or a set of exercises designed to work your entire body.

Age is not a determinant of fitness for overland travel in South America. We met people in their seventies who travel and camp with their own vehicle. Make sure that you're in good health before you leave home, and carry an appropriate first aid kit.

Diet

A balanced diet is crucial to maintaining good health and endurance for doing all that you want. Don't depend on restaurant food to supply nutrients needed by your body. Buy fresh vegetables and fruit in the markets and experiment with a wide range of foods.

Short-term travelers should follow standard health precautions: peel fruit, wash raw vegetables in iodine-treated water, avoid street food (although an expensive restaurant is no guarantee of cleanliness) and buy purified water.

Water is generally safe in urban areas, although excessively chlorinated. If in doubt, put it through a water purification system; treat it with iodine or chlorine, or boil it for one minute.

Bicyclists Cyclists, in particular, will need a diet heavy in complex carbohydrates. Excellent food sources are brown rice, whole grain bread, oatmeal, beans, pasta, potatoes, power bars and fresh fruit, such as bananas and apples. A few cyclists reported problems with maintaining calorie levels. Increased fluid intake should also be a priority. If pedaling long distances, you'll need about 3,000 calories a day. Soup is a healthy way to augment your liquid intake. Make your own or take advantage of midday meals served in restaurants, which usually include a hearty vegetable soup (with meat) and rice. These set meals are inexpensive.

Everyone is vulnerable to dehydration (cyclists in particular) and should monitor their fluid output. The best gauge is urine. When it becomes a dark yellow trickle, rehydration procedures and electrolyte replacement is overdue.

Getting help

Excellent doctors and sophisticated medical facilities cluster in capital cities. There, too, you are likely to find medical personnel who speak your language (contact embassies for recommendations). Many travelers report excellent attention from small town hospitals, particularly in the treatment of common, local complaints. Clinics may not be what you're used to, but chances are that it won't be worse than suffering something easily curable.

Most medicines are available from pharmacies without prescription. They may be manufactured under a different name so you might receive an equivalent drug. (It helps to write it down to avoid misunderstandings.) If unsure of what you need, describe or act out your problem to a certified pharmacist. Mention known allergies or other medications that you might be taking. Few pharmaceuticals are packaged with information regarding appropriate dosages or contra-indications.

Wearers of contact lenses will have no problem finding solutions in pharmacies and in optical stores. Eye doctors are everywhere if you need to replace spectacles or contact lenses.

Sanitary napkins and, usually, tampons can be found everywhere. You don't have to stuff your backpack with a year's supply.

Common medical problems

Until you build a tolerance to different *E. Coli* bacteria you'll occasionally experience intestinal problems, no matter how careful you are. Diarrhea is the most talked about complaint among travelers, but if you want to really start a lively conversation, mention constipation.

Diarrhea

Most attacks last only a day or two but can be debilitating and inconvenient. Find a friendly toilet, drink lots of non-alcoholic fluids, rest and fast. Impossible? Pepto-Bismal is a fast stopper-upper and if that fails, try Lomotil. Boiled rice will quell a growling stomach without feeding the problem.

When the problem persists beyond three days or is accompanied by fever and vomiting, more extreme tactics might be appropriate. First rehydrate. Prepared solutions are sold in most pharmacies, or dissolve ½ teaspoon salt to four teaspoons of sugar per liter of water. Take a wide spectrum antibiotic such as Vibramyacin and/or seek prompt medical attention.

Note: Cyclists, or anyone exposing themselves to the sun, should be cautious about taking antibiotics that increase sun sensitivity.

Constipation

Nobody talks much about constipation, until they get bound up. A bloated, heavy feeling can put a crimp in your activities as surely as diarrhea puts a trot in your step. Constipation is a common problem incurred by many travelers. Exercise, mineral water and fresh fruit (especially coconuts) help.

Altitude sickness

Sorroche strikes when ascending to a higher elevation and can affect people in slow-moving vehicles. Symptoms include a persistent headache, dizziness, respiratory and heart stress, sleeplessness and even nausea. Restrict movement, rest for several hours. Descend to a lower altitude and seek an oxygen tank, if problems persist. *Mate de coca*, a light tea brewed from the coca leaf, can assuage symptoms. Don't overexert until fit enough to dance at an all night *peña*.

First aid

A good first aid kit includes water purification treatment, antiseptic creams, a disinfectant, patches for blisters, different sized bandages and tape, a diarrhea remedy, aspirins, and antibiotics. Also helpful are a sunscreen, vaseline for cracking skin, antifungal powders and a metallic space blanket in case of hypothermia (when the body loses heat more rapidly than it can produce it). We stuffed our kit into a small sack and, luckily, rarely unpacked it.

Take medications for known, pre-existing, health problems, including antidotes to allergic reactions to bee or ant bites. Train a travel companion to recognize symptoms and administer appropriate treatment.

Cuts and abrasions

A common mistake of travelers in the tropics is leaving scrapes and minor cuts untreated. Unfamiliar bacteria enters wounds and can set back travel plans. Treat minor abrasions as if they were major. Clean the site thoroughly and apply an antibiotic ointment or powder. If nothing else, douse it with alcohol. Lightly cover the wound for protection and change the bandage frequently.

Foot problems

Communal showers and sweaty feet bound in closed shoes can breed athlete's foot — a smelly, itchy fungus that causes cracking between the toes. Tinactin powder usually solves the problem, with consistent use. *Bichos de pe* is a burrowing insect attracted to bare feet on the beaches of Brazil, Argentina and elsewhere. They are very painful and must be excised with a needle or knife.

Colds and coughs

Physical stress and extreme temperature changes can bring on simple colds and coughs. Hot days quickly turn chilly in the evening, so be prepared with a sweater or jacket. A cough should be monitored and arrested, via antibiotics if necessary, before it escalates to a bronchial infection.

MONEY

How to get money and how to carry it is the question. I think it safe to generalize that exchange procedures are standardizing within most countries. Before or after business hours, weekends and holidays are bad times to be out of money anywhere. Make every effort to plan ahead or you can spend your leisure time chasing exchange.

Passport cases or money belts are still the best way to carry important documents and money. Wear it under your clothes at all times.

Cash

The American dollar is the most liquid and convertible of all currencies. It is accepted widely throughout Central and South America. In Panama, the American dollar is the official currency. Free zone towns in Paraguay and Uruguay freely trade in dollars. These are all good places to stock up on cash, without forfeiting a commission. Keep a stash of small denomination bills for emergencies. The black market had virtually disappeared in 1995. Licensed *casas de cambio* often paid higher rates than banks. The major drawback to cash is, if robbed, you're unprotected.

Spread money around your body, and even your belongings, in case you should be robbed. I heard several stories of strip robberies. It's not all that common, but it does occur frequently enough to warrant precautions. Thieves know that foreigners wear money belts under their clothing.

In rural areas, carry small denomination of local currency. No-one ever has change for large bills... the equivalent of US$5.

Travelers checks

Spread your financial risk with travelers checks of different denominations — US$50-100 are good, although you may be charged for each check cashed. American Express checks are more widely accepted than any other brand, although VISA and Thomas Cook are becoming popular among banks. (Do not use the two signature checks.)

Unfortunately, travelers checks encumber more deficits than credits. They are difficult to exchange outside major cities. You'll be charged a commission to purchase them, another commission to cash them, and you'll receive a lower rate than for cash. All these charges taken into account, I figure that we received US$80 from every US$100.

Credit cards

A cash advance on credit cards is the easiest and cheapest way to obtain local currency. Commissions are not charged by banks and credit card advances usually receive the highest dollar exchange rate, too. The smartest thing we did was to set up a VISA account with automatic deductions from our savings. We avoided paying commissions, interest or late fees.

Most 24-hour bank machines (ATMs) will not accept foreign credit cards even if you have an international PIN number. Country exceptions are Mexico and Venezuela. You'll have to make withdrawals during regular business hours at designated banks or *casas de cambio*. The most versatile credit card is VISA, at a distant second is Mastercard (particularly popular in Chile), and trailing the pack comes, American Express, Diners Club and all others.

Photocopies

Photocopy all important documents, including credit cards. Keep copies in safe places, separate from the originals. A file copy at home or in the luggage of a friend could be handy. Vehicle documents should be especially well guarded. Their loss can create a bigger headache than losing a passport.

MAPS

Buy as many maps as you can before leaving home. Once on the road, it's virtually impossible to find a road map for any other country but the one you're in, and sometimes that is difficult. City maps too often use pictograms of tourist spots...leaping fish, swimmers and so on. They are not helpful to drivers trying to find their way through a maze of one-way streets.

Regional maps are invaluable for crossing borders and envisioning different routes "further down the road". We used a topographical series prepared by the late Kevin Healey, published by ITM of Canada. Particularly helpful were: No. 153 *North West South America*, No. 154 *North East South America*, No. 155 *South America: South*, and No. 410 *Amazon Basin*.

Long-distance travelers will appreciate a hemispheric map or, at least, one of each continent. They are extremely difficult to find in Latin America. We wore out our National Geographic Central America and South America maps showing where we had traveled and where we were going.

GUIDEBOOKS

The definitive guidebooks are the *South American Handbook*, and the *Mexico and Central American Handbook*, edited by Ben Box, published by Prentice Hall. Travelers by road should reference Lonely Planet's lively guidebooks to individual countries. Other very excellent books in English are listed in the Appendix.

Top-notch guides are locally produced and sold in Mexico, Colombia, Chile and Brazil. Although written in Spanish (or Portuguese), they utilize recognizable international symbols. See individual country chapters.

COMMUNICATIONS

The fastest, surest and most economical way to communicate with friends at home is by fax. Outlets are more common than international phone booths. Of course, a fax is not the same as hearing a loved one's voice for three minutes, but they are cheaper and more reliable than mail.

Mail

Approximately 30% of our mail, both sending and receiving, went awry — gobbled by a black hole. Persistent friends sent multiple copies of their letters to different addresses. Sending mail and packages is costly; postage for a postcard in some countries ran over US$1. Register all packages and don't mail anything terribly valuable. Do not wrap or seal your package before arrival at the post office because it will have to be customs inspected. For really valuable correspondence, use an express delivery service. These companies are proliferating rapidly in the absence of reliable mail service. **DHL** seems to be everywhere in South America.

Your best bet to receive mail is through American Express. Get a copy of their booklet that lists offices and their addresses. They'll also forward mail (for a fee) to other offices.

General delivery

Poste restante is called *Lista de Correos*. Every town of any size has a general post office that will accept and hold mail (theoretically speaking). Choose a town near a large city if you don't want to battle inner-city congestion to do a mail pick-up. Direct friends to mail their letters *at least* two weeks in advance of your projected pick-up date and instruct correspondents to print in block letters. The address form is: SURNAME, FIRST NAME, Lista de Correos, Correo Central, city name, state name (helpful in the advent that there are twenty Vista Alegre's in the country), country name.

Telephones

Be prepared to pay for telephone calls at the phone office. Credit cards are not accepted. From South America, the average cost to the US runs US$7 per minute, with a three-minute minimum charge, more to Europe and elsewhere. If an answering machine intercepts your call, you might as well leave a message as you'll be charged for the connection. (Inquire in advance.) Even for direct calls you'll be asked the name of the person to whom you're calling and your own name. The operator places the call for you. This procedure is a pain. In Peru, I argued and lost when an operator balked over a call to

American Express. A person-to-person collect call was finally placed to Mr Express, from their employee Pam Client. They accepted it.

Phones designated International Direct Dial usually aren't, or they're located on the noisiest street corner in town. Ostensibly AT&T, Sprint, and major European networks have direct-dial codes with which you can use a telephone credit card. In more than half of the phone offices we polled, we were told that direct-dial was "impossible from our country", or from that location, or with that company. Yet it is possible from private phones. That means meeting a local buddy who will trust you. From Central America, IDD credit card calls are not a problem.

CLOTHING

Latin American people are fastidious about appearance. Regardless of their dress, or yours, there is no substitute for cleanliness and neatness. Even while camping, it is usually possible to bathe regularly and to wash clothing.

You will encounter bankers in jeans and even shorts. A Venezuelan, responding to my comment about casual business dress said, "We have two different wardrobes: dress jeans and play jeans". The MTV-style, music video programs have impacted the prior conservatism of South America. Nevertheless, unless you enjoy being stared at, save extreme fashions for nightclubs.

Few beaches tolerate topless or nude sunbathing except in Brazil, where there are eight officially designated naturist beaches. Please abide by local customs. Find a secluded beach to pursue the perfect all-over tan.

It's not a smart idea to walk around wearing camouflage fatigues, although all hunting and camping stores sell them. Many normal people place negative connotations on anything military.

Shoes are always worn, except perhaps on the beach. Bare feet, *descalzado*, is associated with poverty. A solid argument for shoes is that any number of diseases and infections can enter through unshod feet.

PETS

We're convinced that a major trip with an animal friend is selfish and potentially cruel. She/he will have to be immunized against every beastly disease and will be inspected at every agricultural station. (Guatemala allows entry but to leave, a special export permit must be obtained. Panama requires a three-month quarantine.) One day can be frigidly cold and the next so hot that you'll want to peel your skin off, and you can't lock the pup in a hot vehicle. In Chile, pets are not allowed into campgrounds. Commercial boats do not permit pets.

We eventually became willing adoptees to one night stands. Homeless, affection-starved, animal companions guarded our nightly campsites. Be a responsible traveler. When you get home, don't tell your dog about all the others you slept with.

RESPONSIBLE TRAVEL

This is the standard lecture on proper behavior. Unfortunately, it bears repetition. You are a guest. Your actions will impinge on how you, and other travelers who follow, are treated.

If you don't like something, don't do it yourself! If you object to the destruction of the rain forest, don't chop down trees to make a lean-to shelter or a campfire. If you don't like plastic litter in forests or on a beautiful beach, tote waste to a serviced receptacle.

Don't aid the disappearance of sensitive cultures by importing and imposing your own cultural mores. It isn't always easy to distinguish begging from communal sharing, or a gift from a come-on, but try.

Customs

Latins value courtesy. When entering a roomful of people, greet them. A basic *hola* or *buenos dias* will do. A simple greeting helps before requesting services or information. Drink or food sent to your table is a gesture of welcome and should be acknowledged. Yammering loudly in a foreign language intimidates locals.

Gifts

Gifts are not expected except in areas where irresponsible tourists have tried to buy affection instead of earning it. Things to sell or trade are always welcome in out of the way places where money has little value. Useful items include needles and thread, cloth, aspirin, flashlights, bulbs and batteries.

Take a gift if invited to stay or to eat in someone's home. Always appropriate is food, drink or flowers.

Bribes

Personally, we don't appreciate travelers who routinely offer bribes along the way. Not only are bribes illegal, but their payment encourages corruption. We've never paid one, which is not to say that the invitation wasn't clearly extended.

Many times a day we were stopped because our vehicle did not have two license plates. Each country in South America requires two license plates, but Florida, where our car is registered, issues only one. We were threatened with fines, vehicle confiscation and licenses suspended. These were not requests for bribes (although easy money would have absolved the problem), these policemen were enforcing local law. You could do as two Canadians did and photocopy the license plate, laminate it, and mount it.

The best way to protect yourself from extra-legal abuse is to keep documents in order and to obey all local traffic laws. If stopped for an alleged infraction, do not worsen the situation by aggressive argument. Leave the cop a graceful way to backdown. The more advice you ask, the more likely you are to be excused. If in doubt, ask to be taken to a police station. Save bribes for serious incidents.

Firearms

Firearms are illegal except by permit issued in each country and for that country only. You will not need a gun while traveling, unless engaged in nefarious activities. And that's exactly the tack taken by the police and judges who'll try your case.

Drugs

Drugs and armaments are the two most commonly used excuses for searches which can range from cursory to literally dismantling your vehicle. In reality, backpackers and bus passengers are searched more frequently than independent self-propelled travelers.

If you use drugs, do so with extreme caution. The penalty can be as severe for marijuana as for kilos of cocaine.

Law enforcement

Don't get into a traffic accident! Napoleonic laws distribute equal fault to all parties until one is proven innocent. That means you could be detained, or worse jailed and your vehicle confiscated, until you've cleared the court system. Be forewarned that travelers are thought to have deep pockets.

Most borders are well managed. Most police are courteous and professional. In general, a good sense of humor will ease your plight through any situation.

Chapter Two

Your Transport

Freedom is travel with your own vehicle; stopping when you like for picnics or photo opportunities, chasing rainbows or rumors of undiscovered places and making your own schedule. As José Breitsameter says, "The most is important thing is to feel like traveling, the bicycle [vehicle] should just be *a* means of transport, not *the* meaning of your travel".

What are the options?
Nearly any type or size of vehicle can make the journey — even a unicycle or a moped. Ultimately, your choice will reflect your style of travel and your means. This chapter introduces the pros and cons, the upside and the downside of self-propelled vehicles.

Our only advice is to avoid anything that doesn't have high clearance and is broader than a mid-sized car. The old colonial roadways were built for horses and carriages.

MOTORIZED VEHICLES

The most expensive way to travel is by private truck, car or motorcycle.

Besides the purchase price of your car, truck or camper, budget an additional $6,000 for maintenance, fuel, oil and repairs for a year. Expect to pay for *libreta*, tolls, parking and liability insurance. The operating cost of our VW camper van exceeded the cost of public transportation by 20%, not counting repairs. The advantages of having our own vehicle outweighed financial minuses, however.

Motorcycles and cars (and horses) have at least one thing in common, and that is their maintenance always comes first. I complained of engine tune-ups to a Brazilian motorcyclist who admonished me with, "Your vehicle is your life; take care of it and it will take care of you."

Four-wheel drive

Heaven is a one ton, four-wheel drive vehicle with a diesel engine and high clearance. But it is not necessary. Even four-wheel drive trucks bog in the Amazon during rainy season. On the other hand, it gives you a fifth gear option for spurting through mud or sand or for ascending the sheer *tepuy* mesas in Venezuela. Diesel fuel is available everywhere and at a cheaper price than gasoline. Repairs, however, are more expensive than gasoline engines.

A 4X4 is a marketing term for a snazzy 4WD. They are one and the same, lingo wise. You can get sucked into buying optional features faster than you can blink if it's advertised as a 4X4. The best and the newest of cars can break down. We met motorists with 1995 dream-jeeps who had as many mechanical problems as we did with our nineteen-year-old VW. Sophisticated systems, eg: hydraulics, requires sophisticated mechanics and parts that are impossible to find in small towns. In rural areas, a truck mechanic will know more innovative repair strategies than a jeepload of factory-trained mechanics. Keep in mind that you'll be performing routine maintenance and minor repairs yourself.

Diesel 4WD vehicles are very common in Central and South America, but not so in the US. If choosing between a new, gas, turbocharged four-wheel drive vehicle and an older, basic model, we'd choose the old model, pre-fuel injection, GM, Ford, or Toyota Landcruiser. Maybe a Mitsubishi.

Two-wheel drive

Whatever the vehicle, it should have high clearance. You'll encounter deeply rutted tracks, tall speed bumps, rivers, mud, sand, and rock slides. Paved roads can be worse than dirt ones.

With a two-wheel drive car, you simply need to proceed cautiously. Get out and test soft ground before driving over it. Good tire tread aids traction in sand or mud.

A six-cylinder engine yields more power than four, and higher operating costs. In Colombia's mountains and along coastal Peru, the road climbs 2-3,000m, descends into narrow valleys then climbs again. It is repetitive and wearisome. We wished then for six cylinders. Four cylinders will do the job if you don't mind creeping.

We were distressed to learn, by experience, that replacement parts fabricated in South America by Volkswagen and by Ford are machined slightly differently than German Bosch or American Ford. There may be slight differences in other lines. Our information about VW and Ford was confirmed by production engineers, so we can only cite these examples. Don't despair. Most parts can be easily adapted or, in the worse case scenario, hand built. Our VW is still running with a number three piston handcrafted in Peru, and a nasty-looking, pock-marked cylinder head from Chile.

Vehicles for which repairs and parts are economically available are the VW with 1600 engine, Toyota Landcruiser, Ford, and early Mercedes.

Recreational vehicles

There is no place like home. We've been asked if it is possible to drive a motorhome, an RV camper, through Central and South America. The answer is yes, especially if driving on the Pan-Am highway. But the bigger your vehicle, the more restricted you will be as to where you can go. Roads are narrow, especially in cities and towns, and often in bad repair. Many secondary routes are not paved. Low, overhanging shrubbery and low-slung bridges with spanners at the top are two obstacles to high vehicles. Hotel parking lots are typically designed for small, compact cars. Our VW Kombi wouldn't fit under the majority of the entrances.

RVs have been plying the backroads of Central America since the Sixties. They stopped at Panama, not daring a complex ocean crossing. Not any more. You can now ferry a car and trailer for US$180 between Panama and Colombia.

If sixteen-wheel trucks can manoeuver narrow roads, then so can an RV camper. Go slow in the mountains and claim the entire road when easing around hairpin curves. Be prepared to accept scrapes from tree branches and to spend five minutes easing your rig over a single pothole. A patient driving style is the key to manoeuvering your RV through precarious spots.

RVs are popular in southern Brazil, Paraguay, Uruguay, Argentina and Chile. Many are US manufactured campers or converted Mercedes-Benz buses.

Expect to be the focus of local curiosity. People will want to see your rig and will ask embarrassing questions, like how much it is worth. Some people will offer to buy it. Decide your rules about visitors and stick to them. We chose to show our van and sometimes an entire village would line up for what we called "Kombi tours". It got tiresome, yet it was always worth the effort. Once people saw it, they wouldn't gawk anymore; in fact, they would offer protected parking or things that we needed.

Go completely self-sufficient. Carry back-up batteries or a generator. Fill up with water, fuel, and propane whenever you can. Inner-city gas stations may be impossible to reach, due to the narrow streets.

Cheers to the Volkswagen Kombi for compact versatility and economy. The engine is well-known, the frame sturdy, it has relatively high clearance, built-in cabinets hid our belongings and reduced rattles. Best of all, you can set up camp in any weather, anywhere.

Trucks

A sturdy road option is a 425-ton pick-up truck with an attached camping cabin. It is said that modern roads were forged by pick-up trucks following ancient footpaths. You'll see every model, make and year. Parts and mechanical know-how are widely available. They give added versatility for road handling, space to store gear and an inexpensive place to live. One drawback is that many camping cabins do not offer sufficient headroom for anyone taller than five feet. A pop-up cabin is a viable alternative, or do as Latins are now doing and build your own cabin.

Any heavy-duty, commercial rig should be either a Scania or a Mercedes Benz. Service, repairs and parts are widely available for these makes.

Car rental

Renting a car is an option for do-it-yourselfers, with more money than time, and who want to concentrate on one country. We've rented cars in Central and South America with generally satisfying experiences.

Rental cars cannot cross borders without written, notarial permission from the rental agency. Prices vary according to model, with four-wheel drive being the most expensive, but all cost more than in North America. The best fares are usually offered by small, local companies.

Be prepared to show an international driver's license and to pay in cash. Not all rental agencies accept credit cards. What they'll say is they accept them but they don't have a machine. Theory vs reality. Shop around until you find a company that can, and will, accept a credit card charge.

Rental agencies don't offer adequate road service in case of breakdowns. You're on your own. Save repair receipts. Some companies will reimburse, others won't. Inquire in advance their policy for repairs, IVA tax, insurance, deductibles, any discounts, and free mileage *kilometros libres*. Ask and ask again. Write any spoken promise on the face of the contract.

Overland tours

For those who want to experience Latin America by road but not the responsibility of a vehicle, an overland tour might be just the ticket. These, mostly British-owned companies, maintain fleets of customized trucks in Central and South America dedicated to the enjoyment of their passengers. Sign on for one to six months of camping adventure and travel to the highlight spots of the Americas. The best part is the tour company assumes the risks of the vehicle! See *Chapter Four, Organized tours* for details.

Motorcycles

Sturdiness is again the name of the game. Choose a simple but tough bike, up to off-road specifications. Stick with a mainstream Japanese make, like Honda or Yamaha XT600 Tenere or a Kawasaki KLR 650, whose parts are widely available. South of Panama, you'll only occasionally see or hear about a Harley Davidson or BMW. If taking an exotic bike, set up a source for parts before leaving home. Be forewarned that ordering the part is cheaper and easier than receiving it. Weeks can pass while it clears customs and you'll pay import duties that can exceed the cost of the part.

Motor size isn't the limitation it once was. For years, Venezuela prohibited any motorcycle that exceeded the velocity of their police mopeds. Still, not many motors exceed 800cc. Also consider the overall bulk of your bike, including equipment. Will it squeeze through a standard size doorway? Many hotels allow free and safe parking in interior patios.

BICYCLES

The bicycle is the most ubiquitous and cheapest mode of transport in Latin America. It is relatively inexpensive to repair, does not require fuel other than muscle power, nor will you pay heavy shipping charges, tolls or vehicle insurances. On a bicycle, you will live and breathe the world. Avoid major highways, including the Pan-Am, or your view will be colored by noxious truck fumes.

The most versatile aspect of cycling is your ability to hitchhike, bus or fly over undesirable stretches. Bike fares on buses shouldn't exceed half your passenger fare in Central America and much less in South America.

José advises starting with a good quality mountain bike and essential equipment (GORE-TEX), and then improvise. A sturdy but lightweight, mid-priced mountain bike with low gear ratios is an excellent choice. Touring bikes don't fare as well in the sand, mud, and rocks. Quick-release hubs facilitate stowage in the luggage compartment of a bus or canoe.

There are a trillion repair shops that cater to the basic dinosaur. Luckily, the Latin's love of a good race has created a market for the ergonomic-designed mountain bike. Sophisticated components are available in most major cities.

BUYING AND SELLING A VEHICLE

Follow the adage of the stock market: buy low and sell high. We investigated prices for vehicles both new and used, factored in complications, and the market indicators say to buy in North America and sell in South America.

South America

Time-wise it might be more convenient to fly into a South American country and buy a vehicle. On the bonus side, the machinery will have been manufactured by or adapted to regional specifications. Sell it in South America and recover costs. The same vehicle won't be allowed into North America or Europe without expensive modifications.

New, imported vehicles escalate in price within countries that produce their own, eg: Mexico, Venezuela, Brazil, and Argentina. Add US$2-5,000 on to North American prices for a similar, but more basic model. Delivery time averages three months.

Used cars and motorcycles are more reasonable. Putt-putts start at US$1,500. The most restrictive country is Argentina, which prohibits non-residents from leaving with a vehicle purchased there. A good command of Spanish is needed to buy a vehicle. You'll pay taxes, tags, registration, etc.

Cyclists should bring their own machine.

Selling

Unusual, all-purpose or high performance vehicles command the best selling price. For instance, our outfitted 1976, VW Kombi would have fetched US$3,000 more than in the US. Any RV or decent truck is marketable anywhere (Argentines act most blasé). Used motorcycles and bicycles are specialized market niches. Local cycle clubs and adventure tour companies are likely markets.

In South America the vehicle is not stamped into your passport. You can abandon or sell a vehicle with complete impunity from immigration. The buyer should pay all the transfer costs.

Our advice is sell the vehicle in Central or South America, unless you enter the US via a land border. *Do not ship it into US territory* or you'll incur ghastly expenses to bring it back up to current environmental specifications.

North America

The used (and new) vehicle market offers every model. Roads are good, so a used vehicle isn't as beaten up as one purchased in South America. Outfitting is easy.

Used vehicle prices in 1996 are: 1975 Volkswagen US$1,200, 1984 Toyota Landcruiser US$2,500, RV US$3,000, motorcycle US$1,500. Pay the full price up front in order to receive the vehicle title.

Used vehicles are sold by private individuals and by car lots. Car lots charge more and salespeople really don't know the history of the car.

California has a terrific selection of used cars. It could also be the worst place to buy one to take out of the country. Market prices are strong and they have the strictest regulations governing emission control equipment (stuff that you'll want to remove). Florida is excellent for used RVs because retired Canadians motor down and decide to stay.

Sales tax will add at least 6% to the cost. In New York and Massachusetts this will be higher. Sometimes individual sellers will write a bill of sale at a lower amount than that which you paid. This is illegal. If offered, take it. It can save hundreds of dollars.

Insurance is mandatory. The cost varies according to the year of your car (newer models more), your age and driving record, and the type of insurance coverage you desire. Basic, short-term policies are available, eg: US$90 for six months.

Minor charges include title transfer and a license plate for a car, small truck or camper runs approx US$180, for a motorcycle US$75. Again, charges vary from state to state. Florida, Massachusetts and California represent the high end. Contact the Department of Motor Vehicles and inquire about transfer costs in the state where you're thinking of buying the car.

SHIPPING
To or from the US
Europeans buy RVs and camper-trucks in the US, travel around and ship them home for resale. Tiny Delaware State, US east coast, is preferred among foreigners for shipping. Supposedly, a 6% import tax is levied against arriving vehicles. One German motorist squeezed through a New York port without paying any duties.

US import laws
Wash your vehicle. Agriculture inspectors charge US$150 to wash a dirty car.

Vehicles driven outside the US or Mexico for more than 30 days, or vehicles driven on leaded fuel, must have oxygen sensor and emission control systems replaced. Vehicles manufactured prior to 1975 are exempt with a certificate from the manufacturer. Using our 1976 VW as an example, parts were estimated at US$809, inspections US$1,000, and necessary engine work US$2,000. US customs said they do not enforce the law at land borders. Go figure.

Shipping to or from South America

Venezuela is the most viable alternative among the myriad shipping routes. It is a heavy importer and cargo ships routinely include Venezuela because of its cheap fuel. Tourist laws permit unrestricted entry of vehicles and personal belongings. It is also the only country where you can obtain a *libreta*. (Also, if you arrive by air, you won't need a US$30 visa.)

International tariffs

The tariff is computed by the cubic meter of your vehicle, distance and by the carrier. Loose cargo or deck class, called *carga suelta*, starts at US$55 per cubic meter and is the most economical freight category. An option is to pay by the linear foot, which is usually more expensive.

Containerization is the rule, except between South American ports. Containers come in two standard sizes: 20 cubic meters and 40 cubic meters, and you pay for the whole thing. Sample freight charges for a 20-cubic-meter container range from US$600 up to US$1,900 between southern US and northern South America ports. Between Panama and Florida, US$850. From Buenos Aires, Argentina, to Florida, a Land Cruiser ships for US$4,000.

Visitors from the UK can ship a motorcycle to Buenos Aires from Felixstowe. There is one ship a week and the rate is about £100 per cubic meter or tonne, plus £24 customs clearance. Contact **Madison Container Lines Ltd**, Suite 10, Orwell House, Ferry Lane, Felixstowe, Suffolk IP11 8QL; tel: 01394 695560; fax: 01394 693031.

Calculations

Measure the length between the furthest points (usually, outside bumpers) and height from the ground to the highest point. Multiply length times width times height (convert into meters) and cube the sum. You'll need to know linear dimensions, so keep a record. Dimensions for a 20-cubic-meter container are: length 5.91m, width 2.47m, height 2.58m. Negotiable and optional fees are insurance and loading/unloading.

Motorcycles can be shipped economically by cargo plane, and bicycles can go on regular airlines.

Avoid customs brokers, but chances are 90% assured that customs officials won't speak to you without a broker mouthpiece. Broker's fees average US$150-250 at each port. We shipped several times and always got stuck with one. Happily, we were never charged more than direct expenses, eg: faxes, a drug sniffing dog, and US$25 preparation of Bill of Lading. We also sweated side-by-side with the agents, eight to ten hours a day. In one nasty situation, the shipping company took pity and absolved a US$1,300 shipping bill. (We were camping outside their gates while trying to release our van.) Mounds of paperwork justify brokerage fees.

Get your vehicle out of customs as quickly as possible. Fly ahead and lay the groundwork; you will be charged for each minute it sits at dock. The price goes up if it is warehoused.

Vehicle preparation

Shippers require an ignition key, so key all other locks separately. Strip the vehicle of windshield wipers, mirrors, spare tires or anything dangling on the exterior. Hide and lock valuables, tools and spare parts, into sealed compartments inside the vehicle. The more chain, ropes and locks used, the better the deterrent. The idea is to slow down a dilettante thief. Theft is more rampant at port than in transit. We lost a painted stick representing a snake goddess; we hope that it bites the thief.

Your transport

Virtually no maritime company accepts passengers, and we traced every rumor. You'll have to arrange separate passage. The notable exception is the Panama/Colombia ferry, **Crucero Express**, US$50 for a motorcycle, and plush.

Venezuela is the most economical port in South America to ship a vehicle and fly your body. Ship to Puerto Cabello and fly into Maracaibo to save hassle, money and aggravation. Brazilians use this route.

Chapter Three

Preparation & Packing

This chapter addresses vehicle preparation, maintenance and repairs, camping equipment and packing.

FUEL

Unleaded fuel is not widely available outside Mexico, southern Brazil, Chile and Venezuela. Leaded gas is very low octane; near big cities, you can find a range between 91% and 94%. Fill up then and dilute the sludge. Additives are hard to find and they're expensive.

Budget roughly US$2.20 per gallon of gas or US$0.60 per liter. (A liter roughly equates a pint, or four liters to a gallon.) Diesel, the least expensive of all fuels, is readily available. Venezuela is the cheapest country in which to buy fuel — US$0.07 per liter!

VEHICLE REPAIRS

Few mechanics have sophisticated diagnostic equipment; instead they've developed a musician's ear and sense of timing. If they can't fix the problem for lack of parts, they will invent a substitute or a patch. Service is prompt and efficient, better than in the US, and ethical.

Start with the yellow pages of a telephone book (hotels and phone companies usually have copies) and look up *taller* for shops, *repuestos* for repair or parts, and/or *automovil*. Another tactic is to stand on the street and look for models similar to yours and flag down the driver. You don't need eloquent Spanish to get the question across. At a repair shop, any will do, show or explain your problem and they will refer you. Ask a truck driver; they know everything. Don't be surprised if someone insists on leading you to a mechanic; the garage could be tucked in a nook difficult to find without knowledge of local landmarks. A verbal thank you is usually sufficient.

You'll push your vehicle harder and further than at home. For example, US auto insurers demarcate yearly mileage under 5,000 as conservative and over 15,000 as heavy-use. Drive or pedal a straight line from Alaska to Tierra del Fuego and you'll have used two years of your vehicle's normal life.

MAINTENANCE

We guarantee you'll return home with more mechanical skill than when you left. But before you go, learn the basics of your machine and how to perform minor adjustments. Get a mechanic to guide you through the engine and suspension/brake systems and tune-ups. Make a list of commonly replaced parts and their specifications, eg: spark plug sizes and gap, oil filters, etc.

Dirt roads wreak havoc on all vehicles. Walk along a Brazilian road and you'll find scattered evidence — bolts everywhere. Sooner or later, every bolt in your vehicle will jar loose or fall out; check and tighten yours frequently. Heavy duty shock absorbers are a must. If the suspension breaks, your best friend is a welder, a *solderdura*.

Sand, dirt and dusty conditions require extra vigilance. Check and clean filters every few days. Check oil daily in all makes of vehicles and motorcycles. Mechanics in South America recommend an oil change every 1,000-1,800km. Inspect the suspension and boots while your vehicle is on the rack. Lubrication is inexpensive, so grease joints and chains.

Wash the engine and undercarriage whenever it has been in mud or dust. Steam cleaning costs less than US$5. In one small town in Brazil's Pantanal, every business displayed bottles encased in hard drying mud. A curiosity? That's what we thought. Thousands of miles later we were still chipping the hardened mud from the undercarriage, with hammer and chisel.

Consider sealing your engine compartment with a wide tape, as did our Chilean friends in the Atacama. They also put tape around doors and windows to reduced entry of dust.

EQUIPMENT
Emission control systems

Environmentally correct emission control systems are not practical as long as leaded fuels dominate South American pumps. Slowly, Latin American countries are introducing cleaner fuels and establishing regulatory laws, but they're a long way from being able to enforce them. Meanwhile, remove the apparatus south of the US. We hate advocating pollution/contamination, but maintenance problems can dominate your trip. The US Environmental Protection Agency recommends dismantling the system, saving the parts, and installing them before re-entry to US territory.

Carburetors

Fuel injectors are "one more thing to go wrong". Switch to a carburetor system as soon as possible. You'll occasionally take on bad fuel, tainted with water, alcohol or other impurities that will bind fuel injectors.

Check with a dealer regarding special carburetor jets for high altitude driving. We didn't have them and wished we did. Our van suffered respiratory failure in heights above 3,200m although we removed the air filter and advanced the timing. Dual carburetor jets permit finer adjustments.

Converted VWs are typically fitted with a Weber carburetor system. It's finicky and repair parts are hard to find in South America. If you've got a Weber, take a repair manual.

Tires

Mount all-terrain tires on your vehicle and carry at least one spare. A German motorist, in Guatemala, bragged about putting ten thousand miles on tires he'd bought bald. Two of ours, warrantied for 60,000 miles, shredded after 20,000.

Tubeless vs tubed tires (hard to find in the US) is an on-going debate. Having used both, in every combination, the important factor is a multi-plied, all-terrain tread.

Gomerias, vulcanizadores are not generally equipped to repair tubeless tires. Scream "Alto!" (Stop!) before an enthusiastic repairman pokes steel threads through the tire cover, the *cubierto*, destroying all possibility of lining your tire with an inner tube. Carry a complete patching kit.

Oversized tires, or unnecessarily heavy tread, detracts from fuel mileage, speed and open road comfort. Odd-sized tires are difficult to replace. Bald tires slide on a thin veneer of slick sand or mud. (Don't spin your wheels or you'll only dig deeper.)

As you ascend to high altitudes, release the air pressure; air expands and tires explode. As you descend, add air to normal levels. A foot pump and a pressure gauge are indispensable.

Shock absorbers

Heavy duty, light truck shock absorbers won't break easily. A motorist who traveled all the Americas claims that they were the only thing that didn't break at least twice. Ditto for us.

Spare parts, tools and other accessories

Always carry chewing gum in your car's first aid kit. Temporary repairs can be made by sticking a thick wad of gum into a leaking hose. Equally practical are wire of different lengths and gauge, twine, dental floss, epoxy glue and electrical tape.

Carry any part that is prone to weakness and anything consumable: spark plugs, points, condensers, spare filters for oil, air and gas; fuel injectors, fuses, and a jug of oil. Items such as filters and spark plugs, can be cleaned with gasoline or sand paper and re-used. Install at least one in-line fuel filter, if your vehicle isn't already outfitted this way. Check it and change it regularly.

A basic tool kit should include a full range of screw drivers (one enormously oversized flathead was handy), pliers, crescent wrenches and socket wrenches; an assortment of screws and bolts, including carriage bolts, fuses and electrical plugs. A sturdy jack, tow rope, non-flammable "Fix-A-Flat", a rubber mallet, a metal hammer, and flashlights are necessary.

Helpful items are a repair book and a parts catalog. We were fortunate enough to find a repair manual written in Spanish. A parts catalog is helpful, if you have to order something from home. It also provides a ready-made description for customs declarations. One excellent mail order company for automotive and motorcycle parts and accessories is J C Whitney, PO Box 8410, Chicago, Illinois 60680; tel: (312) 431 6102; fax: 312 431 5625.

Brakes

Heavy duty brakes and a strong handbrake is a must. Expect to replace them, pads or cables at least once.

Fuel tanks

A range of two hundred miles will get you between fuel pumps. Auxiliary fuel is necessary if you wander off main roads in the Gran Sabana, Patagonia, the Atacama desert and in southern Bolivia. Periodically rotate spare fuel because it can go bad.

Security alarm systems

Chirps, beeps, honks and sirens are the most common sounds in a South American parking lot and no-one pays them any attention. Our alarm broke early and we never got it working again. Cyclists should use one.

A Brazilian motorist devised what he called a "psychological alarm". It was a battery-operated, blinking red light that sat on his dashboard. It was connected to nothing, but no-one approaching his van knew that. He swore to its effectiveness.

Towing points
These are two metal rings welded on to the undercarriage of a car or truck. You probably have them. They're required safety features in many countries.

Winch
A winch is an unnecessary accessory. Most places where you might need to winch usually lack anything to winch against. Mounted winches add extra weight and decrease fuel efficiency.

Windshield protectors
Do you really want to look at the world through metal grates? If so, armorize your windshield before leaving home. We couldn't find any place that sold protectors or the materials to manufacture one. You'll need a stiff, fine mesh wire stretched on rigid supports that extend at least five inches from the vehicle's body. Buses use plexiglass which scars easily and requires cleaning four window surfaces, inside-outside.

A new windshield can cost less than buying or building a protector. A Brazilian talked us into buying a new windshield after ours acquired star rays. We paid US$110 for tinted, non-shatter glass, new gaskets and installation. Five days later, another rock hit it. (Eventually we'll name our windshield after a constellation.)

Spare keys
We lost a Volkswagen key and never did find a blank in all of South America to cut a new one. Take several sets and hide them in different places. It also helps to have your locks keyed alike in case you lose your back-up set.

Safety belts
Seatbelts are mandatory. Locals don't use them, nor do police. Many times we were arbitrarily stopped and, if the police could find nothing else to fault us, they would claim seatbelts. Imagine their disgust to find us securely strapped. More importantly, seatbelts make good sense, even in remote areas where you might have to come to a sudden stop or swerve to avoid on-coming traffic or a road obstruction.

Roof rack
Use one if you like, but they invite thieves and military/police inspectors. They'll increase your wind resistance and snag on low hanging vegetation. We used our roof for carrying such sundries as firewood, extra water and spare fuel tanks.

Electrical power

When you move into a campground or hotel with exterior power sources, you'll need adapter plugs. Brazil uses both 220 and 110, Argentina uses 220 and so does Chile, but the plug configurations are slightly different. Go to an electrical supply store and describe, or show the male prongs, and the voltage tolerance needed. Check it with your system right away, in case it needs to be exchanged. Individual adapter plugs cost about US$1.

If you throw the switch and the lights don't come on, the problem may be that you've got the wrong light bulb. Light bulbs also need to be changed when converting to a different current. A simple test is to replace a 110 bulb with a 220, or vice versa.

Electronic appliances may require an intermediary power converter, which is not the same thing as a plug adapter. Check the voltage specifications for your electronic equipment before plugging it in.

Lighting

We installed a small power converter (US$80) in our VW to operate my computer, using the spare car battery as the power source. AC lights could also be plugged into it.

DC powered lights are the best. Cigarette lighter plugs installed around the vehicle provide additional lighting flexibility. 12V broad beam workshop lamps and tube lights, fitted with long cords and cigarette plugs, can be used outside the vehicle for night repairs or to illuminate a party scene. Liquid fuel lights are terrific and generate heat; they also break and spill.

Batteries

The most reliable source of power is the battery in your own vehicle. Power greedy components, such as stereos, fans, etc, justify a second battery. Install a battery isolator so you don't drain the starting power from the primary battery. Both batteries will recharge while driving. An isolator must be matched to the electrical system of your car. A Volkswagen, for instance, requires a special diode from the manufacturer.

Fire extinguisher

A fire extinguisher is a required safety item. It's not usually enforced, but the lack of one may be an excuse to write a ticket, a *multa*. I recommend one for every powered vehicle, especially fuel-injected 2000 VWs, which are notorious for engine fires.

Safety triangles

Also required are glow-in-the-dark safety triangles. Most roads do not have shoulders to pull aside on in case of a breakdown, so you definitely need some form of warning sign. Stones piled on the road or small fires are alternative ways to indicate a road obstruction.

Radio

A strong AM-FM radio with a cassette tape player or CD makes a good travel companion. Bolt it into your vehicle or consider a removable unit if staying in hotels. A compact, but strong, shortwave radio would be a nice addition. There are no English AM or FM stations in South America.

Water

Carry as much water as possible. Consider using two separate tanks, one for washing and another for drinking.

Whenever possible, fill up with potable water. Look for water purification plants, *agua purificado*, and ice plants, *hielo*. Gas stations often offer free, unlimited potable water. When the source is doubtful, use a purification/filtration pump or treat your water with iodine, cholorox, or chlorine tablets.

Large containers of water from five to 20 gallons are sold cheaply wherever water is doubtful or foul-tasting. The tanks are interchangeable, once you've paid the deposit. We'd fill up our tank and leave the empty behind.

Note: One gallon of water weighs 8.33 pounds.

Crash helmets

Cyclists, with or without motors, should wear a helmet at all times (just as motorists should stay strapped with seatbelts). Although locals sometimes skip them, that doesn't mean you should or that the police will be as lenient. Wear one, stay alive and whole to return home with tales of your adventure.

Eye goggles

They look stupid, but cyclists should wear some sort of eye protection, even if only sunglasses. Road debris tossed by passing vehicles, wind-borne grit and ultra violet radiation are all good reasons to protect your eyes.

Compass

Knowing what direction you're headed is sometimes helpful. We used a pocket compass to exit cities and verify direction where roads were not marked.

CLOTHING

Space is always a problem and varied climatic conditions compounds the dilemma of what to bring. Choose natural fabrics and styles that lend themselves to layering. Mornings are often chilly, the days torridly hot, and evenings downright cold. Roll clothes like little logs to discourage wrinkles, and wrap each item with an elastic band to keep your packing space neat.

Practical suggestions for clothing include long underwear of non-bulky, wicking fabric; a long-sleeved, lightweight shirt, a pair of durable pants, flexible at the knee and crotch for lounging, climbing or cycling, a windbreaker jacket, a pair of shorts, bathing suit, good walking shoes, GORE-TEX boots, cap and gloves. Padded cycling shorts are appropriate for doing the trip by pedal. A good down, waterproof jacket or cycling jacket (tailored to accommodate the elongated back postures of a cyclist) is a must. They're expensive new and impossible to find used.

CAMPING EQUIPMENT

Machete
Very good ones are sold in hardware stores and markets. Prices range from US$2 to US$10. Use it for digging and trenching, splitting coconuts and sugar cane, or for chopping firewood.

Bucket
A washing machine, a dishwasher, a water scooper, a food soaker, a storage bin, an emergency toilet, a party drum, a small table, a shopping basket — all are ways to describe and utilize a plastic bucket.

Cooking
A two-burner camp stove certainly makes cooking multi-course meals easy. A single burner stove is almost as easy, with a little forethought to food preparation. A pressure cooker is the single most versatile cooking pot ever invented. It requires little fuel, water or cooking oil, and it reduces cooking time. Multi-courses can be cooked simultaneously by layering foods or by inserting a smaller container on top of whatever else you've thrown in.

Cooking fuel
Propane, *gas propano*, is the most common and economical fuel in Central and South America. However each country has different-sized nozzles, which creates refilling problems. Here's how to solve the problem: take your tank or your camper to a big liquid gas plant

and let the chief engineer figure out how to adapt their equipment to yours. 99% of the time they'll succeed. And if you're nice about it, they may not charge you.

We used propane for cooking and to run a catalytic heater. The main tank was stored on the roof. By using an adapter bought from J C Whitney (see page 61 for details), we refilled small camping cartridges from our main tank. It was an extra task, but the small cartridges enabled us to move the stove. I prefer cooking out of doors where we can enjoy panoramic sunsets. (The fresh air sweeps the garlic odors away.)

Small camping cartridges are scarce. They're occasionally sold in hardware stores, for use with small welders. Camping Gaz is available mainly in Chile and Venczuela.

Kerosene or white gas, and alcohol stoves are the best choices for bikers.

Natural materials, such as old wood or dried cactus, can be collected and used for cooking fires. You don't need much. Firewood and charcoal is sold by the roadside and in stores. We have a problem in recommending them, because it encourages wanton tree chopping.

Fire igniters

Take a couple of long-handled igniters. They're terrific for starting fires without scorching your hand and face. They're hard to find on the road. Also, stock up on waterproof matches. In high altitudes, lighter fluids evaporate rapidly and become recalcitrant in the oxygen-rarified air.

Grill

Take a grill top with you, if you can afford the space. A small one with collapsible legs is perfect to set over a campfire. Store it in a plastic or canvas bag.

Plastic bags

Stores dispense plastic bags at the rate of one bag per item, or so it seems. Bag disposal is creating a major ecological problem. We used ours to collect and carry garbage, to wrap food and tools, to take shopping, carry our things when walking, and as a liner for the emergency toilet (see *Bucket*). Large, sturdy bags and sealing, air-tight bags are hard to find.

Tent

Select one that is sturdy but lightweight, free-standing and simple to erect in the dark. One that offers easy access, mosquito netting and screened ventilation is practical for a variety of conditions. Good tents are relatively hard to find and expensive in South America, so it's best to take one with you. Don't forget the flycover. Securely peg the tent if the weather is the least bit uncertain. Bring a patching kit.

Mattresses
Choose one of the new padding systems, like Therm-A-Rest. They're lightweight and roll up small.

Sleeping bags
Down-filled bags are the most compact. One that is weighted down to 20°F should be sufficient. To get the optimum heating efficiency from a bag, remove your clothes and let your body heat warm you up.

Tarpaulin
A handy and versatile tarp can be used as a ground cloth under your tent, when working under your vehicle, to make shade or to deflect rain. Plastic sheeting, sold on rolls, is inexpensive throughout South America.

Waterproofing
Silicon spray is extremely difficult to find in Latin America. And when you find it, it is very expensive. Make sure your equipment is waterproofed before you leave. Test it. Bring extra spray with you. If you spring leaks, try rubbing candle wax into the offending areas.

Curtains
Privacy is more than a frill, it is necessary to your sense of self. Occasional circumstances will require that you camp in a street, a plaza or alongside a busy restaurant. There are few things more wearing on nerves than to have people peering through your windows when you are preparing for bed.

Mosquito net
Choose a lightweight, small-meshed net that's been impregnated with Permethrin. For maximum comfort in your own vehicle, cut netting to fit over windows and doors. Velcro strips work well to secure it in place.

Binoculars
Some people use binoculars to watch beach babes, some people peer at birds and other skittish or far away wildlife, some people hold them up to their camera lens, and some people squint through them in order to read distant road signs.

Refrigeration

An ice box is nice to save leftovers for another meal. Ice can be a luxury in terms of cost (US$0.50-2.50) and availability. Block ice is less expensive and lasts days longer than cubes, *cubitos*. Both are cheaper from an ice plant than from a store. We met a few travelers who outfitted their vehicles with 12-volt refrigerated coolers. They reported poor results and required 30-40 minutes a day charging time, under full engine power. They cost around US$40.

MOTORCYCLE PREPARATION

Bear in mind that the main problems for motorcyclists are the very rough roads, the steep hills of the Andes, and the extremes of heat and cold.

Brakes

Be sure to change your brake fluid regularly, and take spare brake cables. Use your gears as much as possible when going downhill, don't rely on your brakes.

Tires

You will need to change your tires regularly, so make sure you know what you are doing. Bring spare inner tubes, but buy new tires locally. Also bring an air cylinder for inflating inner tubes, as this will work better than a pump.

Carburetor

If you lose the cover you could have real problems, so bring a spare.

Spare parts and tools

The roads are rough, so reinforce front and back shock absorbers. Also take spare bulbs for your lights, and a spare electronic ignition box.

Fuel

Fit the biggest fuel tank possible — you often have to go 400-500 miles without filling up. Fuel is generally of good quality and inexpensive, except in Bolivia (very low octane level) and Ecuador (very dirty — so use an extra air filter). Beware of buying fuel at roadside houses, as this is often mixed with water. In hot conditions, change your oil as frequently as possible.

Head gear

Your helmet should have a chin protector, and goggles should have shatterproof glass. Most helmets only absorb one hit, so if you do have a crash, have your helmet checked — damage to the fibreglass infrastructure may not show but could be dangerous should you get involved in another accident.

Luggage boxes
Buy the best quality you can find; they will get shaken up on the bad roads and cheap ones won't last. Ensure they are waterproof, thiefproof and shockproof.

BICYCLE PREPARATION

Cyclists have to think like minimalists. What's the minimum equipment you can get by with? Very little, as you'll find with time and experience. The one area that you can't scrimp, however, is bike quality.

Spend the time necessary to find a bike that fits you. Talk to a good bike shop and listen to their recommendations, but don't let them sell you something too fancy or you'll find yourself stranded and without repairs. Save the latest hi-tech designs for North American or European roads. Look for a sturdy frame material like chrome-molybdenum. Have the bike shop measure you for the proper seat-tube length which is the most important and basic key to selecting a frame design. Fork rakes and frame angles won't matter if you experience joint and tendon inflammation as a result. You should have 12cm clearance for a mountain bike.

Remember, you'll be living in the saddle so make sure it is a comfortable design: firm but not hard, not too broad, and one which does not chafe your inner thighs. Experiment with the slant of the seat so that you achieve a comfortable distribution of weight.

Tires and wheels
Choose a strong wheel preferably with a 36-spoke lacing system for ease of replacement. Take spare spokes and spoke key. Stick to standard-sized tires. The easiest tires to find in Latin America are 26 and 27-inch. A 1.75 rim will allow you to fit a variety of tire widths to your bike.

Carry a spare tire and at least two spare tubes, a patching kit, and a hand pump, preferably one that can be modified for different valve types.

Chain and gears
The chain is a weak link, so to speak. To extend its life, keep it clean and well lubricated. Ideally, replace the freewheel whenever you

replace your chain and don't wait until they simply wear out. Look in big cities for replacement parts before you need them.

Your derailleurs should optimally have the capacity to compensate in high altitudes, when you are puffing for oxygen. You won't have to wait for the Andes before climbing into the clouds. In Costa Rica, the Pan-Am ascends to its highest, 3491m, the Paso del Muerte. A 34-tooth rear cog is recommended for the job.

Tool kit

Bearings, cables (brake and derailleur), spokes and spoke key, assorted nuts and bolts, an adjustable wrench, allen keys, needle-nose pliers, freewheel remover, crank remover, Y-wrenches, chain breaker, grease, spare tire and tubes, patching kit, and pump.

Equipment

José says don't bring too much stuff, like he did.

> "Thirteen books were too many, it's better to bring maps. Don't forget a helmet, eye protectors, a rear-view mirror, speedometer, compass, and perhaps a wristwatch with an altimeter. You'll need a cooking pot, cooker, tent, sleeping bag, a small water purifying pump (Pur or Katadyn don't require filter changes), a water sack that holds at least 10 liters, and several water bottles. Cyclists need loads of water! The absolute minimum in cold areas is five-six liters augmented by extra liters of beer at night, and up to 15 liters of water in hot regions."

Packing hints

You'll probably have to repack several times until you've got your belongings stuffed into your luggage: Stiff front and rear panniers, and handlebar bag for maps, camera, headlamp, etc. A small backpack and sleeping bag, strapped onto a rear rack, is versatile.

Anything else you've forgotten, you can buy there.

Chapter Four

Organized Tours

The magnitude of preparing a vehicle can overwhelm even the most adventurous spirit. Let's be honest... independent travel by private vehicle isn't right for everyone. Some travelers don't want the responsibility, others are baffled by anything mechanical, and still others are happier with a group of friends. Economics may ultimately play a factor in the decision. Language can be a deterrent; you've tried and tried but Spanish will not stick to your tongue. These may be considerations for not going on your own, but not for staying at home. An organized tour may be the thing for you.

Many reputable tour companies regularly ply the roads of Central and South America in their own trucks, taking in all the most awesome sights. Group size normally varies between 15 and 20 members who share duties of shopping, cooking and cleaning. Driving and vehicle maintenance falls to experienced drivers who also absorb the brunt of border formalities. Tour companies routinely reserve accommodation, in advance, for such events as the Carnival in Brazil.

CHOOSING A TOUR

Research itineraries, accommodation and prices are offered by each company. A typical Central America tour ends (or begins) in Panama. South American routes normally cross Colombia, Ecuador, Peru, Bolivia, Paraguay and Brazil. Alternatively, the route may be reversed through Venezuela or swing south and across the Andes between Santiago, Chile and Bariloche, Argentina. Match trip times and route itineraries with your schedule and interests.

Accommodation
Overland tours normally incorporate camping in their itineraries. The amount of time divided between camping and staying in hotels

varies from company to company. As an average, expect 50% of your nights to be in tents. The company provides the tent (usually two-person), and you provide a sleeping bag, mat and other personal gear. A unique departure from this style is the German-owned and operated company Rotel Tours, which utilizes big trailers racked with 40 individual sleeping compartments. Wall partitions can be moved, so that couples can snuggle together. Within their specialty market, Rotel presents a viable alternative to tent camping.

Because you'll spend a good deal of your time in the vehicle, overland tour companies provide trucks or buses whose interiors have been converted into quasi-living quarters. Each member is assigned a locker to store personal belongings. Seats are usually comfortable and afford ample space for moving around or merely gazing out of the windows. Configurations differ, but they accommodate social activity. They're like mobile living rooms. Kitchens are usually built into the side of the vehicle and open to the exterior. Individual companies can provide a layout of their vehicles.

Alternatives

Toucan, a subsidiary of Top Deck, operates tours by public transportation as does Journey Latin America. They arrange transport and hotel accommodation, and negotiate border crossings. You reap the benefits of a fixed budget, group discounts, reserved travel and a knowledgeable tour guide.

RVers setting off from North America might want to investigate caravaning. The Good Sam Club offers guided tours through Mexico for those traveling in their own RV. Contact this organization if you're apprehensive about Latin America travel. It's a good, secure way to get started on the road south. You might meet other group members who'll want to go further down the road with you.

Group composition

Cultural identification, language and ages vary by group. The British-owned and operated companies tend to attract Brits and Aussies. Other European nationalities and North Americans are increasingly integrating their ranks. English is the dominant group language. Among German and Norwegian companies, you'll like-wise find speakers of those tongues and a shared cultural reference.

Oldsters (those over 40) also toss their backpacks into the overland trucks, although they're still a minority among 20 and early 30-year-olds. One big clue to group composition by age will be found in the brochure. If the company requires proof of health submitted by any-one over 40, you can bet you'll be running with a younger crowd. This is not a problem, and for many people it can be an attraction.

Costs

Count on plunking down an amount between US$4,000-8,000 per person, for a six-month travel period. Additionally, a myriad of other expenses are borne by the individual participant.

It is helpful to make a chart. Brochures explain which costs are company responsibility and which are absorbed by you. Look for fixed costs, approximate costs of hotels and optional tours, insurance, suggested personal budgets and kitty fees collected en route for food; whether air fares are covered between connecting points (if applicable), and your travel costs to meet up with the group and to return home at the end.

Overland tour companies provide knowledgeable and experienced guides and drivers. Their individual capabilities vary, of course, as do personalities. We met up with and interviewed at least ten overland groups during our last trip. All the participants gave their leaders stellar rankings. Many drivers had previously worked in Africa where road conditions and bureaucracy are more challenging than in Latin America.

Organization

Pooled funds are called kitties and they're periodically collected en route. The amount varies dependent on the tastes of the group. Kitties are usually designated to buy food prepared by and shared among the group, however, they can be spent on other items, decided by group consensus.

Hotels are generally used in cities where the sightseeing is terrific and the camping alternatives nil. They're also scheduled to break up the tedium of camping. The cost of a hotel room comes out of your own pocket. This makes sense, because needs differ for personal space and for private time. Overland tour companies have identified agreeable, mid-range hotel accommodation and negotiated group discounts. There is no requirement that you stay in the same place. The leader can generally recommend alternative accommodation from modest up to pampered elegance.

While traveling and camping, the duties of shopping, cooking and cleaning are rotated. How often your turn comes up depends on the number in your group and the itinerary. Participants fix their schedule of duties at the beginning and usually hold to it. Trade-offs can be arranged on an individual basis.

Fitting in

On occasion, familiarity may breed contempt. Coziness inevitably leads to group dynamics and eventually a group personality. (Believe me, it happens between two people.) You'll spend much of your time together and learn more than you ever wanted to know about yourself and 20 other people. Strong individualists and hermits should think twice before joining a gregarious group effort. That's the downside of camaraderie.

You are free to leave the group and return at any point, at your own expense. Permanent exits do not result in refunds, so check the fine print (exclusionary clauses) before taking off. Likewise, it is sometimes possible to jump on to an overland tour while it's in progress. That's nice to know in case you start on your own and change your mind.

If the mode of travel is comfortable but you've found yourself in the wrong personality cluster, you might want to change. In that situation, first inquire within the company for other groups that you can catch up with. You won't lose as much money if making an inner-company transfer. Of course, switching groups is another form of Russian Roulette.

The overland companies

Adventure South America, Top Deck Travel, 131/135 Earls Court Rd, London SW5 9RH, England; tel: 0171 370 4555; fax: 0171 373 6201.

Crosscountry Travels, Postbus 164, 2180 AD Hillegom, Holland; fax: 02520 23670.

Dragoman, Camp Green Farm, Kenton Rd, Debenham, Suffolk IP14 6LA, England; tel: 01728 861133; fax: 01728 861127.

Encounter Overland, 267 Old Brompton Rd, London SW5 9JA, England; tel: 0171 370 6951; fax: 0171 244 9737.

Exodus Expeditions, 9 Weir Rd, London SW12 0LT, England; tel: 0181 675 5550; fax: 0181 673 0779.

Journey Latin America Ltd, 14-16 Devonshire Rd, Chiswick, London W4 2HD, England; tel: 0181 747 8315; fax: 0181 742 1312.

Kumuka Expeditions, 40 Earls Court Rd, London W8 6EJ, England; tel: 0171 937 8855; fax: 0171 937 6664.

Last Frontiers, Swan House, High St, Long Crendon, Bucks HP18 9AF, England; tel: 01844 208405; fax: 01844 201400. For rentals, directions and advice.

Overland Latin America, Worlds Apart Travel, 8 Ormond Terrace, Regent St, Cheltenham, Gloucester GL50 1HR, England; tel: 01242 226578; fax: 01242 242007.

Rotel Tours, Herrenstrasse 11, 94104 Tittling, Passau, Germany; tel: 08504 4040. Plane, bus and sleeping compartments stacked in a trailer.

The Good Sam Club, International Headquarters, PO Box 500, Agoura, California 91301. Call toll free within US (800) 423 5061. In CA dial (800) 382 3455. RVers caravan through Mexico.

Vreemde Kontinenten, Savannstraat 120, B 9000, Gent, Belgium; fax: 329 233 55 49.

Chapter Five

On the Road

You've packed your vehicle, unpacked it, and repacked it again. Friends and family have waved *hasta la vista*. Excitement and anticipation feel more like nervous jitters as you peer towards the horizon of adventure.

This chapter explores more generalities of driving and cycling through the Americas.

NUMBER ONE RULE

Don't take anything that you cannot afford to lose. You want to return home a better person, not a bitter one. Things break, are misplaced or forgotten, accidents happen, a thief outwits you, a million things can intervene between you and your material things. The same rule applies to vehicles. If you can't afford to lose it, don't take it.

Only one thing is truly valuable and irreplaceable... yourself. Maintain it, protect it, and pamper it occasionally.

CAMPING

Campgrounds with electrical hook-ups and sewerage are found in Mexico, Brazil, Uruguay, Argentina and Chile. Occasionally you can plug into private homes or business establishments (offer to pay). Infrastructures range from bare fields to five stars: cabins, hot showers, heated pools, sports facilities, gardens, electricity, washers and dryers, restaurants, markets and even bakeries. Many also have nightclubs, in which case you either join in or plug your ears with tissue.

Campgrounds in southern South America close during the winter, May through November. Often you can talk your way in, or enter national parks for free. These are quiet times and you're likely to see wildlife that would normally hide. Don't expect any services, however.

Latin-style camping

During Holy Week *Semana Santa*, no ground is holy. Families flee cities, restaurants and bars spring up, prices triple, and natural camping takes on an urban look. We've gawked as entire kitchens, beds, TVs and enormous stereo systems were unloaded. Some countries and people, such as Venezuelans, take a *laissez faire* approach. They detest regulation and won't pay to enjoy the great outdoors.

You can camp free on public streets, around plazas, on church grounds; gasoline, police and fire stations, and outside schools (schools start early and you'll be surrounded by inquisitive children). But why choose a noisy thoroughfare, an ugly place, unless you have to? There are billions of lovely places to camp freely and safely, if you just ask.

Choosing a site

It is unsafe to camp alone without taking precautions. Thieves abound, tents are easy targets, as are clothes lines.

Scout the area before dark to find the most agreeable site. Imagine the site in early morning hours; your serene nook might be on a commuter footpath. Don't forget to look overhead. *Do not* camp directly under a coconut tree! Coco bombs are injurious to your health and to your equipment.

Restaurants, *posadas*, and homes offer possible locations for a secure night's sleep. Seek out the owner or nearest land tenant for permission (never ask a gang of kids). The English word "camp" is the same in Spanish but it assumes different meanings depending on points of view. To many it means an organized campground. The simplest approach is to ask permission to spend the night.

The majority of people will extend a welcome or steer you to a better, safer location. They sometimes offer their homes, use of their bathroom, or extend the watchful eye of their guard over your belongings. Hotel owners have given us room keys just so we could shower! No-one expects reciprocity beyond respect for their property, business and lifestyle. Patronize their restaurant or store (if only for a beer or a carrot). Do not leave a mess. José advises, "If they invite you for a meal, pay them back with, for example Maggi soup. Don't be a parasite! Often the poorest people offer you the most."

HOTELS

A hotel or *posada* is a place to spend the night. You'll find five-star Hiltons, Best Westerns, Holiday Inns, independents and lovely, budget accommodations with gracious amenities.

A motel is a place to spend an hour or two. Not all motels are squalid tryst nests; some have pools, jacuzzis and gardens (and closed-circuit porno films). Motels attract married couples seeking privacy from children and extended family, as well as the newly-mets. Unfortunately, our van did not fit through any of the gated-fences surrounding each motel.

José adds, "Often hotels are so cheap that it is not worth it to camp. But always lock your bike in your room (even on the fourth floor)."Indeed, in every cycling report we've read, the authors have reiterated the same advice.

TOILETS, SHOWERS AND LAUNDRY

It is said that all the world is a toilet. Certainly, some campers will exercise the strength of that adage. Make sure you bury your waste.

A more contemporary approach is public toilets. All gas stations have toilets and many have showers. (In Chile, the showers are in the men's restroom.) You can find these same amenities in many restaurants, hotel lobbies or adjacent to their swimming pools, bus stations, and in campgrounds. Beach-side restaurants typically have outdoor showers.

Bathrooms are surprisingly clean. Help keep them that way, *do not throw paper into toilets*. The plumbing and sewerage systems cannot handle it. Use the basket adjacent to the toilet or, if lacking a basket, throw used paper into the corner.

RVs with sewerage tanks will just have to hold it. Organized campgrounds often have dumping stations as do a few gas stations. If you have to dump waste and can't wait, find a remote area and dig a deep hole. Don't forget to cover it up.

Waterfalls make excellent showers. Fresh water springs or streams, *agua dulce*, are sweet, natural bathtubs. Thermal baths are good places to relax and treat your arthritis while soaking away road dirt. Don't pollute the water with soaps. Use a bucket or scoop and rinse on land, especially if bathing in a slow-moving pool.

Laundromats

These are proliferating, but probably not as fast as your dirty clothes. Charges vary from high to so cheap that you'd be a fool not to wash everything you own. They're worth investigating as you go along. For the most part, you'll handwash your own clothes in cold water. A plastic bucket and a brush or rocks are perfect tools. Experienced washers instructed me first to soak the clothes in soapy water, wring them slightly and set them in the sun. Next, dip them in water and scrub like hell. After a few rinsings, hang them out to dry. My clothes never came out as clean as theirs. I was probably too impatient.

Detergents are sold everywhere. Laundry bar soap is economical and very effective; but can make your clothes smell like animal fat.

NIGHT DRIVING

Local motorists, truckers and buses travel at night. Inevitably you will when you get lost or snarled up in a late afternoon traffic jam. Many cyclists start off in the dark hours of morning to avoid gusty daytime winds, heat and traffic.

The main problem with night driving is the amount of obstacles in the road. Local residents know where the problems lurk; you don't. Suddenly, in front of you is a suspension-shattering pothole, a tree branch, a road slide, a detour, a sharp twist in a mountain curve. Traffic signs are unlit. Animals wander into the road, cows, pigs, donkeys and drunks. (In northern Brazil, carcasses of donkeys litter the highway in the wake of night truckers.) Breakdowns occur as easily by night as by day.

You can't see the sights by night anyway, so why do it? Look for a good camping site before the sun sets, tackle cities before they're congested with rush-hour traffic and evening browsers. In small towns, people go to bed early. When the nightlife calls, walk, take a taxi or ride a bus.

PARKING

Many establishments are open air, allowing you to watch your vehicle. Within towns, businesses cluster around the main plaza. Park and run your errands. In larger cities, there are business sectors: parts stores and workshops in one area, markets in another, etc. You can entrust your vehicle to a shopkeeper for a few hours.

Parking lots tend to be fairly secure places, although we don't recommend leaving a key. They'll ask for it if the lot is crowded and they have to move cars around. Express reluctance and the attendant will clear an appropriate space for you.

City employees have replaced grubby-faced children who used to charge motorists for watching (not robbing) their car. These human parking meters wear city licenses and sometimes vests, they carry ticket books, and they'll find you. They'll also fine you, if you are illegally parked.

Consider leaving your vehicle outside congested cities and commuting by public transport. We did this in Guatemala City, Caracas, Rio, Lima and several other big cities. It saved us a lot of anxiety.

Lock bikes to something secure and keep locks on saddlebags. Ask a business owner to store your equipment inside an office. We've left baggage in insurance offices, shipping companies, restaurants, hotels, tourist information booths, libraries, museums, etc.

Vacation from your vehicle is necessary. You can't take it reef diving, deep-sea fishing or to the top of a glacier-packed mountain. And you can't miss the remoter wonders of the Americas! Stash it in a secure location, preferably with a private party. Small, walled hotels are good if you can't find a local's back yard. Put it in a garage for repairs. Some motorists use public lots adjacent to airports, ferry terminals, and even hospitals. The drawback is security guards rotate shifts too frequently for any one guard to accept responsibility.

BORDERS AND POLICE CHECKS

Borders are stationary, even if neighboring countries dispute sovereignty, such as Ecuador and Peru. Other, ancient territorial claims are argued between Guatemala and Belize, Venezuela and Guyana, Chile and Argentina, Paraguay and Bolivia, Bolivia and Chile. For the most part, these rivalries have settled into mutual co-existence.

Approach borders as if on a treasure hunt, where you've got a list of things to find but no clues. If some character, dressed like a reprobate, bosses you around even in a casual way, pay attention and look to cues from the uniformed officers. Chief investigators and tourist police dress down.

Cross borders on weekdays and during daylight hours because they charge for weekends, holidays and after 6pm. Border officials don't maintain posted hours. Technically, a border might be open but during lunch hours and toward the end of the day you'll be ignored or sent on some mission, such as to get a police stamp, and that office will be closed or have moved to a more obscure neighborhood. Even if officials are present and attentive, darkness is not the best time to have people rummaging your belongings and documents.

Central America

Procedures are more confusing than in South America. Typically, offices (customs, immigration, police, agricultural inspection, money exchange, insurance) are not logically located or marked. You'll have to obtain and pay for permits and processing fees which, by the way, are posted and receipts issued. You must accomplish each step in a specific, but secret, sequence and within morning or afternoon hours. The worst is Nicaragua, where they've managed to make deliberate chaos out of order and licensed facilitators are nearly unavoidable. Agree on the price in advance, US$2-5 is sufficient. At other borders, follow someone doing the same thing as you.

South America

Border crossings are orderly, professional and friendly (exceptions are Venezuela, and between Ecuador and Peru). In Chile, Argentina and Brazil, border offices are conducted like tourist information centers. We've been given maps, had reservations made for us, told about local events, and offered food, drink and assistance.

Military/police

Don't put your documents and papers away; they'll be inspected by military/police at least once after you leave the border. These guys aren't as jovial as the border folk.

It's easy to confuse the military and police as their roles are often interchangeable. Many police departments do not have patrol cruisers; instead, they work out of roadside station houses located at entrances to towns. You must stop, or roll to a near stop, and show documents if requested. Let the cop get a look at you. Wait for permission to continue — a nod, a wave, a thumbs up (Brazil), or to be obviously ignored. They are lax on Sundays, holidays, and during the noon siesta hours. Scrutiny intensifies in regions of guerrilla or *bandito* activity, during elections, and preceding Christmas.

Immigration

Thirty to 90 days is standard policy. Choose the maximum stay allowed even if you're thinking of staying three days. Love affairs or time-consuming repairs happen unexpectedly. (Our van spent 23 days in Arequipa, Peru being fitted with handmade pistons.) There is no penalty for leaving a country before your immigration permit expires. Extensions are time-consuming, especially when a vehicle is involved. *Never accept an in-transit visa* because they cannot be changed or extended.

Insularity

Motorists have been criticized for traveling in armored bubbles, insulated from the land and people through which they pass. We feared insularity before we left home, so we decided to drive no more than four hours in a day.

We virtually lived outdoors. Without air conditioning or heat our windows were always wide open and our sleeping quarters, a roof-mounted bed surrounded by screening and porous canvas, made us vulnerable to every fickle change of weather. We got lost and had to repeatedly ask directions and inquire about daily supplies. Our kitchen was the envy of everyone; decorated in sunset hues with 360° views of lakes, beaches or valleys.

Rarely were we alone. We gave rides to walkers in remote areas (women with bundles and children were a favorite). Once we hauled 19 grinning people!

Latins are avid travelers and campers. We met many with whom we shared maps, trip notes and occasionally caravanned. They taught us languages, folk medicine, lore, dances, introduced new foods and recipes, and showed us obscure places. Small-town folk invited us into their homes, to family parties and festivals, to fish or hike.

Being in a vehicle and camping did insulate us from other foreigners, however. We didn't stay in hotels or travel bus routes from city to city; popular, inner-city, gringo hangouts weren't convenient to our campsites. We drove to places that other people reached by paying tour companies.

The vibrancy of the people and land is why we go to South America and it is in abundant supply. At times, we sought seclusion.

SPORTS

Brazilians say that their government could get away with any travesty except taking away their *futebol*. In Latin America, all sports and games are an intricate part of daily life. Stadiums and recreational complexes have become the modern day version of community plazas. Tennis, basketball, volleyball, soccer, swimming and racing of all kinds are popular activities for participants and fans alike. Everywhere are co-ed gyms that specialize in weight-lifting, aerobics, and karate.

Hang gliding, mountain climbing, skiing, surfing, bicycle safaris, horseback riding and scuba diving are examples of sports for which special gear can be rented.

PHOTOGRAPHY

Get your cameras ready. Picturesque is synonymous with Latin America. It is nearly impossible to take a bad picture. The landscape is dramatic and people expect to have their photos snapped. The most hardened *gaucho* will pose.

Courtesy dictates that you first ask permission. Sensitivity should be exercised with indigenous people, particularly highlanders, who may object to photography for reasons of their own.

Camera equipment and film are expensive in Latin America. A roll of 35mm slide film, with 36 exposures, averages US$11-15. Take a variety of lenses. An ultra-violet filter is a must in high altitudes and on water, without one you'll lose color saturation.

Unshot film preserves well in an ice box. We kept ours in a sealed pouch, elevated over ice. Spent film cannot be stored on ice. Use a sealed pouch with silicate gel bags and stow it where it will be least affected by heat, climatic changes, dust and moisture. Protected, film can survive up to three months.

Photo developing labs still aren't up to par. We tried several with disappointing results. The coloration was never quite right. Professional film, such as Kodachrome, is undevelopable or limited to very few processing labs. Use pre-paid processing envelopes and send film home with a friend. Mailing can be chancy and expensive.

Check your camera by shooting a roll of print film and take it to a one-hour developing lab. Newly found local friends are excellent subjects and they'll appreciate a copy of their smiling faces.

Video is all the rage in Latin America. The technology is so familiar to people that they'll be dismayed if you don't have it. Truly, video is the perfect media for capturing a sense of "being there". There are no problems crossing borders with non-professional equipment. Any format video tape is available. Be careful when recharging batteries and in using external power sources or you might burn the circuitry. Use a remote microphone to clarify interviews and on the spot narration; background noise will ruin an otherwise good segment.

Finally, consider outfitting your vehicle as a photo developing studio or video/editing suite. Professionals have done this with good results. French nature photographers, Daniel and Cesily Le Bouringueur, converted their 20-foot sailboat into a dark room. We wired a mini-video editing suite in our VW van when documenting archaeological research in Central America. Gary and Monika Wescott of The Turtle Expedition and *Four Wheeler* magazine are professional photographers who did the same in their 4X4 pick-up truck.

THE SOUTH AMERICAN EXPLORERS CLUB

This is a non-profit organization for anyone interested in South America. First and foremost, the club is a center for members to exchange specialized information on trip planning, scientific expeditions, and more mundane matters like finding a good hotel, travel and seasonal conditions, currency exchange and so on. The club also sells a good selection of books and maps. Members receive a club catalog and discounts on purchases.

The SAEC is entirely member supported. The tax-deductible membership fee is currently (1995) US$40 per year (US$60 per couple) and includes a subscription to the quarterly magazine, the *South American Explorer*. Club members can request trip reports filed by other members, for no fee.

Volunteers staff busy clubhouses located in Lima, Peru and Quito,

CYCLING

When I started my trip in Mexico City, I had absolutely no idea what to expect. I had good equipment and felt like traveling on a bicycle and that's all that's needed for a very special trip.

For me cycling is the best way to travel: you are flexible in every way, you can go wherever you want and if you get sick of it you just continue by bus, truck or boat. Upon reaching a mountain pass, I often had to stop just to look backwards from where I came and forward to the valley I was approaching. It is an indescribable feeling, one I missed when using public transportation. Go one kilometer by bike and you'll see more than going hundreds of kilometers by bus.

Many travelers think cycling is too exhausting and you can't get around all Latin America within one year. They are wrong. It depends on you — just stop for a while if you become tired. All the Alaska-Tierra del Fuego travelers with fixed timetables are really strange people...quantity is not quality.

You'll eat twice or triple your usual amount, but don't worry, you won't get fat! You'll merely change proportions. Quite a few times I'd break for a 'between meal snack': fifteen *platanitos*, several apples, some *guanabas* and so on.

Avoid the gringo routes, the Pan-American and other highways where buses and trucks love to scrape you with their side mirrors. The most beautiful scenery is in the mountains. It's exhausting and takes a lot of time, but is definitely worth it.

Finding maps is the biggest problem. The best topographical maps are the *Instituto Geográfico Militar* (IGM), but you must go to the capital city to get one. I used sun readings, a compass and asked people how to find the road to wherever I wanted to go. (Spanish is absolutely necessary!) You meet many people that way and it's a fantastic way to travel as long as you have *water* and food supplies.

My advice for cyclists is you must feel like traveling. Don't plan too much. Just go as you feel like, have fun and no stress, stay as long as you like and move on when you feel like it. Always expect the unexpected. Improvise, learn to manage problems, and most important...survive.

José Breitsameter, Gerolsbach, Germany

Ecuador (*see country chapters*) where members may store equipment, receive or forward mail, access the libraries, meet other travelers, and much more. You can join at any of the clubhouses but to reap all benefits, sign up in advance, even if you are planning a short trip. Contact headquarters in the US; 126 Indian Creek Rd, Ithaca, New York, 14850; tel: 607 277 0488, or Bradt Publications in England (tel: 01494 873478) — an administrative fee is charged.

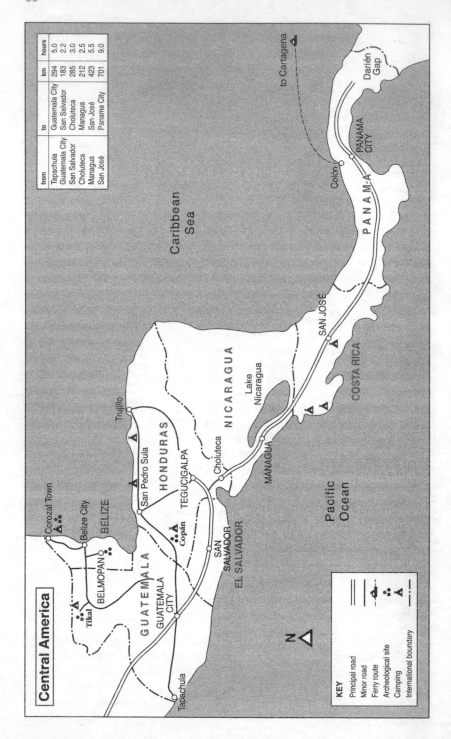

Central America

from	to	km	hours
Tapachula	Guatemala City	294	5.0
Guatemala City	San Salvador	183	2.2
San Salvador	Choluteca	285	3.0
Choluteca	Managua	212	2.5
Managua	San José	423	5.5
San José	Panama City	701	9.0

Caribbean Sea

Pacific Ocean

to Cartagena

Darién Gap

PANAMA

PANAMA CITY

Colón

COSTA RICA

SAN JOSÉ

NICARAGUA

Lake Nicaragua

MANAGUA

Choluteca

HONDURAS

TEGUCIGALPA

Trujillo

San Pedro Sula

Copán

SAN SALVADOR

EL SALVADOR

GUATEMALA

GUATEMALA CITY

BELMOPAN

BELIZE

Belize City

Corozal Town

Tikal

Tapachula

N

KEY

Principal road
Minor route
Ferry route
Archeological site
Camping
International boundary

Chapter Six

Central America

Strictly speaking most of Mexico is part of the North American continent, and seven other distinctly different countries compose the region called Mesoamerica: Guatemala, Belize, El Salvador, Honduras, Nicaragua, Costa Rica and Panama. Each country merits exploration for their cultures, art, histories, geography, ecological preserves, political and economic systems are every bit as diverse and rich as in South America.

Travel is now safe and relatively easy, both within countries and between them. Border procedures are being standardized, thereby reducing the quirks of passage. A ferry links Central America to South America, eliminating the last barrier for north and south travelers.

REGION HIGHLIGHTS

Mexico
The archaeological sites are outstanding. Visit Aztec ruins in and around Mexico City; early Olmec at Monte Alban and Villahermosa on the eastern side; beautiful Palenque in Chiapas, and in the Yucatan it's impossible not to stumble across splendid Maya sites.

Guatemala
The jungle-covered Maya site of Tikal is tops on everyone's list; followed by the lovely crater, Lake Atitlán, surrounded by volcanoes.

Belize
Excellent snorkeling and diving near offshore islands, wildlife reserves and archeological sites make Belize diverse and enjoyable.

El Salvador
Volcanoes and beautiful Pacific beaches highlight this now fairly tranquil country.

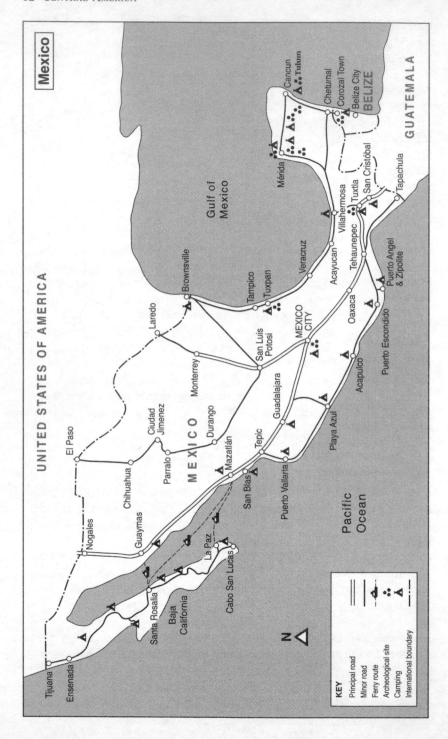

Mexico

UNITED STATES OF AMERICA

Gulf of Mexico

Pacific Ocean

M E X I C O

GUATEMALA

BELIZE

Tijuana
Ensenada
Nogales
Guaymas
El Paso
Chihuahua
Parralo
Ciudad Jimenez
Durango
Santa Rosalia
Baja California
La Paz
Cabo San Lucas
San Blas
Mazatlán
Puerto Vallarta
Tepic
Guadalajara
Playa Azul
Acapulco
Laredo
Brownsville
Monterrey
San Luis Potosi
MEXICO CITY
Oaxaca
Puerto Escondido
Puerto Angel & Zipolite
Tampico
Tuxpan
Veracruz
Acayucan
Tehaunepec
Villahermosa
Tuxtla
San Cristóbal
Tapachula
Mérida
Cancun
Tulum
Chetumal
Corozal Town
Belize City

N

KEY
Principal road
Minor road
Ferry route
Archeological site
Camping
International boundary

Honduras

The peaceful Bay Islands provide aquatic treats and a laid-back Caribbean style of life.

Nicaragua

A visit to the island of Olmetepec in Lago Nicaragua provides a refreshing contrast to the dry, volcano-studded beauty of this interesting country.

Costa Rica

Renowned for its commitment to conservation, more than 12% of the country has been set aside as national parks. Wildlife is abundant throughout peaceful Costa Rica.

Panama

You won't be able to miss the Canal, so don't overlook it. South of the Canal, the Cuna Indians maintain a traditional lifestyle amid rain forest reserves.

POINTS OF ENTRY

By air

The cheapest flights into Central America are consistently from Miami, Florida to Mexico. Typical 1995 single fares to Merida, or Cancun in the Yucatan were US$195, high season, and US$280 to Mexico City.

By land

The only land entry points are between the US and Mexico. The most used borders, from east to west, are Brownsville/Matamoros in the east; Laredo/Nuevo Laredo, Eagle Pass/Piedras Negras and El Paso/Ciudad Juárez in the center; Tucson/Nogales or San Ysidro, California and Tijuana in the west.

The most direct north-south trajectory through Mexico is along the eastern lateral. On the Pacific side is the Baja California peninsula which, together with the mainland, is the longer of the two coastlines. Mountains form the undulating spine of the country.

By sea

Refer to the section on Panama (*this chapter*) for ferry information, and for details of the Darién Gap.

MEXICO

Border formalities

You must, as elsewhere, show a driver's license, license plate and registration, and ownership title. Proof of Mexican insurance is mandatory. Only *one vehicle per person* is permitted entry. Your vehicle is stamped on your tourist card along with receiving a temporary importation permit. Before leaving the border post, make sure that the vehicle permit is for 90 days, as is your tourist card.

Import permits are not required for the Baja, but they are for the mainland. If you enter at Tijuana, obtain the permit at the border if you intend to continue to the mainland. Customs might have you complete a form claiming any expensive accessories. You'll be expected to show it when you leave. Don't sweat over it.

Mexico also requires that you post a 5% bond, based on the Blue Book value of the vehicle. (The Blue Book is a guide to standard retail prices for every model vehicle.) Or you can make a credit card charge for US$11. Make sure that you cancel the charge when you leave.

Mexican insurance

Liability insurance is mandatory and sold all along the border. Coverage for our 1976 VW cost about US$3 a day. We've used several different companies, but the best is Sanborn's, who also produce customized trip guides. The *Travelog* is a superb guide with detailed descriptions of road conditions, interesting sights, and campgrounds. Their main headquarters are: Sanborn's, PO Box 1210, McAllen, Texas 78503; tel: (210) 686 0711.

Recreational vehicles

In recent years, some Mexican border officials have been telling RVers they must drive in a guided convoy through Mexico. This is simply not true. Do not pay US$2,000, or any amount of money, to anyone designated as a "guide" who collects the money then disappears.

On the road

Well-maintained *autopistas* allow fast travel, but primary and secondary roads more closely hug the contours of the terrain. Speed bumps, *topes*, herald every town, both coming and going, and make a washboard out of urban roads.

Be careful during rainy months (June through October), when flash floods inundate roads and sweep away concrete bridges.

Road shoulders are rare and cyclists aren't treated with much respect. Nevertheless, locals commute by bike. Look for parallel bike paths.

Avoid, or caravan by day, the beautiful, but treacherous road Ruta 37, along isolated mountains and sheer cliffs through Michoacán. The 187km between Manzanillo and Puerto Azul is armed *bandito* territory and the most dangerous stretch in all the Americas. Don't stop for road blocks; hit your accelerator pedal, duck and pray.

Traffic is really bad between Mexico City, Mazatlán and Guadalajara. Trucks, commuters, weekenders, business people and toll booths niggle for space along narrow mountainous roads.

The most peaceful roads wend through the eastern side. They can also be boring due to the flatness. The most scenic routes are through the mountains.

Driving style
Trucks set the pace. Truck drivers signal with their left blinker, when they think it's safe for you to pass. Likewise, the right turn signal means to stay put, on-coming traffic. Pass only when you can see the road ahead. Flashing headlights signal on-coming traffic, a loose wire or, more likely, danger on the road ahead of you. Stay alert to your right because drivers also pass on that side.

Fuel
Mexican gas stations, *gasolineras*, are the worst for ripping off foreigners at the gas pump. Few pumps are properly calibrated so it helps to know your fuel capacity in liters (and in gallons). In Mexico watch that the pump is reset to zero, that fuel is not spilled after your tank is filled, and carry small bills to pay the attendant who rarely has change. Use your own calculator. Make sure the gas cap, *el tapón*, is replaced and secure. Check your own oil and watch out for the kids with dirty rags claiming to wash your windshield.

Supplies of unleaded gas, *sin plomo*, are erratic and often dirty. Motorists suggest filtering it through cheesecloth! Propane gas is reportedly difficult to get, owing to restrictions placed on refilling tanks and bottles. Fill up in the US.

Tolls and truck routes
Mexican toll roads, *cuotas*, are more expensive and occur more frequently than in any other country. Non-citizens are charged incredible rates, for example, in 1994 RVers paid US$60 for one 20km stretch between Mexico City and the Pacific coast. To avoid tolls, follow the truck traffic. You'll sometimes go through mesquite and sand, but you'll have detoured around the toll booth.

Seasons

Mexico and much of Central America have similar weather patterns and seasons to those in the southern US. Weather-wise, Central America is delightful between January and April. In general, the rainy season falls between June and late September and the coolest, driest months are between November and April.

Cyclists

Wind patterns depend on which side of the central mountain range you cruise. On the north-northwest side of the divide, 40kph winds from the north predominate. From the south, southeast direction, you'll get wind from the southwest.

USEFUL INFORMATION

Public holidays

Jan 1 (Happy New Year)
Feb 5 (Constitution Day)
Mar 21 (Birthday of Benito Juárez)
Holy Week *Semana Santa*
May 1 (Labor Day)
May 5 (Battle of Puebla)
Sep 1 (Presidential address to the nation)
Sep 16 (Independence Day)
Oct 12 (Discovery of America; hard feelings surround this commemoration)
Oct 31 (All Souls Day)
Nov 20 (Day of the Revolution)
Dec 25 (Merry Christmas)

Camping

Wild free camping is hard to find outside the Baja and Yucatan peninsula, but elsewhere there are campgrounds. Places come and go, but you can find a designated area, with infrastructure, every 100km.

Country highlights

The Baja California

The long and narrow peninsula (1,698km by Highway 1) on the western fringe of Mexico is dramatic desert nearly surrounded by water: the Pacific to the west and the Sea of Cortez to the east. A range of mountains bisects its length which is crossed seven times by Highway 1. The Baja is very dry and torrid most of the year. Watch out for unpredictable violent storms, *chubascos*, between July and October.

Fishing is easy and you'll have no problem keeping fresh fish and crabs in your cooking pot. Kayaking in the Sea of Cortez is very popular, where uninhabited islands swell from the sea like hump-backed whales. No-one can resist the stunning variety of cactus and wildlife (giant-eared jack rabbits, kangaroo rats, whales and seals).

Scammon's Lagoon Rare whale birthing sights come between January and February. Get supplies in Guerrero Negro and head across the salt flats for camping at Parque Natural de Ballena Gris. Whale-watching boats are cheaper from here, US$10 per person, than from Guerrero Negro. Float among the gentle grey whales and wait for their inquisitive approach.

La Paz This is a condo-stacked, expensive resort city at the tip of the peninsula. The ferry to the mainland is more expensive than at Santa Rosalia, midway down the peninsula.

Santa Rosalia The ferry office is at the waterfront terminal, *Grupo Sematur de California*. To Guaymas on the mainland, a seven-hour crossing will cost US$306 for car and US$30 per person. You'll have to show your immigration card and vehicle permit before leaving the Baja.

Pacific mainland The west coast is not a bargain for long-distance travelers. Resorts like Mazatlán and Acapulco, and agri-business dominate the landscape. Development recedes south of the surfing town of Puerto Escondido.

Guaymas Upon arrival by ferry from the Baja, the smokestack city and anonymously busy streets evoke culture shock.

Navojoa South of Guaymas, we found a noisy and strangely off-beat campground alongside the plush Motel del Rio.

Puerto Escondido This is a user-friendly beachside resort where surfing and fishing have influenced its development more than big investors. There is a good campground on the beach.

Zipolite An hour's drive south of Escondido is the only nude beach in Central America besides Tulum, in the Yucatan. Meditation centers are built along the coastal hills and open-air restaurants double as hotels for those with hammocks.

Chiapas State

San Cristóbal is a crossover juncture for those going south to Guatemala and east-west travelers. To the west is Palenque, a premier Maya archaeological site. Since 1993, mountainous Chiapas has been the center of rebellion by indigenous groups. It is generally safe for travelers who don't get intimately involved in politics and local vendettas/land issues. It is also one of the most beautiful areas of Mexico.

The east coast

Less expensive, less developed, shorter and more direct for south-bound travelers, the arid Yucatan hosts the greatest number of Maya archaeological sites, including famous Uxmal, Chichen-Itzá, Cobá and Tulum. The diversity of people, architecture and ecology span centuries. Maya temples tower over jungle canopies and ritzy hotels in Cancun overlook clear ocean — perfect for snorkeling. In colonial Mérida, Yucatan's quaint capital, contemporary Mayan people walk the cobble streets in traditional, embroidered clothing. Not to be overlooked are the gulf coast beaches with small unspoiled towns and wildlife reserves.

Camping opportunities are excellent. You'll find organized campgrounds with full facilities, hotels, or park rangers at archeological sites often permit camping in the parking lot. On beaches south of Tulum there are many campgrounds.

BELIZE

English-speaking Belize wears the latest crown for eco-tourism in the Americas and the culture is more Caribbean than Latin. It is one of the least populated countries in the hemisphere in spite of an open-door invitation to refugee immigrants from other Central American countries.

Wildlife abounds inside and outside reserves; important archeological sites, such as Altun Ha and Caracol, and marine reserves along the world's second longest barrier reef, contribute to the diversity of this small nation.

Only two major roads cross Belize: one runs north-south from Corozal to Punta Gorda where a ferry occasionally crosses the river to Livingston, Guatemala, and another road extends west from coastal Belize City to San Ignacio and the Guatemalan border, east of Tikal and Flores, Guatemala.

Country highlights

Belize Zoo West of Belize City, this is one of the best zoological parks in the Americas. It's very educational for identifying wildlife habitats.
Caracol Glyphs found in this remote Maya archaeological site record the conquering of Tikal — it could be one of the most extensive sites in Central America.
Offshore islands Leave your vehicle on the mainland (although a bike is handy on the small islands) and head out to one of the cays (pronounced "kees") by boat or air from Belize City. Tourism has nearly spoiled Ambergris Caye and smaller San Pedro but they are still wonderful locations from which to snorkel or dive the coral reef.

GUATEMALA

Our favorite country in Central America continues to heave along a rollercoaster road of human rights abuse and progress. Exercise extreme sensitivity to the indigenous population and avoid flagrant political alignment and you'll love the country and the people.

There are numerous ways in and out of Guatemala and all are scenic adventures. From Chiapas, you can ascend to the highest mountain pass in Central America via the old Pan-Am or choose the newer lowland route along the Pacific. All border formalities are very straightforward.

From the Mexican Yucatan to the northeastern sector of Guatemala, bad roads and river crossings penetrate thick jungle north and west of Tikal. Large vehicles are advised to use the road through Belize to Flores. The road from Flores to Guatemala City is subject to flooding during rainy season.

Country highlights

Tikal In the northeastern quadrant, an ancient Maya city or dwelling lies buried under nearly every mound. The greatest and best known of the cities is Tikal. Excellent anytime, the full moon will create an unforgettable experience for campers. Nearby Flores, a charming island-town surrounded by lake, is the perfect base for day trips.

Lake Atitlán Aldous Huxley called this volcano-rimmed, crater lake the most beautiful in the world. The Indian villages which surround it are particularly colorful but extremely difficult to reach by road. 4WD with high clearance is needed for the many narrow, steep descents.

Panajachel This small, but amenable town has developed into a gringo city and thievery is increasing. Still, it is not to be missed. Camping is possible but dangerous along Lake Atitlán, west of town, unless in a group. Otherwise stay in one of the many hotels.

Near by is the famous Indian market town, **Chichicastenago** where statues of saints and conquistadors ride platforms borne on devotees' shoulders. The *copál* incense carries prayers to the deities.

Antigua Destroyed several times by earthquakes and volcanic eruptions, this colonial town keeps rebuilding. Excellent Spanish language schools are located here.

EL SALVADOR

During the 1980s, lovely El Salvador became an unlucky victim of the Nicaraguan war, its own civil war and a devastating earthquake. The western coast was once the premier resort of Central America, yet today it is hard to find the remnants. Recovery has been painful and costly to the nation and the people. You'll see the toll reflected in high market prices. But here live incredibly friendly people.

The loveliest areas are still north, near the Guatemalan border. Cerro Verde and Lago de Coatepeque, like the nation they represent, aren't completely safe for camping, so check locally for recommended campsites or stay in hotels. The rolling green *cordillera*, the central highlands surrounding San Salvador, the capital, is dotted with placid agricultural villages.

El Salvador is making innovative progress in resolving internal problems and in dismantling the militaristic cadres. Very soon it will once again emerge from being a country between Guatemala and Honduras, to become a traveler's destination.

HONDURAS

Honduras is undergoing an economic crisis which, fortunately for travelers, makes it the best bargain in Central America. There is a lot to see and discover in this bountiful country. If you enter in the south, from El Salvador, you must go north to appreciate the unexpected beauty of this mountainous country. Stop at Lake Yojaba between San Pedro Sula and Tegucigalpa for sweet, fried bass and cool lake breezes. For a change in flavor, go to the Caribbean coast where you'll find Black Carib (Garifuna) villages.

Border formalities
Vehicles will be sprayed with insecticide for which you'll pay a small fee. No major problems reported but the easiest border to cross is west of Copán, adjacent to Guatemala. A narrow dirt road on both sides also makes it treacherous.

Country highlights
Bay islands Fly from La Ceiba to any of these offshore islands for access to an aquatic wonderland (go to Utila for cheap PADI certification).
Copán This beautiful Maya city is located in the northwest corner near the Guatemalan border. After a hiatus, intense archaeological excavation has resumed. Four entire cities lie beneath the surface pyramids! The small town is a marvelous out-of-the-way hang out. We camped at *Los Gauchos* restaurant whose owners adopted our Baja cat, Emilio.
The Mosquitia coast The Atlantic is isolated by mangrove swamps and remains largely untouched by the outside world. Only one causeway penetrates the low land and it is subject to flooding.

NICARAGUA

Volcano-studded beauty and nice people enticed José to nominate Nicaragua as his favorite country. It is an interesting country to get around because place names and streets have been renamed with each political regime, so locals refer to landmarks to avoid confusion among themselves. Economic recovery is slow, hampered by continuing political schisms and strikes, but the people are earnest and optimistic about their future. We've visited western Nicaragua at different times of the year and it was always hot and dry (the official dry season is from November through April). Towns in the northeast are separated by vast distances so carry a supply of water and food with you.

Border formalities

Border crossings are more chaotic than in any other country. Although fees are posted, you must collect vehicle permits in a seemingly random order, and functionaries won't give you a clue. A licensed border guide is absolutely necessary, US$2-5 tip. Additionally, a separate driving permit is required, the cost for which depends on your stay. Cheapest is US$20 for 72 hours! No money exchange at the borders.

Country highlights

Lago Nicaragua Once upon a time, this vast lake opened to the ocean which is why today landlocked sharks still patrol the water. A visit to the island of Olmetepec is a refreshing excursion from the dry, hot land.

COSTA RICA

Everything you've ever heard about Costa Rica is true. Volcanoes spew smoke, the eastern jungles are true jungles, clouds constantly envelop the biospheric cloud forests; wildlife preserves brim over with orchids, birds, monkeys, sloths, tapirs, parrots, frogs, fish and snakes (indeed, the entire country is a quasi-preserve); the surf is always up, and the *Ticos* are the friendliest, most peaceful people anywhere. There are no qualifying "buts" nor exceptions to tag onto Costa Rica's deservedly excellent reputation. Good maps and guides, bike and motor repair shops, high-brow cultural events and free public activities can be found in the clement mountain capital, San José.

Border formalities

Border posts operate like friendly welcome stations.

Country highlights

Monteverde Cloud Forest   Quakers moved here in the 1950s, established cheese factories and fostered a climate conducive to environmental preservation and research. Graduate students from all over the world give nightly presentations on the flora and fauna. With luck, you'll glimpse the rare and iridescent quetzal (national bird of Guatemala). The road is rough at anytime of year but passable with patience.

The entire Pacific coastline   It's impossible to nominate places because each cove is more beautiful than the previous one. Mountains slope to meet the surf, creating visual odysseys. International developers have also discovered the natural beauty and are snatching up prime land, rapidly converting small towns into tourist villas. The lovely beaches are state-owned and protected.

PANAMA

Panamanians describe their melting pot of cultures and races as a stew, *sancocho*. Look into faces and you'll see reflected a long and diverse ethnic history.

North of the canal zone life is placid and agricultural. To the south, jungle encroaches on towns, and the road. South of Yaviza, lianas and swamp strangle further passage by vehicle.

Border formalities

Standard and orderly. Once in the country, convert to dollars without paying a commission.

Country highlights

The Panama Canal   Even though the supertankers can't fit through the "antiquated" 50-mile-long canal, it is still an engineering marvel. Three locks control the depth of water. In the center lock, ships can be elevated as high as 85 feet! Passing boats are required to have line handlers and the number of handlers depends on its size. Yachters are always looking for experienced boaters to fulfill these functions. It is a great way to see the canal.

Panama City   To the west, the Bridge of the Americas spans the canal into Balboa. The Panama/Colombian ferry and all other ships leave from Colón, at the east side of the canal. Due to an increase in crime, Panama City and environs are unsafe. We camped at the yacht clubs at each end of the canal.

Darién Gap   The San Blas Indians live about 100km south of the canal, where the road peters out. Cyclists (in groups) will find detailed information on the route across the Gap in *Backpacking in Central America* (*see Further Reading, page 236*).

A road through the Darién was approved in November 1993 to the howls of protesting environmentalists. An international consortium of shippers then decided to back the ferry which, in turn, preserves the fragile cultures and eco-system of the isthmus.

The ferry

The *Crucero Express* departs Colón to Cartagena, Colombia on Monday, Wednesdays and Fridays at 4.30pm. Overnight fares are US$98 per person for a basic double cabin; motorcycles US$50, Car US$125, RV longer than six meters US$200. Optional excursions through the San Blas islands are available. In Panama City contact the shipping company at Torre Banco Unión, 4th Floor, Zona 7; tel: 633 322 or fax: 633 326. In Colón, Puerto de Cristóbal, Muelle (dock) No 6; tel: 416 311; fax: 411 862.

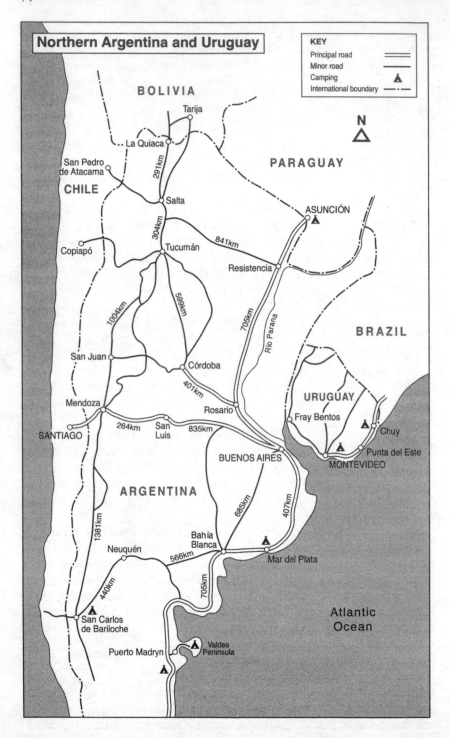

Northern Argentina and Uruguay

KEY
Principal road
Minor road
Camping
International boundary

N

BOLIVIA

Tarija

La Quiaca

San Pedro de Atacama

CHILE

291km

Salta

PARAGUAY

ASUNCIÓN

304km

Copiapó

Tucumán

841km

Resistencia

705km

Río Paraná

BRAZIL

599km

1004km

San Juan

Córdoba

401km

URUGUAY

Mendoza

Rosario

Fray Bentos

Chuy

SANTIAGO

264km

San Luis

835km

Punta del Este

MONTEVIDEO

BUENOS AIRES

ARGENTINA

685km

407km

1381km

Bahía Blanca

Neuquén

566km

Mar del Plata

705km

440km

San Carlos de Bariloche

Atlantic Ocean

Puerto Madryn

Valdes Peninsula

Chapter Seven

Argentina

Argentina stands out in the world book of records for its exaggerated features. Mt Aconcagua at 6,960m is the highest mountain in the Americas. One of the world's lowest points is the Valdés Peninsula at 40m below sea level. Argentina claims the world's most powerful waterfall at Iguazu, shared with Brazil. Just a few years ago, an annual inflation rate of 6,000% earned Argentina a mention in the financial annals of world records. Contemporary travelers cite it as the most expensive country in the Americas.

The extremes of nature have been repeated in Argentina's chequered history. To speak of eco-tourism and not mention, and remember, "the disappeared" people would be remiss. Travelers will be reminded of the difficult years.

Argentina is beautiful and diverse. In the northern third of the country polo farms, agri-industrial towns and European-style cosmopolitan cities flourish. The central sector fluctuates seasonally between coastal resort towns and snowy highlands. Toward the south, in Patagonia and Tierra del Fuego, lies the province of the hardy and determined.

Argentines describe themselves as superficially reserved, aspiring Europeans, but warm and cuddly (friends for life) once "we decide to accept a person". Despite that disclaimer, we encountered welcoming, open-armed greetings, genial people and hardy vivaciousness.

Did we mention that Argentina produces succulent beef steaks and lamb chops? These animals are range grazers and not artificially fattened in confined stalls.

COUNTRY HIGHLIGHTS

Valdés Peninsula
A low point in *tierra firma*, plays ecological hostess to whales, penguins, sea lions, sea elephants, *guanaco*, rheas, foxes, and wildlife voyeurs.

Tierra del Fuego
Also known as both 'the end of the world' and 'the end of the road', Tierra del Fuego is the most southerly land mass with proximity to Antarctica.

Winter skiing
Aficionados of the sport will find few places comparable to the superb slopes of Bariloche (July through October is the season).

Perito Moreno
This is one of the few glaciers in the world that is actually growing; it ranks high among sights for frigid beauty.

Patagonia
The barren and windswept plains of Patagonia attest to the indomitable spirit of life, but Patagonia extends to the mighty Andes and some beautiful national parks.

Iguazú Falls
The most powerful and spectacular water show on earth.

Posadas
Jesuits missions in the 17th century were built in northern Argentina and Paraguay to defend the *Guaraní* Indians, through education, from decimation by greedy land grabbers.

POINTS OF ENTRY

There are so many points of entry that Argentina might as well have open borders. The most commonly used ones follow.

From Uruguay
Toll bridges span the Río Para at several points. There is heavy use at the Friendship Bridge between Frey Bentos and Gualeguaychu.

From Brazil
Entry via Foz do Iguaçu is certainly an impressive introduction to Argentina. The border is open to limited travel within the three frontier region of the falls. If going into the interior, it is absolutely necessary to stop for paperwork formalities.

From Paraguay
Between Encarnación, Paraguay and Posadas, Argentina takes you through the lovely Misiones region that straddles these two countries.

From Bolivia

The Bolivian road to Villazón is receiving a new asphalted face which will eventually make this a more attractive crossing point. La Quiaca is Argentina's border post here.

From Chile

Let me count the ways — twenty? Quite a few require ferry connections. The most traveled land routes are the following.

Completely paved and heavily used is the road from Los Andes (88km north of Santiago) to Mendoza, Argentina another 272km which takes you over a 4,200m mountain pass. Bicyclists note: bikes are not permitted through the tunnel. Hitch a ride on a passing truck.

Crossing from the Lake District, a paved road goes from Osorno, Chile, to Angostura. There is 32km of unpaved road between border posts: the Portezuelo de Puyehue at 1,308m. This has been the traditional pass for land travelers going north and south from southern Chile. Bariloche is 95km south by paved road which bisects Nahuel Haupi National Park.

In the far south, a small trail connects Torres del Paine National Park in Chile and El Calafate, Argentina. Buses and main traffic cross a rough dirt track between Rio Turbio, Chile to Rio Gallegos via La Esperanza. This is the most beautiful crossing.

Tierra del Fuego entails several straightforward border crossings which are discussed in that section (*see page 84*).

Warning: Chile prohibits the entry of any kind of fresh food (meat, vegetables, fruit, etc). Agricultural inspectors will confiscate your valuable supplies.

Border formalities

Travelers requiring visas should obtain multiple entry. They are necessary for Tierra del Fuego which is subdivided at several points with Chile.

ON THE ROAD

As you venture further south into Patagonia and Tierra del Fuego, or west into the Andes, dirt and rock roads, *ripio*, are common. Rocks, spun up by passing vehicles can be lethal to windshields. Wire windshield protectors might help, if you can find one or materials to build a screen. We couldn't.

The *ripio* also tore up our tires. We barely made it between repair shops where we would search through the pile of discards to find something useable. The end result was five different tires, a mix of tubed and tubeless lined with tubes, and five different sizes.

Driving style

Traffic patterns are orderly, signals are obeyed and roads marked. Cyclists do not have to dodge heavy truck traffic except in the vicinity of Buenos Aires.

Fuel

Fuel prices and supply drop dramatically the further south you go. Likewise, prices escalate and supplies increase as you travel north. The dividing line is the northern perimeter of Patagonia.

Carry extra fuel and motor oil in the south. Even on the main coastal road, gas stations were often out of fuel. Oil, when available, costs US$8 a quart and there is nothing but 40W.

Cyclists

Has anyone invented a wire basket that surrounds a bicyclist? Beware and wear protective clothing. Carry spare tires and a repair kit. Wind is vicious much of the year, peaking at 150kph in December. Travel counterclockwise through southern Chile, Tierra del Fuego and Patagonia to keep the wind to your back. The terrain is rather flat except in the Andes, of course.

Argentines are avid fans of bicycle races and motocross competition. This good news means more sophisticated bikes are being imported along with parts and repair know-how. In small towns you'll now see posters or information tables about local bike clubs and their events.

Maps

The *Automovil Club Argentino* (ACA) publishes an excellent road map. They're available from any ACA office or facility. Also, tourist information offices distribute regional and local maps free or for a nominal charge. Some are quite adequate. The tourist offices (and border personnel) get an excellent rating from us for high quality travel and road information.

USEFUL INFORMATION

Public holidays

January 1 (New Year)
Holy Thursday and Good Friday
May 1 (Labor Day)
May 25 (National Anniversary of Cabildo Abierto)
June 20 (Flag Day)
July 9 (Independence Day)
August 17 (Anniversary of San Martín's death)

October 12 (Columbus Day)
November 10 (Dia de la Tradición)
December 25 (Christmas)
December 31 (Nochebuena)

When to visit

Summer months (late December through early April) are the most clement. Everything is open but thronged with vacationing Argentines and surrounding neighbors. The northern pampas sizzles with debilitating heat. Expect snow from winter to early spring and to find many places closed and inhabitants snuggled indoors. September through November is a good time to view nesting sealife in the south.

Camping

Organized campgrounds are open and crowded between mid-December and March. Many campgrounds and some hotels close in the south the rest of the year, when few people travel. Sites for free camping are difficult to find in the populated northeast. Police twice came knocking in the middle of the night to check our documents although we had permission from landowners to camp. Wind in Patagonia buffets sturdy camping vehicles and undoes the best pegged tent; it's like camping in a hurricane.

Reports of armed robberies come from metropolitan Buenos Aires so use precaution as in any other major city. The rest of Argentina is fairly safe.

Money and banks

Inflation was curbed to 4% in 1994. There is little fluctuation in the exchange rate. In 1995 the Argentina peso traded one for one with the US dollar. Banking hours are from 10am until 4pm.

Business hours

The usual siesta break is observed between 1pm and 3pm.

THE NORTHERN PAMPAS

A third of Argentina is pampas: flat, monotonous, agricultural, thickly populated, expansive polo ranches. The tedium is broken by the Misiones region, sprawling Buenos Aires and up-scale Mar de Plata.

Misiones

Located north of the geographically defined pampas is the Misiones region. It begins at Posadas on the Paraguay border and extends east and north to Iguazu falls. Natural waterfalls and ruins left by the Franscians friars are scattered among hills and pleasant scenery. Pick up a map to the sites at any tourism office.

For information on Iguazu and vicinity, see *Chapter 9, Brazil*.

Useful addresses
Paraguay consulate San Lorenzo 179.
Tourist office Colón 1985, Posadas.

Buenos Aires
We heard about the US$5 cup of coffee and US$30 parking lots and nearly 11 million people and so decided to avoid this famous capital city. Residents said it was a shameful omission, that we had missed the most graceful capital in Latin America. We were informed that Argentines, above all, exhibit discriminating good taste. The parks, cinemas, restaurants, museums and cultural life are all on display, and the metro system *Subte* has been called a top-notch bargain. Helpful information kiosks are said to be found throughout the greater metropolitan area. Other travelers were most enthusiastic about the city and, to help you get the best out of it, were able to provide the following recommendations.

Highly recommended for steaks is *La Estancia* at La Valle 941. French restaurants on Carlos Calva. Handicrafts stores with fixed prices on Av Defensa between 372 and 788.

Places to stay
Hotel Phoenix San Martin 780.
Hotel Rana Av de Mayo 1120.
Majestic Libertad y Bartolomé, US$20 double.

Useful addresses
American Express City Service Travel, Florida 890, 4th floor; and at Arenales 707 y Paipú, near Plaza San Martín.
Automovil Club Argentino Av del Libertador 1850.
Brazilian Consulate Pellegrini 1362, 5th floor; open weekdays 10am-6pm.
Chile Tagle 2762; also in Bariloche, Rio Gallegos and Ushuaia.
Paraguay Maipu 464, 3rd floor; open 9am-1pm. Also in Posadas at San Lorenzo 179.
Uruguay Ayacucho 1616.
Tourist office Santa Fe 883.

PATAGONIA

Patagonia begins on the southern bank of the Río Colorado and extends south through Tierra del Fuego. The Atlantic Ocean glimmers on one side and a wall of snowy volcanic peaks shimmers on the other. Anywhere else in the world this would be called a desert. The immensity of this harsh land is exceeded by an inescapably profound sense of loneliness.

The rare meeting with other humans was as startling as looking in a mirror for the first time. We entered Patagonia from the north, in September, and had spent only three days in this zone when we encountered a Swiss traveler coming from the south. He looked normal until we mentioned Patagonia and then a deranged chuckle transformed his face and words, 'You haven't even begun to experience the Patagonia!' I remember backing away, but I've never forgotten him. I wonder if I now get the same crazed look when someone asks me about Patagonia.

Coastal route
Ruta 3, the most heavily traveled north-south route is paved until slightly south of Rio Gallegos.

Valdés Peninsula
Much of this natural wildlife habitat is a privately owned sheep ranch. Besides sheep you'll see the untameable relative of the llama, the *guanaco*, foxes, Patagonian hares, or *Mara* which look like bizarre giant guinea pigs, and the high-stepping local ostrich, rhea, here called *ñandu*. The parks department regulates coastal access to a plethora of marine creatures who beach, nest, breed and raise young ones on shore between late March and November. Penguins, seals and massive sea elephants nurse or flirt while migratory right whales dally in the gulf of Puerto Pirámides. Orca whales thrash onto shore in pursuit of a tasty seal meal January through March. Admission to the peninsula is US$3 per person. Don't miss the very informative exhibit in the park office at the entrance. With only one tiny town, Puerto Pirámides, you'll surely learn that you, as a human, are the invader in this animal kingdom.

The sea colonies can be viewed in a one-day circuit of the peninsula. **Puerto Pirámides** This is the only place where camping is allowed and you should go prepared to spend several days. A small ACA hotel can accommodate 20-40 people and, among the few houses, there are rooms to let. A spacious campground, adjacent to the beach and the ACA hotel, is free off-season.

Good boat tours (US$15 per person) leave here to float among the

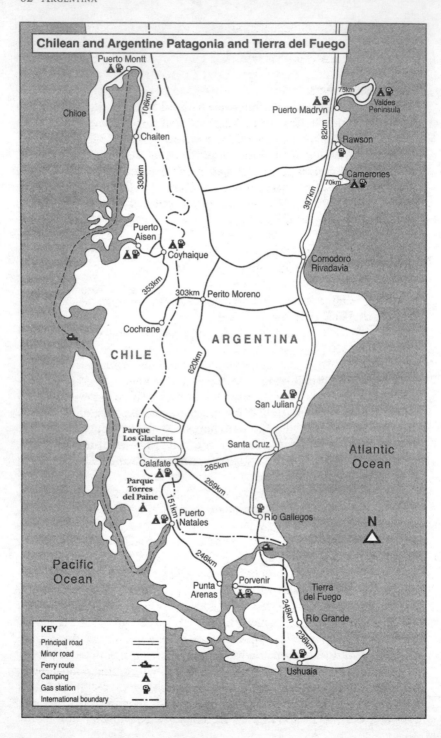

Chilean and Argentine Patagonia and Tierra del Fuego

KEY

Principal road	
Minor road	
Ferry route	
Camping	
Gas station	
International boundary	

whales. Offshore diving excursions to reefs are popular in summer. Boat guides and dive masters are very knowledgeable so don't be shy about asking questions.

Puerto Madryn

Enjoy a feeding frenzy and hob-nob with locals. This is an upmarket mini-resort with all the right places and few drawbacks.

Excellent grocery stores will make you think of heaven and, at heavenly prices (for Argentina), they're cheaper than restaurants.

Hotels, with parking, line the beachside 'cruising strip'. Nightlife is as wild as it's loud. We couldn't find any good camping spots so chose a parking lot at the southern extremity of the beach, near a residential zone.

Comodoro Rivadavia

A big city with good shopping.

Camping   There's an ACA and municipal campgrounds with hot showers at Roda Tilly beach, 14km south.

Rio Gallegos

This is primarily a port and service center for oil and natural gas workers. The military base here was a major launch pad during the war for sovereignty over the Falkland Islands. There isn't much here except a lingering distrust of the military who locals blame for the disappearance of 1,700 of their own.

Stock up on supplies if going south or west. There is little available for the next 599km to Ushuaia. Immediately south of town, the pavement turns to *ripio*.

We stopped at Lago Azul, a crater lake supposedly with a year-round population of ibis, but saw nothing of interest except a hole in the ground.

Border

In the middle of nowhere is Monte Aymond, a lonely border post that serves both Argentina and Chile. The personnel are very helpful. They exchanged money for us and even called for free to Puerto Natales, Chile, for ferry information.

Travelers who wish to bypass Tierra del Fuego and go directly to Punta Arenas, Chile, should continue straight on route 255. Otherwise turn into Punta Delgada to the ferry landing where there are a few small hotels and restaurants. A ferry crosses the Strait of Magellan to Punta Espora every hour or so, costing US$5.50 per person and US$32 for a car. All currencies are accepted.

TIRE TROUBLE

It was a dark and stormy sunset as our ferry nosed into the Strait. We were grinning with excitement for the occasion when someone tapped Robb's shoulder and pointed to a flat tire. It was the third of the day! Land was in sight and our van was first in line to disembark. We set to work with the frenzy of a pit crew in a road race. As the ferry scraped into dock, we twisted the last lug nut in place to cheers and applause from other passengers. We weren't charged, maybe our entertaining plight was toll enough. Win some, lose some. We drove off and quickly got lost in the dark and spent a snowy night camped outside a closed *gomería* (a tire repair shop) which never did open. Luckily, we found one later in the morning, at the next border post. A good thing too, because we were driving on the rim of another flat tire.

TIERRA DEL FUEGO

The extinct Ona indians of Tierra del Fuego asserted that human life began on the island and migrated north and outward. Charles Darwin, perhaps influenced by the Ona stories, began to formulate his theories of *The Origin of Species* on these inhospitable shores. If stories of capsized schooner ships in search of a route around Cape Horn to India, and the lichen-like tree foliage don't convince you that the fittest survive, your arrival will.

Getting there

From Punta Delgada Follow the road through Sombrero. Just west of San Sebastian are border posts, about a kilometer apart. On your way back out, you'll have to repeat the same procedures. There is both an ACA hotel and gas station in San Sebastian. The road then wends along the ocean 97km to Río Grande. Good supplies. Numerous ski lodges and hotels with camping (all expensive) between Río Grande and Ushuaia.

From Punta Arenas A two-to-three hour ferry crosses daily the Strait of Magellan, US$35 per car and US$3.50 per person. It leaves Porvenir for Punta Arenas at 2pm. Small hotels, supplies and gas are available in Porvenir. There is nothing between Porvenir and San Sebastian, 142km to the west.

Ushuaia

Overland travelers earn a night on the town upon reaching Ushuaia. In reality, few ever make it. Many, many times we doubted if we would. It's no wonder that the tourist office dispenses diplomas and shopkeepers liberally stamp passports with official-looking visas for the 'End of the World'. Admittedly the most expensive city in

THE BIG TRIP
Above: The author's route through the Americas (PA)
Below: The end of the world: Argentina (PA)

RELAXING AT THE END OF A HARD DAY
Above: "Maya", the 1976 Volkswagen which carried the authors through the Americas (PA)
Below: After a tough day in the Andes (MG)

RELAXING AT THE END OF A SOFT DAY
Colca Canyon, Peru. The specially outfitted trucks operated by overland companies ensure as much comfort as is possible in these rugged conditions. (SH)

ROAD CONDITIONS
Above: Vehicles are in for a testing time, from the thin air of the altiplano... (MG)
Below: ...to the mud of the jungle (MG)

Argentina, its inhabitants claim to be the friendliest.

Ushuaia nestles on a hillside along the north coast of the Beagle Channel, a scant glance away from Puerto Williams island and Antarctica. In many ways Ushuaia resembles a coastal town in northern Alaska. As though reaching to a distant twin, signboards at the end of the road remind all that Alaska is only 17,383km away (our circuitous route took us over 40,000km to reach the same point!)

The most southerly point, by road, dead-ends in **Parque Nacional Tierra del Fuego** with stupendous scenery and trekking trails. Camping is excellent here, better than the handier municipal park en route from the town. Park rangers at the entrance give information and maps indicating trails, hotels, restaurants, and frigidly cold shower facilities within the park.

Places to stay

Tourist office provides a list of hotels and prices (US$35-150 per double), and camping information. City hotels cluster in the center on or near the Beagle Channel. There are many cheaper guesthouses and rooms in private homes.

Useful addresses

Antarctica cruises   Contact the tourist office for complete schedule of boats to the Antarctica. Costs vary with length of voyage (7-20 days), high tourist season, accommodation, etc, but count on US$1,500 up to US$3,800 per person.

Caminante Adventure Travel   Don Bosco 319; highly recommended outfitters and trekking guides.

Chilean consulate   Malvinas Argentinas 263/244

Tourist office   San Martín 660; tel/fax: (0901) 24550; computerized information, maps and very helpful people.

ANDEAN ROUTE

An alternative route south follows the eastern slopes of the Andes, where Ruta 40 alternates with 17 and 258. Sections are paved, but it's mostly *ripio*. Between Bariloche and El Calafate you'll pass glacier lakes and wooded hills that seasonally burst into bloom with wildflowers. Detours will take you to Los Alecres National Park, Cuevas de las Manos, Parque Nacional de Los Glaciares with Perito Moreno glacier, and the granite pinnacles of Mount Fitzroy.

Bariloche

We have had rave reviews from everyone passing through this city on the southern shore of Lake Nahuel Huapi. Praise goes to the factories of scrumptious chocolate, excellent restaurants and ski slopes, all of which are equally renowned for hefty prices. Bariloche is a year-round resort city resembling a Swiss village set among volcanic peaks. When the snow on the ski slopes melts with the advent of summer, the climate, hiking trails and other attractions entice travelers from the sizzling lowlands.

Useful addresses
Chilean consulate   J M Rosas 180.
Tourist office   Centro Civico.

Places to stay
The tourist office distributes a list of lodging and prices. The following places are recommended.
Hotel Ayelen   Pasaje Libertad 157, near tourist office; three stars.
La Caleta   Tel: 255650. 1.9km on Llao-Llao road with bungalows; extremely popular for excellent value, but often full.

Camping   Good camping in nearby parks. Closer to town there are several sites on the Llao-Llao road, keeping the lake to your right. Try the *ACA* within walking distance of town, and 6km further is *Yeti Camping*, highly recommended.

Parque Argentino Los Alerces
This is an ancient conifer (larch) forest with features similar to the area around Bariloche. It is not heavily touristed, however, and the superb views can be appreciated in solitude. There is good rough camping in designated areas. To get there, follow the paved Ruta 40 south from Bariloche to Esquel. Sixty kilometers to the west of Esquel, unpaved, is the main park entrance. All supplies should be purchased in Esquel for this park and for the onward trip to El Calafate.

Cuevas de los Manos
More stupendous scenery entices you to detour through a valley 56km from Ruta 40. Depicted on the cave walls are handprints left from ancient times. Pass through the town of Perito Moreno (74km east is Chile Chico, an alternate route into Chile) and turn west 118km south, at Bajo Caracoles.

Parque Nacional De Los Glaciares
Perito Moreno glacier is one of few growing glaciers in the world. On the north end is Lago Viedma and to the south is Lago Argentina and El Calafate. This massive blue spectacle measures more than 5km wide and 35km long and moves at the speed of 1.5m per day!

Serenity is rented with the awesome thunder of a huge slab of ice breaking away from the glacial walls and crashing into the lake. Such drama is unbeatable.

Equally breathtaking in its grandeur is Mount Fitz Roy (3,375m) in the western part of the park. The granite spires of this amazing mountain can only be visited by hikers but should not be missed by the fit and well-equipped.

Viedma

Supplies can be found in this town near the northern park entrance. Look for the Supercrop supermarket on the left on the roundabout on the road toward the airport.

El Calafate

On the southern bank of Lago Argentino, El Calafate has been the traditional staging point for excursions to the glacier. It is a small peaceful village with bare necessities and a surprisingly good delicatessen. Souvenir shops and tour operators line the short main street. Giant ice cubes, chunks of Perito Moreno, bob on the lake's surface.

Getting there

This is the Patagonia and distances are exceeded by the loneliness of the roads. There are no supplies between the towns en route. From Viedma go 86km south to Rio Bofe, a modest settlement and turn west for another 35km. From the coast, take the lower fork south of Santa Cruz for 300km or from Rio Gallegos go 302km northwest.

Places to stay

Albergue Del Glaciar, Calle Pioneros, is a youth hostel and there are several nice hotels in town with parking. Municipal campgrounds are by the lake.

88

Chapter Eight

Bolivia

Rolling Andean plains of the *altiplano* plummet to jungle in the north and, in the east, drops to meet the Chaco of Paraguay and the Pantanal of Brazil. The very ruggedness of the terrain has made Bolivia a haven for the likes of Che Guevera, smugglers and trekkers. Until the last decade, coups were more numerous than Bolivia's years as a nation. Modern Bolivia is stable and her beauty attracts many travelers. What it lacks in infrastructure is compensated by heart; after all, landlocked Bolivia is located near the heart of South America.

COUNTRY HIGHLIGHTS

Lake Titicaca
The world's highest navigable lake shimmers at altitudes of 3,810m, on the border with Peru. According to Quechua/Aymara legend, life began here. With luck you'll see a reed boat being paddled to an island.

Mount Illimani
Forbiddingly craggy and snow-crested, this triple-peaked mountain soars above La Paz.

The Yungas
Bolivia is best known for her frigid mountains, yet northeast of La Paz is this tropical garden, a gateway to a little known region of the Amazon jungle.

Tiahuanaco
These fascinating pre-Inca ruins, 72km from La Paz, were the ceremonial center of the Tiwanaku empire, 1,000 BC. Aymara indians still gather here to celebrate the *Pachamama*, the Earth Mother.

Potosí

Silver, and now tin mines burrow deep into the earth. Founded before the Incas and before the Spanish invaders in 1545, it is today a treasure of colonial architecture.

POINTS OF ENTRY

From Chile

The main route skirts Lake Chungará, Chile (at 4,600m) to enter Bolivia at Tambo Quemado. On the Chilean side the road is paved; not so in Bolivia. This is the primary truck route to Bolivia's port in Arica, but is subject to flooding. An alternate entry is at Charaña from Visviri, Chile. The road is unpaved and rough on each side; there is little traffic except for the railroad, few supplies and no bridge on the Bolivian side. Neither route is advisable once the rains begin. If approaching from Chile, take precautions to avoid *soroche* — both the human kind and mechanical. Adapt motors and tires for high altitude; some mountain passes exceed 5,000m. Carry lots of food, water and spare fuel.

From Peru

The most reasonable entry point is Desaguadero, along Lake Titicaca. It's at a lower altitude than the Chilean borders. From Puno, Peru, 35km is paved to the border and another 115km by mostly unpaved road takes you to La Paz.

From Brazil

Good luck. We went into Quijarro, Bolivia from Corumbá, Brazil, and didn't find the road to Santa Cruz as indicated on maps. It is possible to deflate your tires and drive on the railroad tracks, but one motorist ended up in a river when an unscheduled train forced his VW off the rails. A safer alternative is to rent a flatbed. One can be hired to Santa Cruz for about US$140.

From Paraguay

From the middle of nowhere to nowhere. Stop at customs and at the army post for immigration in Boyuibe, Bolivia. In Paraguay, collect stamps at the army office in Fortín General Garay. Supplies are available in Boyuibe, so stock up. It is a five-hour drive to Camiri and another 22 to Sucre over narrow, steep passes.

From Argentina

A newly paved road(!), links Camiri to the Argentine border. It will undoubtably divert travelers from Paraguay's Chaco region.

CULTURE

In landlocked Bolivia, indigenous cultures remain relatively intact. More than two thirds of the population are Indian. Among the many indigenous groups, the highland ones are perhaps best known. These are Aymara or Quechua speaking people. Their colorful costumes, particularly during festivals, are stunning. But don't be too hasty in whipping out your camera. Photos are not appreciated. Ask first or wait for cues from other local people.

Homebrewed beer, *chicha*, can be as benign as Kool-Aid or as potent as Jack Daniels. During festivals and weekends, the latter is the beverage of choice. It's wise to disappear when your drinking companion's eyes begin to glaze and feet stagger, because an aggressive confrontation could be in the making. As a foreigner, an outsider, you become a likely target for pent-up anger.

Coca leaves, from which cocaine is derived, is grown, harvested, transported and consumed. A certain amount of leaves, a *bulto*, is legal. Not only an economic mainstay (more profitable than wizened, freeze-dried potatoes or poor coffee), coca leaves appease hunger between meager meals. Spend several weeks on the *altiplano* and you'll understand their crop dependency.

The leaves are masticated with a hunk of lime or carbon. Most foreigners find it unpleasant and a lackluster experience. It is an acquired taste and the effect is cumulative. Experiment, if you will, but don't travel with a *bulto* of leaves. The DEA has engendered negative feelings and Bolivian police love to bust or fine gringos to prove their crack-down on drugs.

ON THE ROAD

Expect unpaved roads. The harsh extremes of weather and topography makes gravel roads, *ripio*, more practical than pavement. Great care should be taken on steep narrow mountain roads, particularly those with plunging cliffs. First of all, they're often wet from clouds, fog, and rain, so are slippery.

Driving style

Just remember that uphill vehicles have the right away. In Bolivia, the uphill driver clings to the cliff side and downhill drivers take the precarious outside lane.

Off the main roads, traffic is sporadic. In case of a break-down, carry emergency supplies sufficient for two days.

Maps

A topographical map is very helpful, available from the *Instituto Geográfico Militar*, in La Paz, 16 de Julio, 1671.

USEFUL INFORMATION
Public holidays
January 1 (New Year)
Shrove Tuesday and Wednesday (Carnival week)
Thur and Fri preceding Easter
May 1 (Labor Day)
June ? (Corpus Christi Day)
July 16 (Founding of La Paz)
August 5-7 (Independence)
October 12 (Columbus Day)
November 2 (Day of the Dead)
December 25 (Christmas)

When to visit
The highlands are always cold at night, varying between 2-6°C. From November to March violent lightning storms sweep the *altiplano* and thunder resonates between tall peaks. When not raining or snowing, days can be brilliant. Sun protection is an absolute must.

Camping
There are no organized campgrounds, but finding remote sites is no problem. Nearly every town has a public bath, *baños publico*, with lots of hot water for a small fee. Campers are advised to have appropriate cold and wet weather gear.

Money and banks
One dollar equaled 4.3 bolivianos in 1995. The currency is now very stable, with little inflation. *Cambios* in all major cities exchange travelers checks and cash. Visa and Mastercard can be used at banks to make cash advances.

LA PAZ

The real capital of Bolivia is Sucre, judicially speaking. The administrative seat is La Paz. To me, this Bolivian capital looks like a deep cereal bowl. The *altiplano* seemingly breaks off to form a lip encircling the steep-walled valley. Above are the mountain spires of the Cordillera Real and 370m below, at the valley's bottom, is the Prado, the mainstreet, known officially as Avenida 16 de Julio.

No visit to La Paz is complete without a visit to **San Francisco church**, built in 1549. It is a landmark and place to rest after a weary day of shopping in nearby handicrafts markets.

Places to stay

Hot water is a prime consideration for choosing any hotel. Room heat is a bonus.

Hotel Panamericano Turn at second right on freeway to El Alto at Toyota sign and follow to the roundabout, turn right at Manco Kapac. Park in street or in an El Alto car park.

Hotels Vienna and Neumann Av Loayza; near post office.

Residencial Rosario Calle Illampu 704; popular gringo hangout.

Useful addresses

Brazil Consulate Fernando Guachalla 494.

Chile Consulate H Siles 5843, on corner of Calle 13.

Paraguay Consulate Av Acre, Edificio Venus.

Peru Consulate 6 de Agosto 2190 y Calle F Guachalla.

Propane Refill in El Alto station as you approach La Paz from Oruro.

Tourist office Plaza Estudiante 176, corner of Mexico and 16 de Julio.

COPACABANA

A more pleasant city than Puno, Copacabana is popular as a base for trips around Lake Titicaca. Near by is the Island of the Sun and good hiking is available. Restaurants and hotels have recently opened to serve the growing tourist trade. Visit the Virgin de Candelaria, the Dark Virgin of the Lake, Bolivia's patron saint and miracle-worker. On Sundays, vehicles line the roadway before the cathedral to be blessed by the Virgin; smaller ceremonies are held at noon on weekdays. (Don't miss it! We can all use a little extra help.)

PACHAMAMA

More revered than coca is *Pachamama*, Mother Earth. All life springs from her soil and water and returns again. Bad luck can be averted by tributes — a slaughtered llama or the ceremonious burial of its fetus. You'll see dried fetuses sold in markets, along with silver or clay trinkets depicting animals, children, foods, cars, whatever the plaintive wants or gives thanks for. The llama and symbolic offerings are traditionally buried under the corner stone of a new house, to bring good fortune to all who dwell within.

Getting there

From La Paz, take the Rio Seco exit in El Alto. The road is unpaved beyond Tiquina. From Desaguadero go to San Pedro and take a ferry across the straits of Tiquina to San Pablo on the peninsula of Copacabana. Vehicles are carried separately by a rickety barge,

US$3. At times the crossing can be turbulent and very cold. Bundle warmly and expect delays.

Places to stay
Hotel Peregrino Av 16 de Julio.

THE YUNGAS

One of our most memorable trips was crossing La Cumbre pass, 4,725m, to the Yungas. One moment we were in snow and clouds and the next we were descending into the tropical sunny Yungas. Be forewarned that it is a demanding route. From La Paz, you'll climb nearly vertically to the pass. On the other side, the 3,400m descent is more gradual (unpaved). The dramatic views are stunning and worth the whole effort.

Besides growing bananas, peanuts and oranges, the prime cash crop in the Yungas is coca. You really want to avoid "seeing anything you shouldn't see". Chances are you won't.

Coroico
A pleasant hillside town with beautiful scenery, walks, waterfalls, and natural hot springs for bathing. Good hotels and restaurants.

Chulumani
The capital town of the Sud Yungas sits in a picturesque setting amidst jungle valleys, towering mountains, blooming gardens and friendly people. Cool off at one of the many hotels with swimming pools.

POTOSÍ

Another high spot (4,070m) in your Bolivian travels will be a visit to this historic mining city. Before the Spanish arrived in 1545, Indians were already working the silver mines. In the not too subtle way of the conquistadors, the mines and the indigenous miners were exploited to near extinction. Today the silver veins run thin and, instead, tin is extracted by co-operatives of professionals. Still, experts charge that safety has not improved and little of the profits jangle in workers' pockets. (We have always boycotted the mine tours and products for those reasons.) Other travelers report that their mine tours have been eye-opening and educational.

A walking tour of Potosí is definitely in order. With aid from UNESCO, fabulous 16th- and 17th-century buildings have been preserved. The mint, *Casa Real de Moneda*, the Royal Treasury, *Las*

Casas Reales and cathedral stand among several thousand, identified, colonial buildings. Try to arrange for a tour of the intriguing catacombs and tunnels that once connected every part of the city like subterranean roadways.

ON LOCAL TRANSPORT

We once rode for a whole day atop a truck filled with empty Coke bottles, oranges and people. The police searched several times by poking long lances through all the bundles, into the truck bed. At that time, Indians needed permission to travel so we were also subjected to internal migration inspections. With all the official harassment, nervousness seemed appropriate. As we neared our destination everyone but us scrambled to move bundles and bottles to reveal nearly a ton of coca leaf underneath us! Our shock made the confederates laugh so hard that tears leaked from every eye. The ringleader waded through the bags of leaves to embrace us. "Hey *compadres*," he said, "didn't you know that there's a reason gringos never ride on Indian trucks?" And all along we thought that people were just being friendly when they smiled and waved at us on the truck.

Getting there

From La Paz   Good paved road to Oruro, 225km south then becomes twisty but decent for the remaining 316km. Oruro is a good supply stop, decent camping approx 10km south of town at Tarapaya, Km 25. Thermal baths.

From Sucre   Steep and curvaceous but paved, plan six to seven hours' driving time to cover the 163 km.

Useful addresses

Mine tours   Recommended is the **Pailauri** tin mine on the edge of town. Get there before office opens at 8.30am. US$8 per person, hard hats included.

Tourist office   On main square, *Plaza 10 de Noviembre*, and at Cámara de Minería, Calle Quijarro, second floor. Helpful, when open, in arranging tunnel tours.

Places to stay

Hotel Colonial   Hoyos 8; ranked three stars, on the *plaza mayor*.

Sumaj   Fortunato Gumiel 12; at bottom of a long hill, highly recommended and economical, with parking.

96

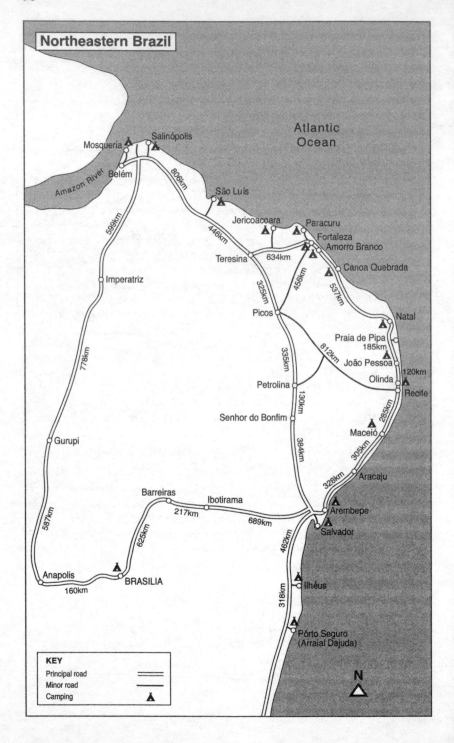

Chapter Nine

Brazil

The Portuguese colonized Brazil and established a legacy that distinguishes this country from all others in the Americas. Romanticized versions of the conquest describe it as an act of love. Stranded Portuguese sailors married the most beautiful of the women. In turn, a tribe of women warriors who initially defeated the colonial soldiers in the Amazon heartland, took the heartiest men to their beds. Black slaves were brought here from Africa and others were dumped after the British and North Americans forbade their trade as commodities. During the mid to late 1800s, white Europeans arrived to work the *fazendas* as indentured laborers. So it goes that love, not guns, created the unique racial blend and cultural harmony that is the hallmark of Brazil.

Brazilians often describe their country as a continent. We first thought this a hyperbole emanating from national pride; likewise, we thought a three-month visa to be generous. We were wrong on both counts. Brazil is not a continent geographically speaking, but its 8,511,965km square absorbs more than half of South America within its borders. From north to south you can travel 4,320km, and east to west 4,328km without leaving the country. Seductive beaches stretch for 7,408km making a life-time project for anyone wanting to visit all of them. The Amazon region, with travel by boat instead of by road, covers more than 40% of Brazil. In all, three months is barely sufficient time to traverse the country.

COUNTRY HIGHLIGHTS
Amazon region
The lungs of the world, the medicine cabinet of pharmacists, the mecca of travelers' dreams.

Beaches
The finest beaches on the continent sprawl along the northeast sector. Surfers should head south, toward Garapaba for world-class waves.

Pantanal
This quasi-aquatic ecosystem attracts fishing enthusiasts and such wildlife as caiman, capybara, giant anaconda and the tall jabiru stork.

Foz do Iguaçu
These mighty waterfalls are simply awesome.

POINTS OF ENTRY
From Venezuela
From Santa Elena de Uairén, Venezuela, you'll enter Brazil at Pacaraima. Your vehicle will be sprayed with a pesticide upon crossing the border. Customs and immigration are housed together on your immediate left. Formalities are conducted in a civil manner in Brazilian Pacaraima. **Everyone** who leaves or enters Venezuela with a vehicle is snagged by bureaucratic complications (*see Chapter Sixteen, Venezuela*). The nearest Venezuelan consulates are in Boa Vista and Manaus, Brazil.

From Bolivia
A bridge spans the Río Paraguay, connecting the border towns of Corumbá, Brazil (the Pantanal) and Quijarro, Bolivia. Standard border hours are observed on both sides (8am-5.30pm, closed for lunch, Saturday afternoons, Sundays and holidays). The port captain's office handles customs entry of vehicles and the office of the Brazilian *Policia Federal* processes immigration at the bus station, the *Rodoviária*.

From Paraguay
There are two entry points: one is between Ponto Porá, Brazil and Pedro Juan Caballero, Paraguay (operational hours are as above, also *see Ponto Porá, page 123* for details), but the main border is between Foz, Brazil and Ciudad del Este which is always open.

From Argentina
The main border point is through Foz do Iguaçu and is open 24 hours. The road is very good. For details refer to this chapter section, *Foz do Iguaçu, page 123*.

From Uruguay

The main border is between Chui and Chuy and is more or less open 24 hours. You can also cross at Rivera, see *Southern Brazil* and *Uruguay* for details.

From Guyana

Over two hundred kilometers of very difficult road connect Letham and Boa Vista, Brazil, to the southwest. Reportedly, the only north-south trail through Guyana is laced by rivers. (We heard a rumor of two motorcyclists who succeeded during the dry season.) Customs and immigration service each border, but the nearest Guyana consulate is in Boa Vista (supposedly).

Border formalities

A *libreta* is not necessary. A simple permit will be issued at no charge for temporary import of your vehicle. However, you must state your point of exit. Choose the furthest point in your route and don't worry. Customs will amend the form at whichever point you depart. **Visa extensions** Brazil is so enormous that your visa might expire. Extensions of tourist visa are at the discretion of the *Policia Federal*, who maintain offices in every sizeable city. (You'll have to ask around to find them.) Vehicle extensions are made by the *Departamento de Fiscalização*. The cheapest and easiest procedure is to exit Brazil with your vehicle and then re-enter with new paperwork.

ON THE ROAD

Roads in the north and northeast are extremely challenging. There are potholes as deep as a truck, mountainous *lombadas*, bottomless *depressões* and broken tarmac. Expect any dirt road to challenge the structural integrity of your vehicle. The famous Trans-Amazonian highway no longer exists. Roads south of Fortaleza are generally good. Roads and superhighways are excellent from Rio de Janeiro south.

Driving style

Brazilian truck drivers are such infamously aggressive drivers that they're referred to as *os touros*, the bulls. They run over horses, donkeys — anything in the road, leaving a horrendous wake of carcasses. It is not only a nasty sight but is very dangerous to motorists.

Fuel

Unleaded, high-octane gas, (US$0.55 per liter) is available south of São Paulo, at **Ipiranga** stations.

Word of warning...alcohol may taint your fuel! Brazil manufactures alcohol-combustion engines, the fuel for which is derived from sugar cane. Although we carefully monitored our fuel sources, and all our rubber seals and gaskets had been replaced three months earlier, alcohol-tainted Brazilian fuel disintegrated everything made of rubber. All petrol and diesel in Brazil has a percentage (about 20%) of alcohol.

Maps and guides

Quatro Rodas publishes excellent road maps and informative guides, from US$15, in easy-to-decipher Portuguese. The *Guia Brasil* lists repair shops, hotels, camping, banks, festivals and even ranks beaches. Elevations are not indicated on their maps.

USEFUL INFORMATION

Public Holidays

January 1 (New Year)
Shrove Tuesday and the three preceding days
Ash Wednesday (*Terca-feira de cinzas*)
Good Friday and Easter Monday
April 21 (Tiradentes Day)
May 1 (Labor Day)
June (Corpus Christi), three saints are celebrated for varying lengths of time in different regions.
September 7 (Independence Day)
October 12 (*Nossa Senhora Aparecida*)
November 1 (All Saints Day)
November 15 (Proclamation of the Republic)
December 25-26 (Christmas)

When to visit

Regardless of when you visit Brazil, you'll probably catch a rainy season, winter cold or summer heat. The equator cuts through Brazil 3° north of Manaus. There is little temperature variance in the equatorial zone with a steady 27°C. Rainfall (3,187mm annual average) is most constant between April and August. As you move south and away from this zone, you'll find the seasons more pronounced and opposite those above the equator. The southern states, such as São Paulo and Rio Grande do Sul, are very cold from July through September with nightly temperatures possibly dipping to 8°C).

Camping

The Brazilian network of campgrounds encompasses everything from those with no facilities to five star luxury resorts. The *Camping Clube do Brasil* is a confederation of regional clubs with sites scattered in remote niches throughout the nation. Sites can accommodate RV campers, trucks and long-term vacationers. Non-members may utilize a campground at (US$12-25 per site) while members benefit from discounts. Membership costs approximately US$160 for six months. For more detailed information contact: Camping Clube do Brasil, Divisão de Campings, R Senador Dantas 75-29° andar, Rio de Janeiro.

Many *postos* (gas stations) are tree-shaded parks which offer restaurants, drinking water and free showers. They cater to the repeat business of long-distance truckers, many of whom travel with family, wives or girlfriends.

The Naturist Federation of Brazil also allows camping at each of their nine official sites. (Single men must be card-carrying members of one of the internationally recognized naturist associations.)

Money and banks

The new *real* was overvalued to the dollar at its introduction in 1994. Nevertheless, this latest currency is proving rather stable. Prices for basic commodities make Brazil the second most expensive country, after Argentina.

The **Banco do Brasil**, located in the capital of each state, changes travelers checks; all other branches allow cash advances on Visa. *Câmbios* are found only in major tourist centers, such as Foz, Rio, São Paolo and Manaus. It is nearly impossible to buy dollars. Street-side money changers don't exist.

Personal security

The countryside is very safe, and cities require standard precautions. Don't be misled by provocative, seemingly open sensuality, conservatism reigns each town.

There are three branches of police: the plain-clothed *Policia Federal* are in charge of immigration and investigation; the uniformed *Policia Federal Rodoviária* are the traffic cops; and the *Policia Militar* patrol streets.

Language

Here are a few words and phrases that can help your day. See the glossary on page 232 for specific terms that apply to road signs.

| Good day | *Bom dia* |
| Arrive | *Chegar* |

Bad	*Mau, grave*
Beach	*Praia*
Broken	*Ruptura. In northeast, quebrada, designates a road broken by flooding.*
Chicken	*Frango*
Do, to make	*Fazer*
Distant, far	*Longe*
Go, I go	*Vou*
Left	*Esquerda*
Leave, Exit	*Saida*
Too much money	*Muito dinheiro*
Near	*Perto*
No	*Não*
Oil change	*Troca de Óleo*
Perhaps	*Tal vez*
Please	*Por Favor*
River	*Rio*
Road	*Estrada*
Right	*Direita*
Straight	*Direito*
Talk, speak	*Falar*
Thank you	*Obrigado* (male person speaking), *Obrigada* (female person speaking)
To be	*Ser*
Turn	*Virar*
Want, I want…	*Quero*
Where is	*Onde fica…?*
Yes	*Sim*
You take a left as	*Vôce pega a esquerada*

NORTHERN BRAZIL

More than a third of the country is encompassed in the region known as *Amazonia*.

We've hiked and canoed into and through the Amazon in all of the surrounding countries. In our estimation, the Brazilian territory north of Manaus is the best for flora and fauna. This is an undiscovered five-star *explor-a-rama*. Brazil provides the *only* "thoroughfares" for travel through the Amazon, by road.

A very good asphalt road extends from the Venezuela border to Caracaraí, 361km to the south. From there it is another 644km to Manaus by a bad dirt road. The road is passable, when dry, usually between late July and February, and motorists make the trip in two days. Once the rainy season begins, count on eight days of travel through mud holes deep enough to swallow a bus. Then the more reasonable option is to take a river barge from Caracaraí to Manaus.

For travel west of Manaus or east to Belém, plan to travel by river boat.

About 900km south of Manaus along BR319 is Pôrto Velho on the Rio Madeira and from there the road is very good, but between Manaus and Pôrto Velho it is terrible, even during dry season when the several ferries and dilapidated wood bridges do not compensate for all the necessary river fords. A 4WD, winch and companion vehicle is strongly advised unless you're prepared to be stuck for days, as there is very little traffic. At best, it is a three-day trip by road. The most economical option is river travel. (Transport details are listed under appropriate city headings.)

Note: The Perimetral Norte road does not exist. Much of BR364, the famous east-west Trans-Amazonian highway, has been abandoned to the jungle.

Pacaraima

This is a tiny, quiet border town, not much more than a clearing in the thick, orchid-tangled jungle. Locals refer to it as "nowhere". The nearest place to change money is in Boa Vista, 220km south, via a newly constructed road (1995). The road is slightly elevated to prevent road flooding in the rainy season, so exit from it is difficult except at a *posto* midway, or into a cattle *fazenda* or homesite of a displaced Yanomani family.

Boa Vista

The capital of the state of Roraima is expensive because everything must be either flown in or transported by boat to Caracaraí and then distributed by truck. Residents claim they produce nothing for export, but in truth, Roirama is a major producer of "uncounted" gold. Smuggled gold from this region alone is estimated at 70,000 tons annually!

Boa Vista is a modern planned community of 143,000 that thrives on an influx of pioneers from other parts of Brazil. The diverse immigrant families contribute their heritage of musical culture at the **Big Star** *Casa do Pagode* on Av Cap Júlio Bezerra, a neighborhood-style bar and restaurant where musicians drop in for jam sessions.

Places to stay

For camping, go north 3km toward Venezuela to Km 765 by the bridge spanning the **Rio Caviné**; good bathing in the river, quiet and safe.

Busy on weekends (live bands) are free sites at the end of Av Cap Júlio Bezerra that dwindles to a dirt road. Follow the signs to

Rio Curupira.
Alpana Plaza   In the very center, very nice with private parking.
Eusébio's   Cecilia Brasil 1107, near the center. For motorcycles.
F Hotel Brasil or **Hotel Monte Libano**   Av Benjamin Constant, can safely accommodate bicyclists. Air conditioned and very cheap.
Praia Palace   Av Floriano Peixoto 352, river's edge, near center; with parking.

Useful addresses
Banco do Brasil   is located on the rotary in the center of town. There is no other money exchange between here and Manaus.
Embratel,   the telephone company (no direct dial access), is one block north of the rotary.
Ice plant   *Gelo* sells bar and cubed ice alongside the Rio Branco, open every day.
Repairs   *Borracharias* for cars, motorcycles (especially Yamaha), and bicycles are scattered all over town. Repair everything on your vehicle before traveling south.
Venezuela Consulate   Benjamin Constant 525.

Caracaraí
A town of 8,000 inhabitants, located along the Rio Branco gives the appearance of being a hot, muggy pot-hole. If the dirt road to Manaus is impassable (usually April to July), you'll spend time here hunting up a boat, as we did.

Places to stay
Hotel Marcia   Opposite the bus station; air conditioning, baths, clean; can accommodate bikes.
Hotel Maroca   Av President Kennedy; air conditioning and bath.
Pizzaria Delicia.   Owner, Margarida Arruda, speaks English and allows camping in the lot adjacent to her pizzeria. If you use her facilities, please be considerate of her restaurant clientele.

Useful addresses
See Aloisio Pissol at **Padaria Pão del Mel** on the main street, Av Dr Zany. He knows everything and everyone.
Propane Fogás   on the dirt road at the north end of Av President Kennedy is very helpful. We had been without cooking gas for a month when the people at Fogás undertook our refilling problem. Three hours later we received a full tank and no bill!
Other supplies   One BR gas station (no alcohol fuel sold). Two ice plants on barges at south end of town. Supplies are available but more expensive than in Boa Vista. Produce is sold from private gardens.

Boats

The "dock" area covers a long strip of river bank. Access is by trails jutting from Av Dr Zany to the water's edge, (the large, modern-looking dock has been abandoned). You have to speak to each captain to learn his schedules and fares. Fares, including food and vehicle transport for the four-day trip to Manaus, run from US$333 with SANAVE to as low as US$83 with independent operators (expect around US$200). One way to bring down the fare is to bargain with a driver of an empty truck willing to piggy-back your vehicle.

Places to visit

Brecan Agua This houseboat behind the *padaria* is a friendly spot to enjoy sunsets with a fishing line and a cold drink. Manuel, the owner, sometimes plays the guitar.

Río Branco See Aliosio at the **Padaria Pão del Mel** for canoe trips. Close to Caracaraí are clean swimming beaches (no *piranha*), *garimpeiros* who mine the river for gold from their *dragas*, and an abundance of monkeys, macaws, toucans, jaguars, margueys and crocodiles. Indian groups that can be visited are Macuxi, Apixana, Way-way, and the Yanomani. Aliosio and Bernardo Mosler own a sort of jungle lodge for groups of four to eight participants on their 16-day excursion by river, foot, horse and jeep. Price US$5,800 per group. Reserve by tel or fax: 0952321536 or 0952321353.

Manaus

Population 1,010,544. This was the center of the great rubber boom that ended in 1920, after Asia began cultivation of rubber from seeds stolen from the Amazon. Manaus today is the capital of the Amazon and primary transport center for people, industry, petroleum refineries and saw mills. Its importance as a commercial free port for Brazilian bargain hunters is waning as imported products via Uruguay become competitive. Historical sites within the city are well marked.

Getting there

Crossing the Amazon is one of the great concerns of self-propelled travelers, therefore this section is more detailed than others. (Also *see Northern Brazil, page 102*).

To or from Caracaraí by road The road between Manaus and Caracaraí takes two days, but several motorists report doing it in one by getting an early start. Under the best of conditions, the road is deeply rutted, hilly and strung with dilapidated plank bridges. Fill up with fuel in Caracaraí and you should make it to Presidente Figueiro (gas, hotels, restaurants). Midway is an Indian reservation where the road is closed between 6pm and 6am. If you get caught on the north side, you'll have to camp as there is nowhere to stay. On the south side, stay at Presidente Figueiro. Some asphalted sections begin 100km north of Manaus.

OUR ROUTE TO MANAUS

At the cusp of the rainy season, mud on the Manaus road was too deep for trucks and the Rio Branco was too low for river traffic. We were again stuck at the end of a road. One thing we've learned while traveling, besides patience, is that we have a habit of getting stuck in towns described as "nothing here, move on as quickly as possible".

Portuguese was an unfamiliar language but we understood gesturing boat captains who wagged their heads, pointed to the sky and shrugged their shoulders. For a week we slogged through the muddy streets of Caracaraí, waiting for their shrugs to turn into thumbs up.

In a short time we'd met nearly everyone and although the river didn't flood, invitations did. Soon we were fishing from canoes, visiting gold prospectors on their river barges or trudging jungle paths with macaws as guides and chattering monkeys swinging by our shoulders. Five foot giant otters frolicked at our knees.

Then, one night it rained and the river swelled 19 feet. A boat captain found us hunkered under a tin roof out of the rain and stuck his thumb up — the "let's go" sign.

A bulldozer pushed a mound of mud to the lip of a barge *balsa*. Someone whistled that we were to drive on and we quaked with hesitation.

It turned out that we were the only cargo on three empty barges pushed by a family-operated tug. Delicious meals were served from the family's galley, followed by raucous card games played on hammock swings. At dusk, Paganini operas blared from loud speakers while I made popcorn for all to share. We even played soccer, with dogs acting as goalies.

The jungle enveloped us with sounds and flocks of the parrots, macaws, cranes, dolphins that accompanied the boat, but nary another person. The incredible Río Negro is like an obsidian mirror reflecting the jungle walls and calico sunsets and sunrises.

It was all so perfect that Robb and I hoped the tug would break down, delaying our arrival in Manaus. No such luck. On the fifth day the urban skyline of Manaus glimmered like Oz. It had been a goal more than a destination but after the serenity of the rivers, it looked too big, too noisy, confusing and scary. Our new boat friends must have read our hesitation because they presented us with a wonderful gift: an invitation to camp on the barge while in Manaus! We bought *cervejas* for all and watched the lights of the city twinkle from the comfort of our floating hotel. Already the city seemed a friendlier place.

To Caracaraí by boat   Hitching a barge north to Caracaraí is complicated simply because there are so many docks in Manaus. Go to the first bridge on the western end, a section known as **Aparecida**. Inquire under the bridge for tug boats with the identifying logo *Gobierno do Roraima*. *SANAVE* also offers barge services, although US$133 more. Their offices are west of Aparecida in the section called **Compensa**, Entrada do Bombeamento 20, tel 234-4803.

From Pôrto Velho by boat   The *Rio Madeira* connects Manaus to Pôrto Velho. Costs for the 901km, four-day barge trip averages US$250 for a car, US$350 for large truck, US$50 per passenger with food. UNINAV is recommended. Cyclists can get a ride on any of the passenger ferries (in Manaus go to the floating dock). The fare for a motorcycle is US$40.

In Pôrto Velho   A recommended hotel is *Floresta P*, Prudente de Morais 2313, safe parking, pool. Fill propane tanks at *FOGAS*, 3km from truck dock. Camping is possible around the dock area.

To Belém   *SANAVE* offers weekly barge service to Belém, departing on Thursday evenings. They charge US$625 per vehicle and US$40 per passenger. *Bertolini* also operates barges and will ship vehicles for US$666 and US$30 per passenger. (Note: Neither company allow you to stay on the barge with your vehicle). Bertolini offices are located beyond Compensa on the road to Punta Negra. Jonasa is located next to Bertolini, but they've been bought out by Bertolini and no longer operate their own barges. *Transnav*, another company, refers everyone to government run *ENASA*.

You can choose among the smaller boats that berth at the floating dock if the height of your vehicle does not exceed one and a half meters. *Cisne Branco*, for example, charges US$58 for a motorcycle and US$67 per passenger. Be aware that all boats are crowded, quality of food and sanitation is inconsistent and a hammock will be absolutely necessary. Take your own drinking water and food.

The worst of the transport companies, but also the cheapest for shipping to or from **Belém** is *ENASA*. The dingy, ill-marked office is located at Rua Marechal Deodoro 61, Ed. Galeria, 6th floor; tel: 232 7084. Ships depart from Manaus every Friday at 10pm. Freight for a VW Kombi is US$220 and US$35 per person for the four-day trip (fares are posted but there are many discrepancies between what people actually pay).

Pilfering is not unheard of but *ENASA* will permit you to stay in your vehicle which will be stored in the stuffy cargo hold. (Ask the crew to open the cargo doors during the trip.) Hammock space is provided in the deck called *Clase Regional*. Sleeping on the cooler upper decks is prohibited. The two expensive passenger cabins are

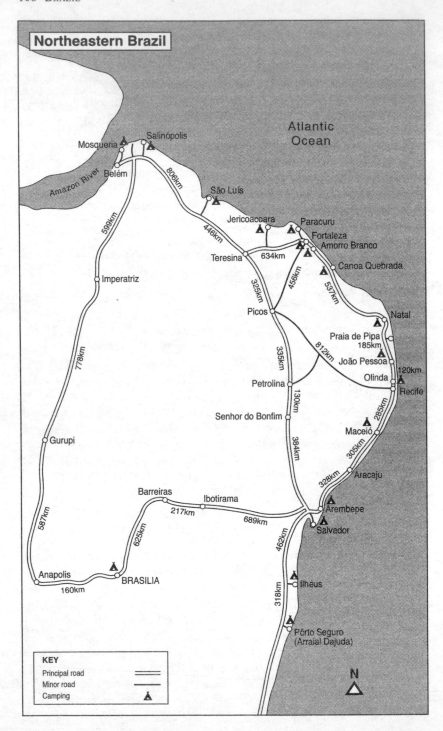

Northeastern Brazil

Atlantic Ocean

Mosqueria
Salinópolis
Belém
Amazon River
806km
599km
São Luís
446km
Jericoacoara
Paracuru
Fortaleza
Amorro Branco
Teresina
634km
Canoa Quebrada
Imperatriz
325km
456km
537km
778km
Picos
Natal
Praia de Pipa
185km
812km
335km
João Pessoa
Olinda
120km
Petrolina
130km
Recife
Senhor do Bonfim
285km
Gurupi
384km
Maceió
305km
Aracaju
Barreiras
Ibotirama
328km
587km
625km
217km
689km
Arembepe
462km
Salvador
Anapolis
BRASILIA
318km
Ilhéus
160km
Pôrto Seguro
(Arraial Dajuda)

N

KEY

Principal road	
Minor road	
Camping	⛺

usually reserved. Passenger capacity is 600 but even at 100 the infrastructure is strained. Toilets and showers are foul. One set of plastic utensils is issued to each passenger for the duration of the trip. Large portions of food are served on metal trays but no-one eats more than necessary. Brazilian passengers described the boat as "an insult, an offense against the people".

If your boat departs from, or arrives at, the floating dock in Manaus you will be charged a dock tax of US$15 per vehicle. In Belém you will have to pay another US$25 in taxes (US$12 for a motorcycle). In Belém, the tide can fluctuate three meters. We docked there at the bottom of low tide and had to wait six hours for the water to raise our ship so we could disembark our vehicles.

Useful addresses

Banco do Brasil   Ag. Center, Rua Guilmermc Moreira 315. It is located on one of the narrow streets that has been closed to vehicle traffic near the Hotel Amazonas. Rates are not as good at **Cortez Cambio e Turismo**, 1199 7 de Setembro, open 9am-5pm daily, and Saturdays until 12.30pm.

Water and ice   Purified drinking water is free at two Manaus locations: on the west corner of the wall surrounding the Brahama brewery in Aparecida, and at the Crimgelo ice plant in Compensa. Ice is sold at most gas stations.

Capitan do Porto   Save time and go directly to the appropriate dock. The posted list of ships does not give destinations or berthing information. The information officer knows nothing.

Venezuelan Consulate   Rua Recife 1620, morning hours, Mon-Fri. Overland trucks that need permits and insurance in Venezuela are advised to obtain them at the consulate in Rio.

Places to stay

You have the choice of an expensive hotel with low clearance, underground parking or cheaper accommodation and a public parking lot. A private, all-night guard charges about US$5 per night.

Hotel Anaconda   Three blocks east of **Pensão Sulista**, in the backpackers section. Inexpensive, institutional but the management can arrange safe parking nearby.

Pensão Sulista   On the corner of Quintino Bocaiuva and Nabuco; cheap, basic, laundry facilities and private baths with secure but limited parking. This was the only place we found that could accommodate the height of our VW.

Camping   Owing to the vast urban sprawl of industrial Manaus, camping is nearly impossible. The beach area known as Ponta Negra is now a narrow, cement parking area. Good swimming, very popular but no security.

Places to visit

Tour companies barrage foreigners with brochures for jungle trips whose boats depart from the floating dock at the center of the city. Overland travelers will see nothing new but nevertheless, **Amazon Wild Tours** (US$125 per day), Rua Quintino Bocaiuva 425, Room 102, has been recommended by budget travelers.

A walking tour will take you past many fine structures preserved from the days of the rubber boom. Look for dates imprinted over the lintels and imagine the barons who sent their dirty clothes to Europe for launder. Of course, no visit to Manaus is complete without touring the ornate opera house, the **Teatro Amazonas** constructed in 1896 and restored in 1990. The nightly theatrical productions are reasonably priced.

Belém

A leviathan city with a population of 1,244,688, Belém is first a port and secondly a commercial center for the northeast. It sprawls on the southern bank of the Amazon near its aperture to the Atlantic Ocean, and serves as the capital of Pará, the second largest state behind Amazonas.

River distance from Manaus is 1,713km. By land from Teresina, in the south, BR316 shoots through 947km of parched land.

To the west is Santarém, a charming river port, one day out of Belém. If the weather permits road travel, Santarém is an ideal port to load or unload a vehicle and for circumventing customs fees, hassles and tidal delays in Belém. The road juncture to Santarém is through Marabá, to the south of Belém.

Places to stay

Boat operators will sometimes let you stay on the boat. Lack of parking in the city center is a problem. Less expensive and pleasant hotels can be found immediately outside Belém on the road south toward Teresina, or east toward Salinópolis.

THE NORTHEAST COAST

Savvy travelers and Brazilians nominate these beaches as the best in all Latin America. They aren't well known because they are difficult to reach by all except the self-propelled traveler.

Ilha de Mosqueiro

Fresh-water lagoons lace Mosqueiro Island, 86km east and north of Belém by road, where you'll find good bathing, free camping, cheap fish restaurants and tranquil *pousadas* (just follow the road signs).

Cyclists can utilize a twice-daily passenger ferry between Belém and Bispo, Praia Grande, on the island. Popular vacation spots are Farol, Grande, Chapéu Virado and San Francisco. Illuminated by night, quiet on weekdays, safe camping is possible all along the tree-shaded beach road.

Further afield

Recommended beaches in Pará state are the island of **Bahia do Maracaná** near the town of Maruda 93km north of Castanhal, **Salinópolis**, and **Ajuruteua**, northeast of Bragança.

Salinópolis

Also known as Salinas, is on the Atlantic Ocean, 223km north and east of Belém. It is a sleepy resort town except during holidays when the population swells to nearly 23,000. Off-season, many expensive houses stand empty.

Places to stay/eat

Salinópolis' beach access is limited: there's a saltwater marsh on one end and houses on the other. Camping is possible in the public parking lot fronting the marsh at the end of the road, known as Macarico, also a military drill field. The many restaurants liven up with bands and dancing at weekends when local farmers come to town.

Two hotels offer secure private parking and cheap rooms. **Hotel Florida**, owner Claude Grenier speaks English and French and serves excellent food. Also try **Hotel Salinas**.

Buy supplies in Pôrto Grande, the fishing village on the west end of Salinópolis. Ice, fresh vegetables and fruit, fish and crab are abundant and less expensive than anywhere else. Excellent meals are available at **Casa do Caranguejo**, on the lagoon.

Two kilometers before Salinópolis is a cloverleaf turn off to **Ilha do Atalaia**, 7km, another high-rise resort town but with sand-dunes and hard beach sand. Fish restaurants are a bit overpriced but conveniently extend over 2km of beachfront. Campers beware: a very high tide floods the entire beach.

Another popular location is along the river. One kilometer past the *Posto do Policia Militar* is a turn-off to the fishing village of Cuiarana. Look for the signs to **Gringo Louco** that caters to tour groups, with a restaurant and *pousada*, US$40, double.

CEARÁ AND MARANHÃO STATES

Ceará state is one of the most scenic in all Brazil. Mountains and jungle-covered escarpments carve the inland terrain surrounding

Ubajara. Crested sand-dunes sculpt coco-palm fishing villages. The state is ideal for anyone seeking get-away coves.

BR316 was one of the original roads to nowhere that paved the way for settlers. The jungle was hacked away, exposing poor soil, and droughts ensued along with governmental neglect. Narrow and monotonously poor, strip towns cling to the roadside as if the road itself were a the trunk root for survival. Through Maranhão BR316 is deeply rutted with unmarked *lombadas*, and BR222 between Teresina and Piripiri is impossibly worse.

Places to visit
Santa Ines
There are two hotels with parking, but **Restaurante Sabors do Nordeste** on the road west, allows camping and serves good fish dinners.

Bacabal
On the banks of the Río Meraim, this shady town is a mecca of repairs for almost any make vehicle. The banks do not change money, you'll have to go to São Luis or Teresina.

Campo Major
A military camp borders the picturesque lake at the center of town. Join the joggers and walkers for a break from routine.

Piripiri
We stopped to ask directions and almost didn't leave. Ultra-friendly residents gave us a town tour and supplies, we gave them a Kombi tour. Their library needs reference books.

Parque Nacional de Sete Cidades
Past Piripiri 26km, open daily until 6pm, admission US$1. Bizarre rock formations entertain your imagination, natural swimming pools and ancient ocher paintings on the rock walls are attributed to Vikings or Phoenicians but were most likely made by early, indigenous *Tabajaras*. Within the park is a hotel. Camping in the grass field costs US$3 per site. Outside the gates is Hotel **Fazenda Sete Cidades**, US$18 per room. We camped here free.

Parque Nacional de Ubajara
Ferns and palms cover steep escarpments with plunging waterfalls. A *teleferico* (1991) descends to the entrance of many spectacular caverns. Admission US$2 per person. No camping within the park.

Camping permitted (US$10) in the floral gardens of **Hotel Pousada da Neblina** 1km from the park entrance; swimming pool.

Jericoacoara

The most northerly of popular beach towns in Ceará state is surrounded by ocean, towering sand-dunes and saltwater marsh. It is the latest "in spot" for Brazilian weekend partiers and backpacking gringos. *Pousadas* and restaurants fill early despite the difficulty in reaching Jericoacoara.

Custom built, high-rise trucks traverse the final 1.5km into town. Likewise, 4WD vehicles can make it at low tide, dry season. Nearby towns specialize in storage of private vehicles, but be wary of hard-sell hustlers. Exercise care in choosing storage for your vehicle and, once in Jericoacoara, with your hotel. Theft is on the increase.

To get to Jericoacoara, follow BR222 through Itapipoca and north to Marco where you'll hit pitted dirt roads. Fortaleza is 317km to the south. Supplies are very basic en route, take water.

From the north take CE071 to Sobral and follow CE161 to Morrinhos. A truly wretched 72km dirt road splits off at Granja (very low bridge clearance). There are interesting farm communities en route.

Praia da Laguinha

Just over 100km north of Fortaleza and south of Jericoacoara is this well-known secret; a tranquil beach surrounded by sand-dunes. *Jangadas*, raft-shaped sailing boats, come in at sunset laden with fish. Lobster, crab and shrimp, cheaper than fish, are very popular and disappear quickly (inquire at the white house with stairs, behind the church on the plaza). There is excellent free camping among the palms along the beach.

O Milton Bar Restô, E Pousada is always open. Owner Jaoazinho Gois gave us a room key so we could do our "necessaries". Fresh water bathing is under a pipe where the fishing *jangadas* beach.

Paracuru

It is small enough to be attractive to seekers of the off-beat. For us coming from the northeast, the restaurants, bakeries and markets were marvels. This is also the first place we found 20 liter bottled water, a reassuring find considering cholera epidemics are rampant in the north. Camping is available at the beach front *pousadas*. High tides prohibit beach camping.

Fortaleza

The capital of Ceará, is home to 1,765,800 people who boast they live at "The Beach of the Future". As population spills from the south and meets with the unemployed laborers from the northeast, Fortaleza could well be a "wanna-be" Rio de Janeiro by the year 2000. In spite of its pretentions, it retains a laid-back, unhurried charm. Restaurants, grocery stores and chic clothing boutiques offer almost anything that a tired road traveler could wish for.

Places to stay
There are many hotels with parking in the mid-to-expensive range. Camping is difficult along the beach. Northward, the beachfront is industrial/commercial. Going south from the center of town is **The Beach**, a string of cosmopolitan restaurants and half-built, concrete condominiums.

South of Fortaleza
The beach road from Fortaleza does not connect to the southerly beaches. You must pick up BR116 and turn off at Aquiraz. Highly recommended beach camping can be found at **Iguape** and **Caponga**, fed by a freshwater river.

Morro Branco
Distinctly amenable for cobblestone streets, fresh sand-filtered water that flows on to the beach from pipes that stud seashore cliffs, sand-dunes and colorful clay ravines is Morro Branco. *Jangada* boats glide in at sunset laden with fish, lobster, crab and shrimp. The beach-side restaurants close by 6pm, after the last tourist bus departs to Fortaleza, so make eating arrangements early with **Restó Do Riba** or **Bar do Sandro**.

Canóa Quebrada
Tiny Canóa is perched on a cliff strewn with inexpensive *pousadas*, restaurants and *forro* bars. Since getting electricity in 1990, the fishing village has emerged as a popular spot for foreigners and Brazilians alike. During July, the sandy streets of town are jammed with visiting traffic. Off-season, Canóa is tranquil, but weekend nightlife greets the dawn. Locals nap frequently during the day in order to maintain the pace. Noon action unfolds on the central beach among a medley of small fish restaurants, *barracas*. Sunsets are superb from atop the pink sand-dunes that sweep skyward behind the town.

If you want to stay here, there is a *pousada* at the end of each sand alley, and at points in between. Camping is possible on the beach but access is through such soft sand that it bogs 4WD. We camped alongside a small *pousada* where, once again, we were given a free room key for showering. You would be well advised to avoid a *pousada* near the center of town unless your heart pounds to the beat of loud disco music.

Pizza lovers should buy tidbits of seafood at the beach and take their ingredients to **Pizzaria** on Broadway (the main street) for the **best** white seafood pizza in the New World.

Aracati
Just 13km north of Canóa, you will find supplies, markets, repairs and exchange are abundant in this city of 61,700. (Exchange travelers checks at **Bancesa** Rua Col Alexandrino; two doors down, Banco do Brasil accepts only Visa cards).

Natal
Boasting a population of 607,000, industrial Natal is the capital of Rio Grande de Norte. Pleasant, as far as cities go, with extensive beaches, it is fairly easy to get around thanks to signs indicating routes, but there isn't much to see. Most people head out to the smaller, outlying beaches. **Genipabu**, slightly north, has been taken over by dune buggy enthusiasts who race the huge sand-dunes and compete to break the sound barrier.

Praia de Pipa
South of Natal, this village is *pousada* central for several gorgeous beaches. To reach Pipa, take BR101, 69km south of Natal and turn east at Goianinha (where Banco do Brasil accepts Visa). Another 19km along a well-populated dirt road takes you to **Tibau do Sul** where the Río Jactí spills into the ocean. (Shrimp farmers sell shrimp here at bargain prices.) Pipa is another 8km to the south.

Places to stay
Espaço Verde   Located on the mainstreet, is a regional restaurant and campground, US$1 per person. *Tamarin* monkeys chatter in the coco palms. Pipa beach is very rocky and not good for swimming or camping but a short walk north will take you to numerous sandy coves.

Praia dos Golfinhos   Tent camping is possible beneath the sheer, colored cliffs that embrace this beach where dolphins chase their breakfasts.

Praia do Madeiro   Fringed with coco palms. On the cliff above is the lovely *Village Naturez*, US$20 cabin for two, pool, gardens and overpriced restaurant.

The beaches south of Pipa are developing rapidly. *Barracas* and pricey *pousadas* at Praia do Amor. Sibaúma, 10km south of Pipa, is a poor village of sugar cane workers and a site for new beachfront homes whose owners arrive and depart by private planes.

REAL OR IMAGINARY

Umbanda is one of a score of diverse religious practices that similarly incorporates Christian elements with rituals imported from West Africa, and embraces spiritualism. Subtle differences in ritual or between deities distinguish one center or church from another, just as different regions recognize *Umbanda* by such names as *Candomblé, Xangô* and *Macumba*.

Every Brazilian knows something about *Umbanda* and, in one way or another, acknowledges its influence in society whether they believe or not. We met detractors who carried amulets or avoided disturbing a ceremonial site.

The astute traveler will recognize evidence of *Umbanda* throughout Brazil. Paraphernalia shops are in every town or market, some churches even advertise; many *samba* dances at *Carnaval* derive their inspiration from the rites. Your first brush with *Umbanda* may be similar to ours.

On the morning of our second night in Brazil, we went down to the river to bathe. Not 20 feet from our camping spot was what looked to be the remnants of a beach party. However, the empty liquor bottles, scattered cigarettes and half-burnt, multi-colored candles seemed to be intentionally arranged. It had not been there the night before nor had we heard anything that night but frogs. Honestly, it gave us the creeps.

I asked in Boa Vista about what we'd seen. Everyone flushed pale and asked if we had touched it. When I assured them that we had not disturbed the site, color returned to their faces. Other than to say that it was *Umbanda*, no-one would explain the significance.

Such unexplained occurrences continued as we traveled. In Olinda, we met and queried two Brazilian anthropologists, Paula and Nelson, who admitted to *Umbanda's* powerful influence in all strata of society, but confessed personal skepticism and curiosity. Together we visited a local church, Sodalicio da Divina Profecia.

The inner sanctum must have held a thousand statues of everything from mermaids and *Mãe de Santo* who looks like an old black man, to *Xangô* who looks like a white conquistador. Tawdry colored beads draped the statues and the offerings of cigars, candles and liquor. The Priest and Priestess looked like gypsies.

Paula and Nelson went for private council with Priestess Mme Edth Torquato, an uncommonly ugly woman wearing a gold-gilded tiara, leaving us alone with Priest Andre Assis and the statues. He entertained us with photo albums of ritual offerings and spirit possessions. Very interesting stuff until we linked explicit photos of bare-handed "surgeries" with Andre's claim to be the reincarnation of a Doctor Adolph Fritz, a German physician who died in 1940. Andre wanted to perform surgery on us in order to demonstrate his prowess. Robb and I immediately decided to wait for Paula and Nelson, outside.

ARGENTINA
La Boca, a section of Buenos Aires, Argentina (EP)

BRAZIL
Above: Brazilian rodeo (EP)
Below: Foz do Iguaçu (EP)

A BIRDWATCHER'S PARADISE
Left: Blue and gold macaw (EP)
Right: Common egret (EP)

BEWARE! There are some nasty, and cheeky, characters in Latin America. (EP)

João Pessoa
The capital of the state of Paraíba, population 497,306, is surrounded by lush fields of sugar cane, pineapple, manioc and beans. The city is industrial, with belching smoke stacks. Good supplies are available for campers headed south to better beaches.

Praias Jacumã
Tabatinga, Coqueirinho, and the official nude beach, Tambaba, are all reached via Conde. From BR101, 13km south of João Pessoa turn off to Conde, population 10,396. Provision here and in Jacumã (14km) for primitive camping.

Tambaba
An excellent beach with coco palms, tropically lush covered dunes, craggy clay valleys sculpted by wind and sea, trees draped with flowering vines and an official, nude sector, offers something for every nature lover. The road from Coqueirinho is very nasty and washes out in the rainy season.

Olinda and Recife
A very popular *carnaval* and Foundation Day festival, March 12-15, spurs rival dance groups to practice year round. The narrow beach is not attractive and it's polluted. Do something different here, like investigate the religious arts imported from Africa. Practitioners of *candomblé* and *umbanda* open their church ceremonies to walk-ins throughout the historic district of Olinda. Artisan shops are housed in colonial convents constructed soon after the city founding in 1582.

Take public transport into Recife, population 1,300,000. Beachside is Boa Viagem, where you'll find money exchange, Banco do Brasil, vehicle repairs and a McDonalds.

Places to stay
Stay in Olinda and commute into Recife.

Camping Olinda   Rua Bom Succeso 262, Amparo tel 429 1365, located at the center of old Olinda, several blocks from the ocean. It is a picturesque area with narrow cobblestone streets but difficult navigation for oversized vehicles.

Hotel Alberque de Juventud, Rua do Sol 233; tel: 429 1592. A youth hostel, US$12 double room, some parking, safe, popular.

Very nice but very expensive hotels are strung along the north end of the beach. In Recife, the beach community of Boa Viagem is popular, but with high-rise condos and shopping districts, it is not easy to find lodging with parking.

GOING SOUTH

An alternative to BR101 runs south 285km to Maceió. AL-101 takes you through sugar cane fields and small towns, some of which are located on the beaches and only spring to life during summer vacation, such as Tamandaré. Maceió's beach is a popular destination for Brazilian tourists. On the north end is Jatiúca with an oceanfront campground, *Camping Jatiúca*, US$8 per site, electricity and showers. Heading south toward Salvador (632km) and Rio (2,131km), BR101 takes on the ruggedness of a bombed zone. For 100km, locals dig up the pitted road with hoes and then pretend to refill them in exchange for money. It is a pitiful and disconcerting sight.

Arembepe

The first really good beach south of Recife is tiny Arembepe, with surf foaming over the ubiquitous reef into a natural swimming pool. Slightly north of town, where the dunes begin, there is good swimming and surfing. Follow the dirt road north of town that runs between dunes and freshwater lakes to the amazing *Aldea de Hippies*. This Tahitian-looking village was founded by hippies in 1975 and today receives government support. Camping is free.

Ilheus

Eight hours south of Salvador takes you to Ilheus, the setting for Jorge Amado's book, *Golden Harvest*, which documents the cacao boom and bust. Surprisingly, it looked as the book described, even the people seemed familiar characters. The road is hilly but bamboo-shaded. There are inexpensive campgrounds on the beach south of the inlet.

Pôrto Seguro

Seguro attracts jetsetters on their way to up-market **Arraial D'ajuda**, across the inlet. Prices are better in Seguro and many budget travelers stay here, browse the souvenir shops, outdoor restaurants and money exchange.

The ferry to Arraial charges US$4 for a vehicle, US$2 for a *moto*. At the summit of a slippery incline is the town. It descends sharply on the other side and there you'll find outdoor malls, restaurants and hotels as swanky as in Europe.

Places to stay

Most hotels and campgrounds in both Pôrto Seguro and Arraial operate during *carnaval* only. Year round campgrounds follow.

Campina dos Marajaás   In the center of Seguro, US$3 per person, fenced.
Camping de Jussara   At base of Arraial, same price, hot showers, shady.

There are beautiful beaches for camping, north of **Vitria** where BR101 swings west toward Belo Horizonte. Continuing south on BR101 from Vitria, you'll pass through the lovely state of Espirto Santo.

Ouro Preto
Anyone headed to Brasilia, the nation's capital, or Belo Horizonte, or those tired of the coastal route, should definitely detour into Ouro Preto. Most of the gem-studded jewelry and giant crystals that you'll see in Brazil are extracted from this hill country. Ouro Preto is an ageless mining town with stunning colonial architecture preserved as a national monument. The 20th-century American poet and traveler, Elizabeth Bishop, lived and wrote here (*see Further Reading, page 263*).

RÍO DE JANEIRO

The world-famous *Carnaval* has elevated this city to one of the wonders of the world. During the three days preceding Shrove Tuesday and several days thereafter, bacchanalian festivities reign. Advance reservations are absolutely necessary and tickets to the judging area, at the *Sambadrome* arena, can be inflated 20 times. Street parades are rowdy but free. Check out Av Rio Branco after 9pm. Rio is busy all year; congested with vacationers between June and August when it's coldest down south, and unfettered bodies strut the surrounding beaches of Flamengo, Copacabana, Ipanema and Leblon. Otherwise, Rio is easy to get through and easy to navigate around. Buses and a metro system link far-flung areas with an efficient, frequent and cheap service. Pick up a copy of the free booklet, *Riotour*, for complete information on anything you might need to know.

Getting there
From the north   From **Arrial do Cabo** (overrated but a good place to re-group before or after the city traffic) cross the six-lane bridge, avoiding rush-hour traffic. Follow signs to the beaches which will take you to the center of the tourism strip: Flamenco, Copacabana, Ipanema/Leblon, Botafogo, etc. Immediately after the bridge, there is a tricky clover-leaf exit. Head east, no matter where you exit.
From the south   Don't miss the small, colonial town of **Parati**,

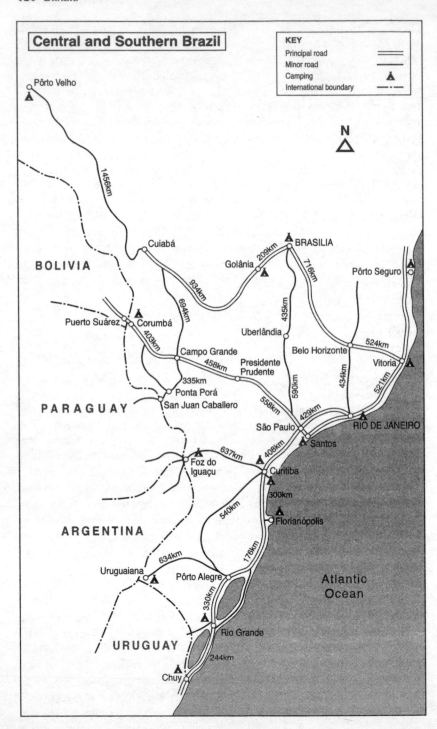

Central and Southern Brazil

KEY
Principal road
Minor road
Camping
International boundary

N

Pôrto Velho

1456km

Cuiabá

BOLIVIA

Golânia 209km BRASILIA

716km

Pôrto Seguro

934km

694km

Uberlândia

435km

524km

Puerto Suárez Corumbá

403km

Campo Grande

458km

Belo Horizonte

Vitoria

590km

434km

521km

Presidente
Prudente

335km

Ponta Porá

558km

San Juan Caballero

429km

PARAGUAY

São Paulo

RIO DE JANEIRO

637km

408km

Santos

Foz do
Iguaçu

Curitiba

300km

540km

Florianópolis

ARGENTINA

634km

176km

Uruguaiana

Pôrto Alegre

Atlantic
Ocean

330km

Rio Grande

URUGUAY

244km

Chuy

186km south of Rio. Turn onto RJ07 at Itaguai. There are several good campgrounds in this relaxing town or free camp 2km north of town, by the ocean. Hug the alternative, coastal highway, SP55, with hillside vistas (altitude 1,119m) of turquoise-blue ocean and long, brilliantly white beaches. The SP55 will lead you north to BR101 and **Praia Recreio dos Bandeirantes** with several campgrounds, restaurants and a regular bus service (30-45 minutes each way) into Rio.
From São Paulo BR 116 is signposted but more congested than the above route.
From Belo Horizonte BR040 leads directly into Av Brasil. There are excellent supermarkets on this road.

Places to stay
Hotel Florida Rua Ferreira Viana and Catete; beachside, breakfast and guarded parking.
Hotel Marajo Rua Joaquim Silva, **Victoria**, **Imperial**, and **Hispano Americano,** all in the beachside area north of the Hotel Florida. Recommended parking lots are at Rua dos Toneleiros with Av Henrique Veladares which runs into Av Chile, and also at the corner of Av Invalidos and Relagao.
Ingles 20 Rua Siliera Martins; popular with overland groups.

Campgrounds are located south of the city in Bandeirantes beach. Leave your vehicle, or tent, at one of these places and use public transport. Nearby shopping at the Barra Shopping Center has supermarkets, movies, ice skating, bowling, etc.

Camping Clube do Brasil Several kilometers south of Ostal on Av das Américas. Full facilities, wooded, but not on the beach.
Novo Rio Almost adjacent to the above; nice and less expensive than at the club.
Ostal Corner of Av Sernambetiba directly in front of ocean. This is a modest trailer park with camping space.

São Paulo
We planned a fact-finding mission into this enormous city but once we got on the fast, multi-lane highways, we couldn't get off. And when we did, we were too dazed to turn around and try it again. Brazilians gave us the following helpful advice, "First you must know where you're going and how to get there. Then you grit your teeth, stomp on the pedal and pray".
Nor did we meet any foreigners who could coherently elucidate road directions. We won't add to the confusion by inventing information.

From São Paolo, 400km to the north, BR116 is bumpy and dangerous because of the many fast drivers. BR277 goes through Curitiba and west to Foz do Iguaçu.

THE WESTERN REGION
The Pantanal
There are several ways to enter the wetlands of the Pantanal, but whatever means you select, the Pantanal should not be missed. Here you'll see flora and fauna that is unrivalled by most wildlife refuges worldwide. Foremost is the *capybara*, a giant-sized relative of the guinea pig, that wallows in herds in shallow water, resembling miniature hippos. Alongside the *capybara*, you'll usually see alligators (*jacaré*) sunning their spiny three-meter-long backs. Flocks of pink flamingo dip their bills in the clear, black water while groups of what are called speckled-emu strut on shore. Anteaters, tapir, jaguars, birds of prey, giant slithering snakes and freshwater fish make this an animal lover's paradise.

The best time to visit is May through October when it is fairly dry and hot. The dirt roads, which provide the best vistas for watching wildlife, are passable. This is also the period when birds nest. In the wet season, December through April, the dirt causeways are subject to flooding and animals pitifully cling to small knolls of dry land and hummocks. Mosquitoes voraciously suck blood all year long. Take strong repellent and apply liberally.

Getting there
From the north Descending from *Pôrto Velho*, it is a straight shot south on BR174 (good infrastructure via Cuiabá) into **Pocone**, the northern entrance to the reserve. Travelers suggest this route as the easiest and quickest way to traverse Brazil. Stock up in Pocone, the next stop is 145km south at Pôrto Jofre. The Transpantaneira is a raised dirt road through a corner of the 77 square mile reserve. There are occasional fish camps and *fazendas* that put up guests.

From the south Leaving São Paulo State, there are any number of fast, superhighways leading into Campo Grande. Take BR262 west from Campo Grande to **Miranda**, the southern gateway to the Pantanal. Get supplies in Miranda. Camping is permitted 12km west of town on the grounds of the hotel **Fazenda Salobra**.

From the west Coming from Bolivia, Corumbá is the border town and the western gateway to the Pantanal.

Bonito

For western travelers this and **Aquidauana** are the only sizeable towns between Miranda and Ponto Porá. In this sector, roads are mainly lonely dirt arteries skirting cattle *fazendas*. You're likely to meet the last of the true cowboy *gauchos* here, but not much else.

Pretty Bonito though, is surrounded by gentle hills, rivers and natural springs which are attracting domestic tourists. Certified divers can explore a labyrinth of underwater caves while non-divers refresh themselves under waterfalls.

Tour companies, campgrounds and inexpensive *pousadas* abound amid what is still a rustic, unspoiled area.

Caution: This is the area that our van was slathered in a ceramic-like mud.

Ponto Porá

Ponto Porá on the Brazil border is divided from Pedro Juan Caballero, Paraguay, by an imaginary line running through the center of Rua Independencia (called Rua Dr Francia on the Paraguay side). You can pass freely between these two towns, but not beyond. Both currencies, Brazilian reals and Paraguayan guaranís (and dollars) are freely exchanged in shops on each side of the border; in fact, this is a good place to stock up on dollars without forfeiting a discount or commission. Groceries are cheaper in Ponto Porá and manufactured goods cheaper in Pedro Juan Caballero. There are no amenable camping areas in either town.

Useful information

Customs   Go to the airport in southeast quadrant of town. The staff is very helpful.

Immigration   The office of the *Policia Federal*, is located in a dowdy, smelly, two-story building on Rua Mal Floriána 1483.

Money exchange   All *cambios* are located in Pedro Juan Caballero. In Ponta Porá go to the **Banco do Brasil**.

Paraguay consulate   The office is located next to the *Hotel Internacional*.

FOZ DO IGUAÇU

Brazil, Paraguay and Argentina meet at this corner of the world. The two main attractions are The Falls and Itaipú Dam. Eco-tourism has effected a positive impact; much of the lush surrounding countryside is protected. This area definitely deserves a minimum three-day stop. The borders are user-friendly. You do not need visas, exit or entry stamps, in order to cross the different borders temporarily. Border officials told us that there isn't a time limit for such excursions, but you must stay within a restricted area. This means you can go with a vehicle to the Brazilian side of the falls one day, the Argentine side another or cross into Paraguay to visit Itaipú Dam or shop without surrendering documents.

We formally entered Brazil from Paraguay when our time expired in that country, but then returned to Ciudad del Este, Paraguay for five days of car repairs, local sightseeing, money exchange and, again, for shopping. Staple goods such as food and fuel cost half of what is charged in Brazil and Argentina. Another time we camped alongside the Argentine side of the falls and several days later returned to the Brazil side.

Travelers to the interior of any of these countries must go through formalities. Customs and immigration between Brazil and Argentina are housed in one building alongside the Río Paraná. The Friendship Bridge also spans the Rio Paraná but between Paraguay and Brazil. Pertinent offices are located on each side of the congested bridge. On the Brazil side all traffic funnels past "the buildings". On the Paraguay side only one building services all functions.

Places to stay

Accommodation, restaurant and camping are better and cheaper in Foz do Iguaçu than in neighboring Paraguay and Argentina.

There are many hotels in Foz and a billion hotel "guides" who advertise accommodation. Do not let anyone accompany you. One unfortunate and serious note is the increasing crime in Foz city. Incidences of armed-robbery in parking lots and drive-by shootings of tourists on city streets indicate the need for conservative precautions. The following campgrounds are very safe.

Brazil

Camping Clube do Brasil   At the entrance to the Iguaçu national park. Beautiful but a remote site; no restaurant or food supplies; US$15 per person.

Camping International   Tucked at the end of a side street on the outskirts of Foz, going toward the falls. Look for the turn-off to Porto Meira, 3km before Rafhians restaurant. Look for signs. Very popular. US$4 per person with hot showers, 110 electricity, gardens, security, cabins, swimming pool and small restaurant. Management is thinking of changing names to *Piscina do Bosque*.

Camping International   Further out of town on the main highway toward the falls. This site is exposed and unsafe.

Argentina

There are two campgrounds on the road south from Brazil to the park:
El Pindo   Near the forked turn-off to Ciudad de Puerto Iguazu, is simple but adequate.
Camping Viejo Americana   Further on, just outside the park entrance; US$4 per person plus US$6 for the site; pools, gardens, grills, restaurants, etc.
Ciudad del Puerto Iguazu   Within the town of the same name this municipal campground often doubles as a *futebol* field.
National Park   Free, primitive camping is permitted in Argentina at a site above *Garganta del Diablo* (The Devil's Throat). To reach this scenic location, turn on to a dirt road about 1,000m beyond the Argentine park gates, toward Puerto Canoa and El Ñandu. Ask the park rangers if in doubt. There are bathrooms but no drinking water or food.

Useful addresses

American Express   STTC Turismo is located in the Hotel Bourbon on the road to the falls.
Argentine Consulate   Rua Don Pedro II.
Banco do Brasil   Av Brasil, changes travelers checks and Visa cards.
Paraguay Consulate   Bartolmeu de Gusmão 480.
Tourist offices   One is located on Av Brasil approximately 1,000m east of the *aduana*, near the Friendship Bridge. Another is at the eastern entrance to the city, on the Curitiba road. Both stock city maps and are extremely helpful.

Places to visit
The Falls

Admission to the falls on the Brazil side is accepted in reals only, US$2 per person. (The Argentina side accepts pesos, reals and dollars at US$5 per person.) The Brazil side has been called the most scenic, due to the panoramic view of the falls from the sheer cement-pathed cliffs. It will evoke gasps from the dullest of travelers.

Soon after entering the park, you can find vendors of jungle hikes and boat trips. Helicopter rides cost US$30 per person for approximately 20 minutes. The massive falls are loud, but not so loud as to drown out the helicopters and the intrusive whine of boat motors.

Aside an unforgettable experience with a troop of *coatamundis* (extremely aggressive beggars that look and act like pointed-nosed raccoons), we preferred the Argentine side of the falls for a *sense-a-rama* experience. Take a bathing suit as there are many fern-laced pools. Trails are excellently marked with descriptive signposts of flora and fauna, picnic areas, and expensive food/souvenir/beer kiosks.

Take the free boat-shuttle to the island San Martin for swimming, hiking, and unique views of the *Garganta del Diablo*. Depending on the force of the water, you can climb along the lip of some of the falls.

Itaipú Dam The most impressive time to view the workings of this hydro-electric plant is during or immediately after the rainy season. The alleged most powerful dam in the world is otherwise so disappointing that the video tape at the information centers is a highlight.

THE SOUTH

Highways are signposted and maps are fairly accurate from São Paulo south.

Southern Brazil is very organized and architecturally reminiscent of the early European settlers' influence. It is a culturally rich sector of Brazil and the infrastructure requires little elaboration except to note that the chocolate, sausages and cheese are scrumptious. Also, don't miss **Blumenau** in October when the city hosts the biggest beer bash outside of Munich.

Curitiba

One of the few remaining railroads in South America connects Curitiba with Paranagua, on the coast. The rail tracks, and a road, wend through mountainous rain forests with views of deep gorges. It is truly spectacular and should not be missed.

Places to stay

The 400km stretch between Curitiba and São Paulo is notoriously bumpy and dangerous with many fast drivers. It is safer to stay near Curitiba than to attempt a late start after your train ride. The city was too congested with traffic for us to find a hotel.

Camping Clube do Brasil Located 14km north of Curitiba on BR116.
Municipal campground Located 7km north of Curitiba on BR116.
South of Parangua Campgrounds and hotels cluster around Montinhos (a surfing beach) and Garatuba (a ferry crossing).

Vila Velha

BR277 connects Foz with Curitiba. The 631km stretch takes about ten hours to drive over hilly, long inclines. A good place to break lies 94km west of Curitiba on BR277. **Vila Velha** is a national park with strange rock formations and grottos. The modest admission price also includes admission into Furnas, giant sink holes, and Lagoa Dourada. Swimming is possible at both sites.

Places to stay

Camping Clube do Brasil Full facilities, very expensive but easy to find along BR277.

The forestry station Located 10km from the park entrance where they'll give you directions. It is secure and free.

Lagoa Dourada This location is free although less secure than the others.

Porto Alegre

South of this sprawling city, the road narrows and population thins out. Brazilians recommend the beaches as the best camping spots in the country. Keep supplies topped up because there are long stretches with nothing. If you follow the western side of the lake, stop at **São Lourenço do Sul**, a pleasant resort community with good campgrounds in and around the yacht club. Roads are subject to flooding to each side of **Lagoa dos Patos** which is a popular fishing and sailing lagoon.

Pelotas

Users of propane gas should refill tanks before going into Uruguay and Argentina, where it is more expensive. Go to *Agip Liquigas*, Av Fernando Osorio, at the north end of town, 1.5km from BR116.

128

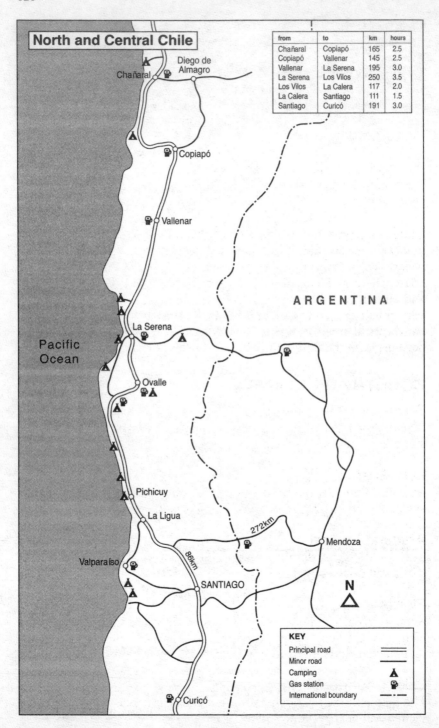

North and Central Chile

from	to	km	hours
Chañaral	Copiapó	165	2.5
Copiapó	Vallenar	145	2.5
Vallenar	La Serena	195	3.0
La Serena	Los Vilos	250	3.5
Los Vilos	La Calera	117	2.0
La Calera	Santiago	111	1.5
Santiago	Curicó	191	3.0

Diego de Almagro

Chañaral

Copiapó

Vallenar

ARGENTINA

La Serena

Pacific Ocean

Ovalle

Pichicuy

La Ligua

272km

86km

Mendoza

Valparaíso

SANTIAGO

N

Curicó

KEY

Principal road	═══
Minor road	═══
Camping	⛺
Gas station	⛽
International boundary	·—·—·

Chapter Ten

Chile

Chile is a stringbean of a country, 4,300km long and so narrow that you can see across its width, from the snowy *cordillera* to the Pacific ocean. Volcanoes puff with promise and fjords lace the southern coast where glaciers glimmer like sapphires. Chile is at once wild and tamed, very European and North American, but the people are very much their own. Roman numerals designate states instead of names, as in other countries. Region I covers the far north and Tierra del Fuego; in the far south is Region X.

COUNTRY HIGHLIGHTS

Torres del Paine National Park
A natural wonder of menthol-blue glaciers and lakes, golden tundra and craggy peaks. The hiking is fantastic.

Lake District
Volcanoes interlaced by a myriad of lakes, Swiss-style chalets surrounded by neat gardens, is nothing less than picturesque.

Atacama desert
The world's driest desert is a seemingly endless panorama of baked rocks and dried salt lakes.

Fjords
Snow-covered and heavily forested fjords lace the southern coast of Chile. A four-day ferry trip through 2,090km of ocean bound mountains is a continental highlight.

Lake Chungará
The lake is home to flocks of pink flamingos, herds of endangered vicuña and nearly extinct flora.

POINTS OF ENTRY

From Argentina
See *Chapter Seven, Argentina, Points of entry*.

From Bolivia
There are at least three points of entry to Chile. The most southern is at 5,000m between **Laguna Verde**, Bolivia and 25km later to **San Pedro de Atacama**. One motorcyclist described the Bolivian connection as, "a bunch of rugged dirt trails, smuggler's routes. I rode a full day between towns without seeing anyone else. Be prepared for bitter cold at night and carry extra supplies".

Chungará   Peaking above 5,200m, this truck route is paved and mostly downhill on the Chilean side. It offers the best infrastructure between Bolivia and Chile.

Visviri   At the corner of Bolivia and Peru, this crossing is very remote and difficult (see *Chapter Eight, Bolivia*).

From Peru
There is only one border point with Peru and that is on the Pan-Am highway: Santa Rosa (Tacna), Peru and Chacalluta (Arica).

ON THE ROAD

Primary roads are generally good but, unfortunately for cyclists, there is not much of a road shoulder. The Pan-Am highway bisects Chile from north to south and is known as the *Longitudinal*. It bypasses nearly every town and city, so expect to detour, east or west, as much as 80km to reach attractive destinations.

South of Puerto Montt, the unfinished Pan-Am, Ruta 7, is called the Trans-Austral Highway. The *ripio* road is passable only during January and February and ends in Chaitén. Travelers to or from Chile's Tierra del Fuego must either zig-zag through Argentina (see *Chapter Seven, Argentina, Andean routes*), or ferry through the fjords.

Kilometer markings along roads are sometimes wrong by 100km.

Driving style
All traffic laws are strictly enforced. Motorists come to complete stops at yield signs, in the dead of night, and at defunct railroad crossings. The police *Carabinero* monitor traffic with radar guns.

The following regulations apply. Maximum speed on highways is 100kph (60mph) and in towns 50kph (30mph), unless otherwise posted, which it usually is. No right turn on red (maybe five intersections in all Chile are posted to allow this shortcut). Make complete stops at red lights, stop signs, railroad crossings, and at yield signs. Headlight low beams must be used within 100 meters of on-coming traffic. Turn signals are mandatory as are seatbelts, or helmets for motorcyclists.

In Region X, the far south, one paved lane parallels a lane of *ripio*. Right of pavement goes to whomsoever has the paved lane in their direction.

Fuel

Spare fuel tanks are a necessity. Factors such as wind and altitude are aggravated by dire shortages of fuel in some regions. Region X in the south and Regions I and II in the north offer motorists vast distances with no infrastructure.

Propane tanks can be filled in every major city. Ask for AGIP gas.

Border formalities

Vehicles are admitted for 60 days only and extensions are not granted within the country.

At a few borders (mostly in the north) you might be required to file a profile of passengers called a *Relación de Pasajeros*. You'll need four copies of this form and, inconveniently, offices do not stock it. If stuck, ask the driver of a commercial carrier (bus, truck, taxi) to sell them to you, US$0.50.

Cyclists

Definitely consider tossing your bike into a bus or truck in the Atacama. Hundreds of kilometers separate scarce water sources and supplies. Chilean cyclists travel in teams accompanied by supply trucks.

Maps

The *Turis Tel* maps and guidebooks are invaluable (*see Further Reading, page 236*). Don't rely on the accuracy of the kilometer charts because the sums don't add up.

Police

The police *Carabineros* (and there are a trillion of them) maintain traffic order. Bribes and payment for services are completely unacceptable but they are the most helpful and courteous of any in all of Latin America. Chilenos consult with them as if they were travel agents.

Agricultural inspection

Chile does not permit the entry or inter-country transport of any fresh food. This includes meat, seafood, vegetables, fruit, dairy

products and even firewood. These items will be confiscated. The only ways to prevent loss are to eat well in advance of inspection stations, or to pre-cook, dry or can your food supply.

Rigid searches are also conducted at SAG stations within the country. Most internal inspection stations are confined to the regions north of Santiago: at **Cuya**, **Quillagua** and **Caldera** which, unfortunately, are in the Atacama where very basic supplies can be found as far apart as 300km. Leniency is granted to northbound travelers and those with private vehicles. (Commercial vehicles, buses and overland trucks are thoroughly searched.)

USEFUL INFORMATION
Public holidays
January 1 (New Year)
Easter Holy Week (Semana Santa)
May 1 (Labor Day)
May 21 (Naval battle of Iquique)
End of May (Corpus Cristi)
June 29 (Saints Peter and Paul)
August 15 (Asunción de la Virgen)
September 18 (Fiestas Patrias)
September 19 (Army Day)
October 12 (Día de la Raza)
November 1 (All Saints Day — cemetery festivities)
December 25 (Christmas)

When to visit
In the north, you'll find beach weather between August and October. In November, the *altiplano* rages with thunder and lightning storms, snow and hail. The central valley basks in nearly clement temperatures and mild winds for much of the year. The far south is best visited between November and March when northwest winds are at their lowest ebb. Winters start late-April and hang around for skiers through September when rains, mixed with snow flurries, don't seem to end.

Camping
Many campgrounds and national parks are open only during high season, December through February. When closed, some places will allow you to enter or camp free, but there are no facilities.

Public toilets are staffed and charge. **Copec** service centers offer showers for US$1.50, but *for men only*. Several times, late at night, I was allowed access to the men's shower accompanied by my husband. Showers are almost always cold, tepid at best. Perhaps that attests to the popularity of thermal baths in this country.

Money and banking
Banking hours are 9am-2pm, Monday through Friday. The Chilean peso has remained fairly stable in recent years. *Casas de cambio* give a slightly better rate than banks but many don't accept travelers checks or credit cards. **Banco A Edwards** doesn't charge for travelers checks, **Banco de Concepción** accepts Visa; **Fincard** banks accept Mastercard. Exchange rates are lower in Arica than elsewhere.

Business Hours
Santiago is the only city that is said to remain open throughout the *siesta* hours. Generally speaking, there are local and individual variances to the noon break. In Arica for example, many shops are open between 9am-12.30pm and from 4.30pm until 7pm, or maybe 10pm.

Personal security
Perhaps because crime often goes unreported and criminals unprosecuted, a false impression of security has emerged. Owing to this illusion of safety, we place Chile in the caution zone.

National character
The Chilean people are different. They accurately describe themselves as reserved and sticklers for order. Their somber and formal fashions reflect these attitudes. Social and personal problems are shrouded by a conspiracy of silence, of shame, with roots in the terror years of the Pinochet regime. As a result, people are cautious in speech and in forming associations.

Culturally, Chile is the most *macho* society in Latin America. We endured insufferable discourses on men's natural superiority over women.

THE ATACAMA

Unlike Peru's coastal desert, Chile's Atacama offers few rewards beyond basic survival. Nearly 1,500km of sun-baked rock and eery "ex-towns", ghost towns adjacent to "ex-cemeteries", intervene between Arica and Santiago.

In the northern third, the Pan-Am redundantly plunges and climbs through barren canyons of 2,500m in depth. Ancient travelers scraped giant geometric designs and stylized human and animal forms on these rocky hillsides. Experts think they might have been similar to travel bulletins, not unlike the contemporary Coca-Cola *geoglyph* near Arica.

There is no fuel in the entire northern sector of Chile from Arica until Pozo Almante near the junction to Iquique, 49km to the west. The road flattens south to Santiago via dry salt flats, a pitted lunar-like landscape and abandoned nitrate mining towns.

Travel fully-supplied through this region.

Arica

This desert oasis and ocean-side port city survives due to an underground irrigation system fed by the Andes. Until recently, Lake Chungará slaked the thirst of an expanding coastal population. When the lake nearly dried up, environmentalists won international protection of the Andean biosphere. Although water shortages concern residents, swimming pools are weekly emptied of water and refilled. (International aid in the form of chlorine and pool brushes might not be a silly idea.)

Nearly everything is here. The provincial outskirts melt at the center (banks, *cambios*, phone companies). By night these same streets are closed to traffic while pedestrians browse the ultra-sophisticated shops and restaurants. South of the center and along the coast, discos and jet skis vie for the rocky coastline. Slightly north you'll find extensive beaches, surfers and local families.

Places to stay
Hotel Res Madrid Av Banquedano.
Residencial Venecia Av Banquedano 739.
Camping Gallinazo 13km north of Arica, near turn-off to Bolivia; full facilities and pool.
Camping El Refugio Valle de Azapa, a garden-like suburb southwest of Arica; full facilities.

To Lake Chungará and Bolivia

Chilenos refer to the steep and rapid 4,700m ascent to the *altiplano* as "the climb". The road actually peaks at higher elevations. Upon descent, a motor is not necessary but good brakes are. Adapt your engine and tires for altitude regardless of direction and carry supplies to last for days. Aymara and Quechua-speaking Indians herd llama and cultivate tubers (a very low-fat, low-calorie diet) and depend on weekly markets for other nourishment. They have nothing to share with drop-in company.

Putre

This valley plateau is the last supply stop. *Bencina* is sold out of barrels from the main, but modest, grocery store. An excellent hotel is at the entrance to the town. Residents rent rooms and welcome campers.

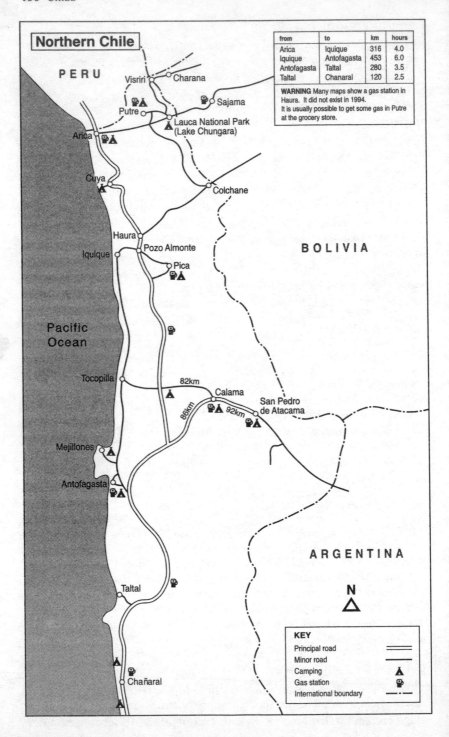

Northern Chile

PERU

BOLIVIA

Pacific Ocean

ARGENTINA

from	to	km	hours
Arica	Iquique	316	4.0
Iquique	Antofagasta	453	6.0
Antofagasta	Taltal	280	3.5
Taltal	Chanaral	120	2.5

WARNING Many maps show a gas station in Haura. It did not exist in 1994.
It is usually possible to get some gas in Putre at the grocery store.

Visriri
Charana
Putre
Sajama
Lauca National Park
(Lake Chungara)
Arica
Cuya
Colchane
Haura
Pozo Almonte
Iquique
Pica
Tocopilla
82km
Calama
San Pedro
de Atacama
86km
92km
Mejillones
Antofagasta
Taltal
Chañaral

N

KEY
Principal road
Minor road
Camping
Gas station
International boundary

Parque Nacional Lauca

Between Putre and Lake Chungará, this park is successfully conserving nearly extinct flora and vicuña from human exploitation.

Chungará

Shelter and hot showers are available at the park office and at nearby border facilities. Scenery, birds, hiking trails exceed the superb.

Visviri

This is an outpost town bordering Peru and Bolivia. Although the Chile/Bolivia railroad bisects the *altiplano* here, there is little else. We were broken down for three days without a mammal sighting before a truck came by and carried a help message to *carabineros* who towed us four hours over frost-hoven roads to their less-remote station.

WHEN TOURISM CAME TO PUTRE

In November 1994, Putre's 800 inhabitants hosted the premier site for a total solar eclipse. Fifteen thousand scientists, celebrities and tourists gathered overnight and left the next morning. The Chilean press called it a Woodstock.

The preceding year had been a flurry of preparations for the onslaught of tourists. Surrounding Aymara villagers had trekked into Putre for weekly English lessons and organizational meetings, and had delayed several local celebrations to create an extravaganza around the solar eclipse.

Traditionally, celebrations begin early and last until the last celebrant drops, in order to accommodate people who have walked far. And this was no exception. Putre sprang to life five days before the tourists arrived with the eclipse and literally fell asleep on its feet a day later.

We nudged one vendor of hand-made fabrics from a standing sleep. "Hello, welcome to my village, how are you," she said in bold English before lapsing into Aymara and nodding off again.

Her university educated son translated the Aymara language into Spanish which I'm now translating into English.

"My mother says she had to walk two days over mountains in order to attend the English lessons. Sometimes her work at home is so great that she didn't come. She says that she loves the English language and she will study harder for the next year."

We asked others about the sudden impact of tourists on their lives. Responses ran the gamut from shyly evasive to politely scornful. "Shirtless, purple haired people are not what we expected. We are poor and modest. But we're learning a lot!"

South of Arica
Salar de Atacama and Valle de Lunar
At the foothills to the Andes, crater-sized pits scar the barren land. Endless salt fields mesmerize daylight travelers. At sunset and sunrise, this area glows with reflected colors. Good supplies are available in Calama and San Pedro de Atacama.

Excellent camping is to be found on the way to San Pedro from Calama. Look for the sign to Peina, turn toward the valley and continue approximately 2km.

La Serena
A large international population resides in and around La Serena. Many are associated with the La Silla observatory and others with the university. This is one of the more pleasant coastal cities in northern Chile. Full facility campgrounds are on the ocean road.

Central Valley
The central garden valley starts approximately 50km north of Santiago and ends above Puerto Montt, in the Lake Region. Living off the land and sea is never easier. Artichokes, asparagus, lettuce, onions, peppers and fruit are abundant and cheaper than elsewhere.

Coastal towns serve up an incredible variety of tasty shell-fish. Succulent giant crab claws are both overpriced and overrated when compared to giant barnacles. Defying the gustatory imagination are mussels, clams and oysters.

SANTIAGO

A rapid metro connects the far-flung suburbs with the center. Find a parking lot and explore using public transport. After stuffing your face, you'll need to walk around before again indulging in culinary delights.

Both educational and worthwhile is the **Museo Chileno de Arte Precolombiano**, Bandera 361. Or stroll along Avenida O'Higgins to Santa Lucia hill for a panoramic vista of the city and mountains.

Smog is a problem. Dangerously high levels are recorded between May and August.

Places to stay
There is no camping in or around Santiago.

Residencial Londres Londres, near the San Francisco church.
Hotel Cervantes Morande 631.
Residencial Mery Pasaje Republica 36, good but expensive.

Useful addresses

Argentina consulate Vicuña Mackenna 41. (Multiple-entry visa is needed if going south to Tierra del Fuego.)
Bolivian consulate Av Santa Maria 2796.
Peruvian consulate Av Providencia 2653, Room 808.
Tourist office Av Providencia 1550, between metro stops Manuel Montt and Pedro de Valdivia.

Places to visit

Decent winter skiing is right outside Santiago, if you happen to be there then. On the coast, popular posh beach resorts are in Valparaíso and Viña del Mar.

Going South

South from Santiago on Ruta 5, the next 150km cuts through the valley. We scouted a number of urban centers and pleasant towns. Quinchamil and Chillán which are both famed artisan centers.

Puente Alto   Stop 40km south of Santiago at the Concha Y Toro vineyard. Free tour and wine tasting. Good prices.
Los Lingues   The famous horse breeding ranch is located 120km south of Santiago on Ruta 5.

Concepción

Detour from Ruta 5 to this large coastal city where you'll find just about anything you need (repairs, etc). Fine grocery stores in new shopping malls lead to the point, Punta el Bosque where the Rio Biobío meets the Pacific. (Camping is permitted but bring supplies.) Weekend vendors sell cooked shellfish.

There are good sandy beaches south of Concepción, beyond the belching coal mines and stinky fishmeal plants. Popular seafood restaurants provide some security and facilities for campers.

Continuing south, you'll pass through the territory of the Mapuche Indians. Once fierce warriors who defeated Incan armies and Valdivia, they're now reduced to poverty.

Loop back to the Pan-Am via scenic **Lago Lanalhue.** There you can stay overnight at one of a number of guesthouses, but there are few possibilities for camping. The road gets rougher from this point, so you will need to take extra care when driving, but gentle mountain scenery and countrified folkways make it a pleasant excursion.

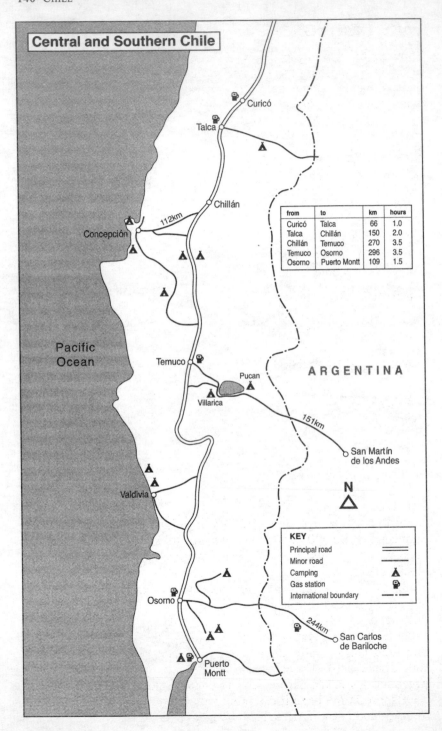

Central and Southern Chile

Pacific Ocean

Concepción

Curicó

Talca

Chillán

112km

Temuco

Pucan

Villarica

151km

San Martín de los Andes

ARGENTINA

Valdivia

Osorno

San Carlos de Bariloche

244km

Puerto Montt

N

from	to	km	hours
Curicó	Talca	66	1.0
Talca	Chillán	150	2.0
Chillán	Temuco	270	3.5
Temuco	Osorno	296	3.5
Osorno	Puerto Montt	109	1.5

KEY

Principal road
Minor road
Camping
Gas station
International boundary

LAKE DISTRICT

South of Temuco begins the Lake District. You'll need several weeks to enjoy meandering through this beautiful country. Don't skip the thermal baths! *Termas* are all over and typically out of the way but when you dunk yourself in one, all your travel aches melt away.

Parque Nacional Villarrica

The smoking *volcán* Villarrica gives its name to the nearby lake and this fantastic park. The 2,800m high volcano takes only eight hours to climb and return. During the open season, river rafts, bikes and horses can be rented.

The easiest access is via the southern shore of Lago Villarrica to Pucon. Shop for the park in the charming town of Villarrica (money changers accept travelers checks), where there are artisan shops, street musicians). Pucon is more expensive and chic.

Petrohues National Park

Stunning year-round beauty lies below the lava fields of Volcán Osorno. Chilly lake Todos Los Santos feeds into bigger Llanguihue via menthol-blue waterfalls, rapids and creeks. Orchids bloom among ferns and lichen-encrusted trees. Great hiking trails! There is an official campground, hotel and restaurant on Lago Todos Los Santos, otherwise rough camp in designated areas.

Paved access is along the southern shore of **Llanquihue**. We were here off-season while the many lakeside hotels, restaurants and campgrounds were closed, the pace of life slow.

Ox-carts creak over the unpaved and deeply rutted northern shore road past peaked houses and golf-course green pastures.

Puerto Montt

Nothing bad has ever been said by travelers about Puerto Montt. Supposedly 100,000 people live here but they must be tucked away in surrounding hills. A small-town flavor prevails over the concrete blocks of central downtown. Souvenir shops line the *malecón*. At the north end is one of the best fish markets in Latin America. Don't be put off by its rudimentary appearance; all the best restaurants buy their supplies from here.

Puerto Montt is nearly the end of Chile's Pan-Am. It's possible to travel the Trans-Austral as far as Chaitén (some say to Puerto Aisen and Chacabuco). From Puerto Montt, go north to cross into Argentina by road or take the ferry through the fjords to Puerto Natales.

Offshore is the beautiful **Chiloe** island which can be reached by frequent and cheap ferries from the mainland.

Places to stay

Hotel Central Benavente 550.
Hostal Panorama San Felipe 192.
Camping North of town, toward the yacht club, are several unnamed backyard lots with full facilities.

Fjords

An absolutely stupendous boat voyage ranks high on list of scenic travel. Puerto Montt is at the northern head of the journey that finishes in Puerto Natales. *Navimag* operates the ferry, four nights and days covering 2,090km (1,300 miles) each way. At times the boat scrapes ice-capped island walls. It heaves during a six-hour crossing of open seas, where (if you're not seasick) you might see migrating whales and seals.

Fares Off-season (May-Oct) rates for vehicles run about US$250 for a Volkswagen or small truck, US$23 for a motorcycle, and US$12 for a bike. Delicious and filling meals are included in passage: US$120 per person in hull bunks or up to US$250 per person for a private room and bath, exterior window. This is neither a hardship cruise nor the Queen Elizabeth, but something in between.
Contact:
Navimag Punta Arenas, Av Independencia 840; tel: (56061) 224256;
Puerto Natales, Av Pedro Montt 380 (the port office with blue tile roof); tel: (56061) 411421;
Puerto Montt, Angelmó 2187; tel: (56065) 253318; and in Santiago, Av El Bosque Norte 0440; tel: (562) 2035030. Reconfirm reservations.

Puerto Natales

Like many homes in the far south, modest-looking doors open into warm interiors and friendly people. Trekkers from all over gather in Puerto Natales before and after their assault on Torres del Paine, about 150km up the road.

Places to stay

There are no formal campgrounds near Puerto Natales. You can camp free along the coast (with permission of *estancia* owners), but beware of fierce wind chilled by the water and sudden snow flurries.

Casa Cecilia US$7 per person, non-smoking, no parking. This is the definitive place to forming hiking groups into the park.
Casa Familia Señoret 322 (three houses from Cecilia), US$6 per person; very nice, enclosed parking, kitchen privileges, hot showers.

Parque Nacional Torres del Paine

Superb views of glaciers, snow-capped peaks, blue lakes, wildlife and flora are accessible even to the day-tripper. But to experience this unique biosphere properly, you must trek it. Paths are clearly marked and camping is permitted in designated sites. Guides (US$50 per day) are now mandatory for all but the most accessible routes around the administration center and hotels.

Punta Arenas

The most southerly city in Chile and capital of the Magellan province, Region X, supports 119,692 friendly people, plus operas, museums, and a free-trade zone, and supplies ships to the Antarctica. It is windy year round, with an average mean temperature of 6.5°C.

Getting there

There are no supplies nor fuel along any of the following routes. For more complete information on borders and the "Land of Fire", including Porvenir, see *Chapter Seven, Argentina*, especially *Points of entry* and *Tierra del Fuego*.

From Puerto Natales, there are 246km of alternating *ripio* and paved road. The Strait of Magellan separates this colonial town from Porvenir on Tierra del Fuego by 22 miles of water. There is daily ferry service.

From Argentina A land route of 192km leads to Puerto Aymon on the Argentina border.

Places to stay

Guesthouses are excellent value. Breakfast and tea are usually included; often private parking. Every traveler claims to have stayed at the best. Simply browse the streets south of the center and you'll see signs posted on nearly every house advertising rooms to rent. If one is full, the owner will direct you to a neighbor.

Useful addresses

Argentine Consulate 21 de Mayo 1878.
Banco Concepción Av Magallanes, takes Visa.
Casas de cambio In the center, the *cambios* offer higher rates than in banks plus change travelers checks.
Correo Central Bories 911 (first floor).
Fincard Av Pedro Montt accepts Mastercard. Processing time is very slow, it could take 24-hours to receive authorization.
Laundromat Libertador Bernardo O'Higgins 969.
Navimag Av Independencia 840.
Tourist office Sernatur at Waldo Seguel 689, helpful, little printed material.

144

Chapter Eleven

Colombia

The people of a country and good experiences shape travelers' opinions, perhaps, more than pretty sights. For all reasons, Colombia is nearly every traveler's favorite country.

Mountains, more than any other feature, sum up Colombia. Travel through them takes weeks of rewarding work. Roads scale 3,800m in 40km! From the bottom, you'll face a nearly vertical wall. Pause at each summit and the beauty will enrapture your senses. Look then to where you're going — the next pinnacle of your journey.

COUNTRY HIGHLIGHTS

Above all, Colombia is to be enjoyed. The people deserve top awards for warmth and hospitality. Just lean back, relax and follow the *merengue* beat.

Cartagena
A port, a resort and historical treasure trove of Colonial architecture.

San Agustín
The scenery is a marvel and the ancient stone sculptures are a wonder; together they create a gawker's paradise.

POINTS OF ENTRY
From Panama
The ferry, *Crucero Express*, docks in Cartagena after an overnight passage from Colon, Panama. Entry formalities for a vehicle have thus far been reported to be standard and simple. (*Bienvenidos* to South America!)

The ferry departs from Cartagena on Sunday, Tuesday and Thursdays to Panama. (Reserve through any travel agency in Colombia.)

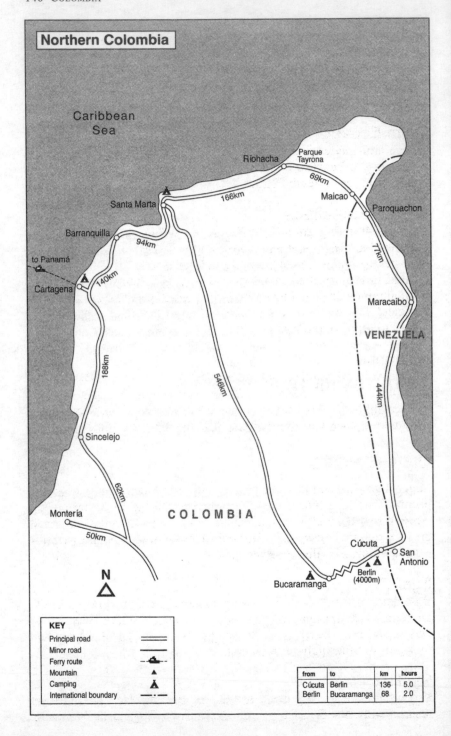

Northern Colombia

Caribbean
Sea

Riohacha

Parque
Tayrona

69km

Maicao

Paroquachon

166km

Santa Marta

77km

Barranquilla

94km

to Panamá

Cartagena

140km

Maracaibo

VENEZUELA

188km

546km

444km

Sincelejo

62km

COLOMBIA

Montería

50km

Cúcuta

San
Antonio

Berlin
(4000m)

Bucaramanga

N

KEY

Principal road	
Minor road	
Ferry route	
Mountain	▲
Camping	▲
International boundary	

from	to	km	hours
Cúcuta	Berlin	136	5.0
Berlin	Bucaramanga	68	2.0

From Venezuela

There have been no recent problems reported along the lowland of the Santa Marta border post. However, the preferred route remains through the more scenic highlands surrounding Cúcuta, Colombia and San Antonia/San Cristobal, Venezuela. Money exchange is more favorable in Cúcuta than in Venezuela.

From Ecuador

Tulcán and Ipiales is a friendly and efficient border, although slow upon entry to Ecuador. Money changers offer much lower rates than border bank or in nearby Ipiales.

Border formalities

As of 1994, immigration (DAS) limits tourist visits to 30 days. If you enter with a *libreta*, get the longest time possible for your vehicle. It is easier to apply for an immigration extension (DAS offices are located in major cities) than to extend entry of your vehicle. The official policy has been that a *libreta* or bond is required for entry of vehicles. The trend is toward relaxation of the rule, especially in regard to the Panama ferry.

Insurance

All motorized vehicles must be insured. Police stringently enforce this rule. It isn't expensive. *Seguro obligatorio* is available to foreigners for a one-month period, US$7. Don't be bullied by insurance agents who might insist on a resident's six-month policy.

ON THE ROAD

Super-highways connect every major city from nearly every compass point. Truck traffic roars throughout the night creating an omnipresent decibel level unequaled in any other country. You must go very remote to escape it. Strive for the secondary, back roads, for a more enjoyable, albeit bumpier ride.

Fuel

It is easier to fill non-standard propane tanks here than in Venezuela or Ecuador. White gas for cooking is widely available here and in Venezuela, but elsewhere is difficult to find. All grades of motor fuels are sold throughout the country.

Cyclists

Colombia is frequently cited as tops for cycling. José Breitsameter recommends his favorite biking thrill: from Bogotá to Manizales through the scenic Parque Nacional Los Nevados. He chose a rugged route, virtually impassible to motorized vehicles, where the road dips to 300m at the Río Magdalena then topples over a 4,800m pass and back down again. "It takes some time but is worth every second!!"

On normal roads, it's not unusual to see bicyclists grabbing the rear bumper of a truck for uphill tows. Bike shops in every big town carry the latest equipment and parts.

Bicyclists pass free on toll roads. Stay to the right.

Maps

An unfortunate dearth of maps exists. We found an auto guide at a bookstore, *Auto Guia, Guía turística y automotriz*. It was addictive reading with excellent route maps facing colored profiles illustrating the altitudes. Good maps are available from tourist offices in major cities.

USEFUL INFORMATION

Public holidays

January 1 (New Year)
January 6 (Epiphany)
March 19 (St Josée's Day)
Thursday and Good Friday
May 1 (Labor Day)
May 24 (Ascension Day)
June 29 (Sts Peter and Paul)
July 20 (Independence Day)
August 7 (Battle of Boyaca)
August 15 (Assumption Day)
October 12 (Discovery of America Day)
November 1 (All Saints)
November 11 (Independence of Cartagena)
December 8 (Immaculate Conception)
December 25 (Christmas)

When to visit

There is a chance of rain year round in the Amazon region and in the misty mountains. The heaviest showers generally fall between April and October. Temperatures are consistent with the altitude.

Money and banks

Banco de República   cashes travelers checks. *Cambios* are located in border cities and tourist centers. You may encounter difficulties in exchanging more than US$200 in any one day.

THE FAMILY
Above: The Highland Maya of Guatemala (HB)
Below: Cuna children, Panama (HB)

MODES OF TRANSPORT
Above: River ferries take many forms (MA)
Below: Cycling through Argentina (MA)

BEASTS OF BURDEN
Above: In a Guatemalan market (PA)
Below: On the trail, Venezuela (EP)

CHILDREN, URBAN AND RURAL
Above: A girl and her friend, Peru (PA)
Below: The morning bath, Ecuador (EP)

Personal security

Put aside exaggerated fears generated by bad press. True, guns are nearly as common as toothpicks and crime in major cities is a problem (sounds like the US), and being at the wrong place can be devastating. It is still best to get through police check points as quickly as possible as these are favored targets of armed guerrillas. Kidnapping for ransom cyclically peaks and wanes. The best defence is political and associative neutrality. Tourists are rarely targets or victims.

Colombians are ultra-sensitive on the subjects of the drug cartels and guerrillas. Avoid pontificating negatively or you'll surely offend your hosts, perhaps to your detriment.

Entire towns and regions ascribe their livelihood and peace to these different groups. Drug cartels have built stadiums, schools, hospitals and have rebuilt towns after natural calamities. Rebel groups have brought law and order to regions neglected by the government. Residents gladly pay "taxes" for their services.

THE CARIBBEAN COAST

Hibiscus flowers, bananas and coconut palms wave like tropical flags over white sand beaches and turquoise water. Sultry and flat, it's easy pedaling between beach coves. West of Cartagena, you'll find the most gorgeous and untouched areas.

Cartagena

When you spy the walls of the old Spanish fort, *San Felipe* and city walls, you'll know that you've arrived in the New World. Luckily, the cannons no longer lob fire balls at travelers. Lining the western bay is swank Bocagrande beach. Opposite is the "every person's beach", La Matuna, where beach volley-ball is more popular than shopping. Boats shuttle between offshore islands and coral reefs. Get lost in the narrow streets of old town, but don't miss the **La Popa** convent on the hill (150m altitude); beautiful and placid, it provides the best view of Cartagena.

Useful addresses

Ferry office   Av 3a No 28-78 Int 1, Manga; tel 607 722.
Tourist office   Av Blas de Lezo, Edificio Muelle de los Pegasos; also at the airport and in Parque Flanagan, Bocagrande.

Places to stay

The safest places to stay are located in Bocagrande. Avoid Calle Media Luna near the center where the cheap *hostelrías* are usually rough and tumble brothels. Further out, toward the airport are secure, reasonably priced beachfront hotels and *pensiones*.

Hotel Bellavista   Av Santander, Playa Marbella; inexpensive, parking.

Santa Marta

For many years, Santa Marta was synonymous with lawlessness. At first a haven for smugglers, it later became a battleground for drug traffickers seeking sea access. It's tamer now, but not yet high on the list for attractive towns. Good supplies are available.

Places to stay

Move west along the coast toward Barranquilla for decent camping.

Hotel Santa Marta   Oriente Santa Marta y Calle 10c; with basic rooms, parking and small charge for camping.

Tayrona National Park

Located on a spit of land 35km north of Santa Marta (the turn-off is signposted west of town). It is a coastal highpoint at 280m. Tayrona's lush vegetation and excellent beaches make this a splendid park to loll around for a few days. There are no food supplies within the park so stock up in advance.

CENTRAL HIGHLANDS

As all roads lead to Rome, in Colombia they lead to Bogotá, the political, commercial and industrial seat of the nation. Bypass routes are fairly well marked so consider using secondary roads through the more placid and beautiful countryside.

Bogotá

The altitude (2,650m) won't disable those arriving by road, but city smog and congestion might. Seemingly on-going new road construction and old road neglect wins Bogotá our nomination for the worst capital city to drive around. The official name is Santa Fe de Bogotá. The 1991 census counted five or six million people crowding this plateau capital. The one million discrepancy must be reflected in the rapid growth rate.

My most impressionable moment in Bogotá was seeing a giant billboard erected over a cemetery and hospital. It depicted the earth as a cup spilling billions of little people into the atmosphere. The message, translated, said, "Don't contaminate the world more. We're waiting. Garden of Peace."

Places to stay

There are several hotels north of town on the road to Bucaramanga, but few to the southwest. The following suggestions are inner-city.

Hotel Residencial Santa Fe Calle 14 y Carrera 4, No 4-48, Candelaria.
Regis C 18 No 6-09, somewhat shabby but with private parking.

Useful addresses

Gold Museum (Museo de Oro) on Parque Santander at corner of C 16, No 5-41; all museums close Mondays.
Propane refill Calle 18a No 50-60 or wait for Neiva where there is a station just south.
Touring y Automóvil Club de Colombia Av Caracas, No 46-64.
Tourist office CNT, C 28, No 13A-59, and at Eldorado airport.

EAST FROM BOGOTÁ

Truck traffic falls off slightly north of Bogotá, decreases through Bucaramanga and pleasantly disappears on the Cúcuta route. Dangerous hairpin curves, sheer cliffs and a collapsed road wrap the ascent from San Gil to Aratoca and the descent to Pescadero. Standing between Bucaramanga and Cúcuta is a nearly vertical 3,000m climb by single-lane road. Thick ferns, orchids and creeks accompany the ascent to the flat, windy *páramo* of **Berlín** (fuel, restaurants and cabins).

Villa de Leiva

Detour 34km west from attractive Tunja and rejoin the highway 22km later at Arcabuco for a delightful, almost obligatory, excursion through quaint Villa de Leiva. It is like stepping back to an earlier century. Narrow cobblestone streets pulsate with Colombian tourists who shop for emeralds and fossils. We camped in the peaceful botanical nursery (*vivero*) at the north end of town. There are two bare campgrounds 3km from town and numerous *pensiones* with parking in town.

Iguaque National Park with lovely hiking trails is reached by a nasty dirt road north of Leiva. There is a hotel and campground on the mountain peak.

Bucaramanga

This is another large commercial city but it is reasonably easy to navigate. Besides finding banks, supplies and repairs in town, there are several outlying areas worth visiting or breaking from the road. (**Note:** The Venezuelan consulate here is difficult to find and has a

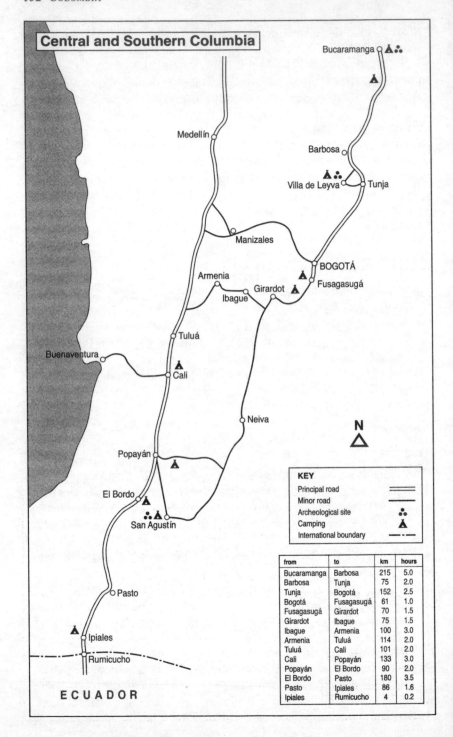

Central and Southern Columbia

Bucaramanga

Medellín

Barbosa

Villa de Leyva   Tunja

Manizales

Armenia   BOGOTÁ

Girardot   Fusagasugá

Ibague

Tuluá

Buenaventura

Cali

Neiva

N

Popayán

El Bordo

San Agustín

KEY

Principal road	
Minor road	
Archeological site	
Camping	
International boundary	

Pasto

Ipiales

Rumicucho

ECUADOR

from	to	km	hours
Bucaramanga	Barbosa	215	5.0
Barbosa	Tunja	75	2.0
Tunja	Bogotá	152	2.5
Bogotá	Fusagasugá	61	1.0
Fusagasugá	Girardot	70	1.5
Girardot	Ibague	75	1.5
Ibague	Armenia	100	3.0
Armenia	Tuluá	114	2.0
Tuluá	Cali	101	2.0
Cali	Popayán	133	3.0
Popayán	El Bordo	90	2.0
El Bordo	Pasto	180	3.5
Pasto	Ipiales	86	1.6
Ipiales	Rumicucho	4	0.2

history of telling travelers that a visa is not needed to enter Venezuela. Skip it.)

Seven kilometers toward the northwest of the center is **Girón**, a popular artisans' town set among conserved colonial architecture. Although less remote than Villa de Leiva, it is less visited.

Places to stay

Centro Recreativo Campo Alegre   Seven kilometers south on the Bogatá road. Good hotel rooms, restaurants, campsites and facilities, all sports fully represented. Convenient to Bucaramanga, without city hassle.

Hotel Camarúu Campestre   Along the road to Girón; with camping.

Cúcuta

Growing Cúcuta is given short shrift by travelers whose main purpose is getting into or out of Venezuela. Visas are needed by everyone entering Venezuela by land and since their more remote consulates deny this is true, you'll be in Cúcuta for several days pursuing your visa.

You might as well enjoy your stay. There are some lovely places to get away to on the outskirts of town. About 20km out on the Bucaramanga road, you'll find rivers, small waterfalls and local restaurants. **Villa Rosario**, toward the border, is also soothing. There is a nice picnic park between Av 0 and the cut-off from the Pan-Am.

Note: *Cambios* give better rates for the Venezuelan bolivar than in that country.

LOSING TO THE SYSTEM

It might seem strange to include Venezuela in the Colombian chapter but overland travelers through this border will form opinions of Cúcuta based on their experience. There are no sneaky or straightforward ways to circumvent the Venezuelan consulate in Cúcuta except to drive, pedal or walk without a visa or car documents (we met two motorists who had done so.)

We have had three "adventures" with the Venezuelan Consulate and they never get better. Once we were ordered to get VD tests for a 72-hour in-transit visa!

Another time I volunteered to watch the reception desk for a few minutes and then copied all the internal phone extension numbers and names. I later made direct phone calls starting with the ambassador and his secretary and posed as a journalist, a US Congress person and a well-connected relative of the president of Venezuela. None of the ploys worked.

Places to stay

There are lovely hotels on the way to the border, in peaceful Villa Antigua del Rosario, 8km from Cúcuta.

Arizona   Av 0 7-62, opposite the Venezuelan consulate, a bit pricey with three stars, low entrance to parking garage. There are other, more expensive hotels on the same street.

Hotel de la Paz   Calle 6 No 3-48; US$12 double, small pool, in-room tv, good parking. Within easy walking distance to the Venezuelan consulate.

Hotel Brena   Calle 6, one block from Paz.

Useful addresses

Venezuelan consulate   Av 0, C 8, on the corner. Opens at 8am but an orderly line begins forming at 5am. They take the first 20 people in line each day. Ultimately, be prepared for a physical brawl when line-breakers and weeping supplicants try to elbow past you. There is no sympathy for the hesitant.

Propane refill   *Gas Rosario*, 3km out of town on Bogotá road. Fill up if going into Venezuela.

Getting to the border

The road that passes in front of the Venezuelan consulate leads directly to the border. All Colombian formalities are now conducted on the left side of the road, before crossing the bridge. It is easier to park on the right side. See *Chapter Sixteen* for further information.

THE SOUTH

Directly south of Bogotá and west through Medellín is the domain of guerrillas and drug lords. A very busy highway leads south from Bogotá to Ibague through Armenia and to Cali. Turn south at Cali approximately 166km from Bogotá, to reach Popayán. The peaceful Río Sumapaz sculpts a narrow, tropical valley between Fusagasuga and Melgar with many campsites en route. Worth a stop.

A more pleasant route bypasses the large cities and fast trucks between Bogotá and Cali. From Melgar go to Espinal and take the road to Neiva where you'll find good shopping and repairs. Continue on to **Garzón** and Pitalito, a good place to buy provisions, before continuing to San Agustín. The Garzón-San Agustín stretch is hilly and pitted, so allow at least four hours by motorized vehicle.

Cali

The third largest city is an expanding industrial center. Follow the highway signs through town south to Popayáan and San Agustín.

San Agustín

Exotic stone figures dating from circa 3300BC mutely guard the surrounding countryside; the best examples are in situ in the Parque Arqueológico, US$8 admission. Hire horses for an excellent day-long tour. Hiking is easy at 1,700m and brings terrific discoveries. This is a very pretty area.

Places to stay

Hotel Yalconia   About one kilometer from town, on hill, convenient to park entrance; pool, rooms, and camping for US$4.
Osoguaico   Closer to the park, similar amenities, but cheaper.

Useful addresses

Tourist office   Center. Maps, lists of hotels, rooms and legitimate guide services.

Popayán

Nearly destroyed in 1983 by an earthquake, sections of Popayán were later restored with financial support from a drug cartel. Charm and friendliness go in hand with narrow, cobblestone streets, antique cars and a jumble of small commercial sectors.

Popayán is adjacent to the Pan-Am, on the Cali to Ipiales route south. The mostly paved road between Popayán and San Augustín, 135km, is rough but beautiful. **Parque Nacional Puracé** lies en route to Pitalito and San Agustín. Stop in Pilimbalá, to camp and/or climb to the summit of Puracé volcano (which will take you approximately seven hours).

Places to stay

La Casona de Virrey   This graceful hotel is a local landmark on Calle 4a. Good parking, but expensive.
Camping   Leave town in direction of San Agustín and at the top of the hill you'll see a gas station — pass it. On the next crest is a cluster of cabins (not family style) and a small but popular restaurant. Although not a perfect site, many campers (including overlanders) stop here for the night. With luck, you'll meet neighbors, Michael (an Aussie) and wife Franny (whose family owns the restaurant/hotel).

Useful addresses

Tourist office   Car 6A 3-74. Very helpful, maps and regional display.
Telephone office   Car 6A, three blocks from the tourist office; very helpful when every other place is closed for siesta.

El Bordo

Tense police checks are at each end of this tiny supply town, 93km south of Popayán. The military and police are very nervous since guerrillas have attacked these posts several times. (In one attack the day after we went through, five police were killed.) Top up supplies in El Bordo for a long trek through deep valleys south to Ipiales.

Places to stay

Parador Turístico Patia About ten minutes' drive south of El Bordo. Hotel rooms cost US$15 double, camping US$2.50 each; big pool, shady gardens, restaurant and a water purification plant. This is the best place to cool off until south of the border.

Ipiales

Ipiales is only 3-4km from the border with Ecuador. Many Otavalan Indians from Ecuador shop here because prices for staples, repairs and exchange are favorable. Follow signs from the main highway to *el centro* on the main plaza, for supplies and exchange.

Many outlying farmers cultivate coca and marijuana among their vegetable fields. Unless traveling in a group, exercise caution and discretion when adventuring far from the main routes.

Places to stay

Hotels Travelers needing parking should stay in one of the full-service hotels between Ipiales and the border. There are no hotels with-in the city of Ipiales with adequate parking, and we investigated many.

Camping You can camp roadside on the Colombian border strip. Likewise camp alongside a restaurant on the north end of town. In town, the bus station lot and Esso truck lot are busy, noisy and greasy pits.

Useful addresses

Banco Anglo Colombiano is located in the shopping complex adjacent to the square and changes travelers checks. Before waiting in line, make three photocopies of your passport, tourist card and checks to be cashed.
The border The Colombian side is housed in a modern cement complex. A bank is located here but opens during normal business hours. Ecuador is in another building, closes at noon, requires a *libreta* for a motorized vehicle and lines are long.
Money exchange Surrounding the plaza are several *cambios* which give good cash rates and are open from early morning to late evening. **Casa de Cambio**, Carrera 6, No 14-09, is reliable.

Chapter Twelve

Ecuador

Renowned for the Galapagos Islands, compact mainland Ecuador bursts with color and Indian tradition centuries old. Ecuador is small enough to sample randomly and savor slowly. Distances between destinations are short in comparison to countries further south and supply centers are all along the way.

Climatic zones are within easy reach. A narrow, not overwhelmingly high, ridge of mountains runs down the center like a spine. To the west, roads slope rapidly to the Pacific and to the east they lead into the Amazon jungle.

COUNTRY HIGHLIGHTS

Otavalo
Deep blue ponchos and wrap skirts, white blouses looped with golden beads, and shiny black braids distinguish the Otavalo Indians who create an unforgettable Saturday market amidst narrow cobblestone streets.

Jungle
The gateway to Ecuador's Amazon is through tiny Mishualli. Getting here is an adventure but the real adventure goes eastward, by foot and canoe, through the territories of "pacified" headhunters, the Jibaro Indians.

POINTS OF ENTRY

There are only three points of entry to Ecuador, not counting sea or jungle.

From Colombia
Tulcán and Ipailes is a friendly and efficient border, although Ecuador side is very slow. Money changers give much lower rates

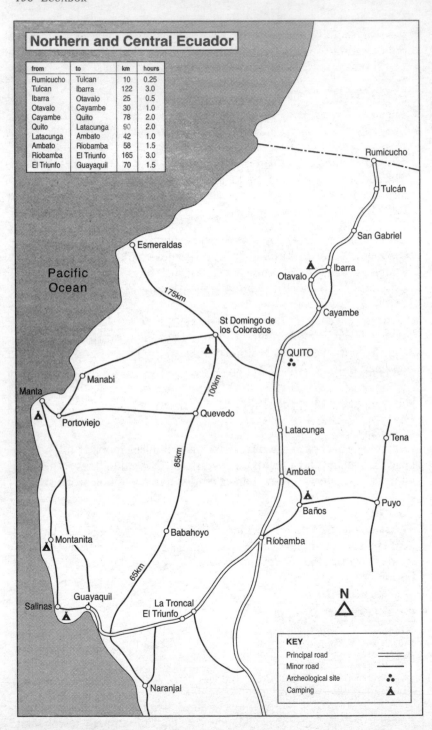

Northern and Central Ecuador

from	to	km	hours
Rumicucho	Tulcan	10	0.25
Tulcan	Ibarra	122	3.0
Ibarra	Otavalo	25	0.5
Otavalo	Cayambe	30	1.0
Cayambe	Quito	78	2.0
Quito	Latacunga	90	2.0
Latacunga	Ambato	42	1.0
Ambato	Riobamba	58	1.5
Riobamba	El Triunfo	165	3.0
El Triunfo	Guayaquil	70	1.5

Rumicucho

Tulcán

San Gabriel

Esmeraldas

Pacific
Ocean

Ibarra

Otavalo

Cayambe

175km

St Domingo de
los Colorados

QUITO

Manabi

Manta

100km

Portoviejo

Quevedo

Latacunga

Tena

85km

Ambato

Baños

Puyo

Montanita

Babahoyo

Ríobamba

65km

Salinas

Guayaquil

La Troncal
El Triunfo

N

Naranjal

KEY

Principal road	
Minor road	
Archeological site	
Camping	

than at the border bank or in nearby cities. There are several police/military check points between Ibarra and the border where you'll have to sign a book and have your tourist card stamped.

From Peru

Through Aguas Verde to Huaquillas is the common crossing point. See *Chapter Fourteen, Peru, Points of entry*. More picturesque scenery and less traffic lies further east between La Tina and Macará. Mutual claims to territorially rich oil fields contribute to the corruption and tension that hallmark both border points. Expect numerous military/police checks on both sides but especially in Ecuador. Foreigners must register and have tourist card stamped at El Telegrafo and Pontazgo.

Border formalities

The *libreta* (*triptico*) is required for any vehicle. Tourists are permitted entry for up to 90 days in any 12-month period. No extensions.

ON THE ROAD

Primary roads are paved but often deeply pitted, as are some secondary routes which, at best, have been described by one bicyclist as bumpy Inca roadways. There are no road shoulders, few kilometer markings and few towns erect their name. Watch out for landslides and flooded roads during wet season. Gigantic potholes mar the road between Misahuallí and Baños.

Police   These are the most brutish in Latin America for requesting "co-operation".

USEFUL INFORMATION
Public holidays
January 1 (New Year)
Good Friday and Maundy Thursday
May 1 (Labor Day)
May 24 (Pinchincha Day)
July 24 (Simon Bolivar Day)
July 25 (Founding of Guayaquil)
August 10 (Independence Day)
October 9 (Guayaquil Day)
October 12 (Columbus Day)
November 1 (Imperial Day)
November 3 (Independence of Cuenca)
December 6 (Founding of Quito)
December 25 (Christmas)

BURN OUT THE OLD
New Year's Eve, *El Nuevo Año*, can't be mentioned without adding *El Año Viejo* in the same sentence. It is the burning of the Old Year that makes the New Year the most loved of all holiday celebrations. Preparations begin months in advance with schemes and giggles and hoarding of materials. By December, the *año viejos* assume definition and shape as effigies.

Effigy building occupies a year-round commercial industry. Every world-famous face is comically reproduced on giant whimsical paper bodies, from soccer star to Disney character to politician. Many people prefer to build their own effigies and these are usually more personalized jabs at local bigwigs or other offensive types.

On New Year's Eve they're brought to their final splendor after a day of sawing and hammering. Elaborate houses are fashioned to showcase imaginative still-life scenes. Kids don masks and close streets in anticipation of horn-honking parades and to extract donations which go to the next year's effigy fund.

At the first stroke of midnight, bonfires lick the sky. Cheers resound as the Old Year is reduced to ashes, inaugurating a new start.

When to visit
Neither wind nor cold are terribly adverse factors in this small equatorial country. Nights are chilly year round under starry skies in mountainous areas. Along coastal areas and in the jungle, heat and humidity wilts those not acclimatized. The driest months fall between July and September.

Money and banks
The Sucre is pegged to the dollar but the economy fluctuates seasonably. Generally, Ecuador is one of the cheapest countries for travel behind Bolivia and Venezuela.

Filanbanco is consistently your best option for financial transaction. Accepts Visa cards.

THE NORTH

The better of the roads is Ruta 35 between Tulcán and Ibarra. South of the hot tropical Chota Valley, the descents are steep and the terrain is dry. The mainly black populace has cultivated rich agriculturally productive pockets. Luckily, there are places to stop and refresh your body with a swim. Clustered 44km north of Ibarra, are various *hosterias* with pools and water parks. Camping is permitted alongside busy **Oasis Hosteria**, US$4 per person.

Ibarra
Almost sterile in comparison to surrounding villages, Colonial Ibarra bustles with truly genial people. This is a good place to stock up for the northern journey and get repairs.

Otavalo
Visit during the week when serenity is restored to this placid mountain community. The Saturday market attracts both Ecuadorians and foreigners. Prices zoom skyward with the arrival of the first Saturday bus, and escalate until sunset. The Otavalo Indians are noted not only for their lustrous black braids and distinctive costumes, but also for business acumen. Few articles are of local origin; most items come from Colombia, Panama and even Taiwan. Vendors cram **Poncho Plaza** during the more leisurely week days.

The most exciting festival of St John we've ever experienced, occured here when the entire town split in half and threw rocks at each other! The Pan-Am became a dangerous battle field where blood and laughter flowed in equal proportions. (Can you imagine the cleansing feeling from lobbing small boulders at nasty neighbors?) The *chicha*-aided ritual dates to pre-Inca times.

Excursions
San Antonia de Ibarra This small town lies between Ibarra and Otavalo and is renowned for wood carvings. Even if not buying, ramble through the many shops to see the different carving

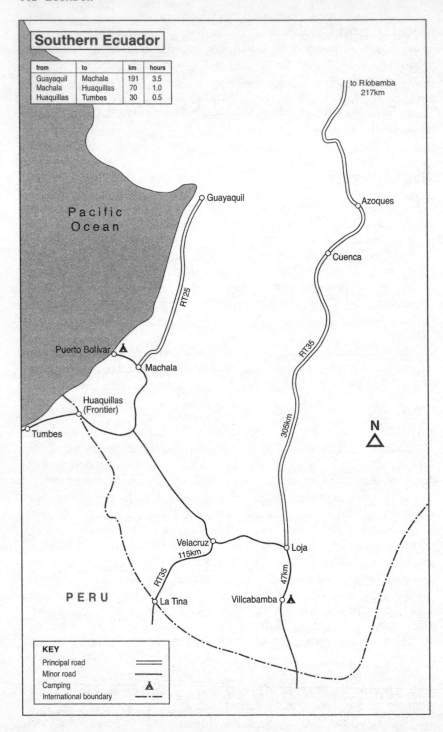

Southern Ecuador

from	to	km	hours
Guayaquil	Machala	191	3.5
Machala	Huaquillas	70	1.0
Huaquillas	Tumbes	30	0.5

Pacific
Ocean

to Ríobamba
217km

Guayaquil

Azoques

Cuenca

RT25

RT35

Puerto Bolívar

Machala

Huaquillas
(Frontier)

Tumbes

305km

N

Velacruz
115km

Loja

RT35

47km

PERU

La Tina

Villcabamba

KEY
Principal road	═══
Minor road	───
Camping	⛺
International boundary	─·─·─

techniques which range from crude to exquisite, but always entertaining.
Cotacachi   Near by, this is another town that specializes in leather products.
Lake Cuicocha   A rough, steep road leads from Quiroga (14km north of Cotacachi) to this crater *laguna* nestled among glacieral peaks. Camping, hotels and restaurants.
Lago de San Pablo   Southwest of Otavalo, along the Pan-Am, is this Otavalo resort lake, with splendid walks and fine views.

Places to stay

Hotel Yamor Continental   On Pan-Am, north end of town; luxurious rooms, gardens, pool, safe parking. US$35-40 double.
Residencial Centenario   One half block from Poncho Plaza, US$11 double with private bath; good enclosed parking for one truck or several cars.
Residencial Isabelita   Roca 11-87; they'll direct you to a private parking lot.

From Otavalo to Quito

Along the 110km mountainous stretch, several delightful towns will divert you from any other mission. Valleys are spectacularly scenic and you'll have to stop frequently to reflect on life. It is a slow, cliff-hanging road, often wrapped in wet mist, so allow plenty of time. There is a good photo opportunity at the equator monument south of Cayambe, or detour through **San Antonio** with a better equator marker, small museum and the Incan ruins of Rumicucho.

Quito

Poised between towering mountains at 2,850m, Quito is the second highest capital city in Latin America. Once an Inca city, the cobble-stone streets of the colonial center date from 1534. Unfortunately, this splendid section has lapsed into shabbiness and crime. To the north lies the new, safer and more cosmopolitan downtown.

Places to stay

The following places are located in the northern **ciudad nueva**.
Hotel Embajador   9 de Octubre y Colon; with parking.
Hotel Pickett   Juan Leon Mera y Calle Presidente Wilson, off Amazonia.
Amazonas Inn   Pinto 471 Y Amazonas, near the Pickett; small and friendly.

Useful addresses

Colombian Consulate   Av Amazonas 353.
Peruvian consulate   Av Colon Y Amazonas, Edificio Espagne, 2nd floor.
Propane refill   Liquigas, 7km north of Quito on the Pan-Am.
Repairs   At the north end of 10 Agosto (Pan-Am), you'll find repairs and parts for most motorized vehicles.

South of Quito
Cuenca
The latest convention spot on the gringo trail is the third largest city in Ecuador, Cuenca. Popular markets crowd the colonial streets on Thursdays and Saturdays. The Christmas Day parade is the best in all Ecuador.

Places to stay
Hostal Duran   Five kilometers north at hot springs, Baños. Camping permitted.
Hotel Crespo   Av Cordero, near the river with parking.

Useful addresses
Tourist office   Beningo Malo 735.

Vilcabamba
The celebrated drinking water is said to be the secret of these residents' long life (100 years plus). True or not, the agreeable mountain climate will entice you to prolong your visit.

    Podocarpus National Park is near by and affords good hiking and bird watching in a cloud forest environment. Find it by taking Ruta 35 south from Cuenca to Loja. The road from the Macará border connects to Loja, as well. This is a beautiful region and not heavily touristed.

THE AMAZON JUNGLE
The Rio Napo forms a waterway route that eventually spills into the Amazon River. High jungle canopies shade the ground, nature's own greenhouse where miraculous medicines are still being discovered, but few animals roam. The hilly land, having been hunted out, and rivers dynamited for fish dinners, is nearly silent. Rewards of nature increase the further you venture from civilization. At the very least, a three to five-day jaunt by foot and canoe will introduce you to the mysterious world beneath the jungle canopy.

Misahuallí
After a downpour, rainbows arch over the gateway town to the Amazon, Misahuallí. Dirt streets turn into boot-sucking mud and termites nibble at the foundations of modest wood houses.

Getting there
Misahuallí can be reached from Tumbaco via Bacza and Tena (153km) or from Ambato via Baños. The roads are rough and deeply

pitted from any direction. They've been ravaged by earthquakes, land slides, torrential rain and baked by the sun.

Excursions

The standard three-day, two-night circuit combines boats, jungle walks and time to relax. Expect to pay at least US$20 per day per person; guide, food and Wellingtons included. Good guides emphasize the educational component and are sensitive to contact with endangered Waoraní Indians. Recommended guides are Carlos, Douglas Clarke and Héctor Fiallos.

We took a two-week hike with Carlos who imposed strict rules, such as no noise, and led us over such demanding trails that the only noise we could make was the sound of our own puffing. During rest breaks and after dinner he lectured on plants and local lore. Before we knew it, we were surviving off the land using our new knowledge.

Baños

Bubbly hot mineral baths make this the perfect place to go after the jungle to clean off the last of the mud. The town is pleasant in spite of a great influx of tourists.

Places to stay

Res Alborada On church plaza.
Res Magdalena More upscale but still a good value.
Residencial Paty The gringo hangout. A good place to leave messages.

THE COAST

There are many more accessible beaches in the central region than in the north. Below Guayaquil, it is marshy with mangroves. At any rate, you'll have to descend from the cool mountains. Start early in the morning so you can soak in the surf by afternoon. It is a spectacular trip by way of Ruta 30 to **Santo Domingo de los Colorados**, where the road splits. (Uphill, it is a long, slow climb.) Not much is en route.

From **Santo Domingo de los Colorados**, Ruta 25 goes northwest to Esmeraldas which has never received rave reviews from travelers. South from there, however, are several pleasant beach communities.

Continue on Ruta 30 through Santo Domingo to reach the central beaches. The lush tropical scenery envelopes the narrow road to the coast.

Montecristi

Stop for a Panama, hat that is. They're made between here and **Jipijapa**, but the selection is much better on Montecristi's main street. The *finos* are soft as silk and carry fine price tags (several hundred dollars). A decent *Panama* can still be found for about US$10.

Manta

The beaches of this bustling port city improve north of town where they are less crowded. More secure camping sites lay nearer Crucita.

Puerto Lopez

A few hours' drive south of Manta brings you to this quiet fishing village. Besides being the supply center for coastal areas further south, seafood restaurants and boat trips to **Isla de la Plata** are the primary economic activities. The island is part of the **Manchilla National Park**. A visit costs US$20 per person for the boat and US$22 for park admission (valid for ten days). The park ranges just south and west of Puerto Lopez. Take advantage of the good market in the center of town and fuel-up if headed south, or later buy it out of the barrel for double the price.

Alandaluz

Plans are to turn this haven into an ecological town. The foundations are laid. Tourist *palapas* (US$15 per person), a restaurant, bars, gardens and pristine beaches greet the eye. The effect is soothing and the behind-the-scenes story is exciting. All construction and the infrastructure utilizes natural materials and recycling principles. (Check out the bathrooms.) It all works, they've converted a sub-desert into a garden paradise.

Montañita

If you didn't bring your surfboard, rent one. Long tube rides are excellent, making it the primary surf spot of Ecuador. It's a tropical mini-town with a few overpriced hotels and cheap campgrounds. Non-camping, budget travelers stay in **Manglaralto**, 3km to the south, and hike the beach back and forth. For camping and small, basic rooms, try **Vito's** on the beach, or **El Rincón de los Amigos**.

Night time parties rove from place to place. Invitations are not required to join the multi-national fests.

Ballenista

The coastal road passes through many small, unattractive fishing villages. Get fish fresh from the boats as sanitary conditions are not up to par in these towns. A truly beautiful, secluded beach with one inn stretches south of tiny Ballenista.

From Santa Elena, turn right at the *Ballenista Inn* and then left on to a dirt road for 1.5km. The elegant *Hosteria Farallón Dillon*, with a marine museum, tennis courts, gym, etc, might entice you to splurge for a longer stay, US$20 per person for a double room.

Guayaquil

Approaching Guayaquil from the east gives the impression of a wealthy, thriving city that's moved on and up from its reputation for squalor and crime. Then you meet the traffic snarl when all ambition translates to just getting through.

Residents of Guayaquil escape to beach resorts at **Salinas** (charming but busy) and **Playas** on the southern shore of the peninsula.

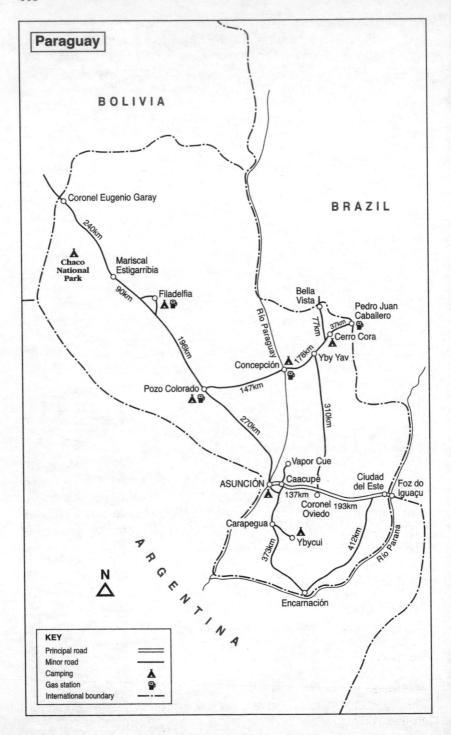

Chapter Thirteen

Paraguay

For many visitors, landlocked Paraguay is a place to pass through quickly. One overlander commented, "The Chaco is an adventure, but after that there isn't much here."

Yet, Paraguay is one of the last emerging countries where many traditions are still intact. Ox-carts are as common as cars. People are kind and resilient within a deceptively fragile culture.

The history of Paraguay is a military chronicle. National heroes are all generals, national parks are military monuments, as is public art. The Paraguayan people have a right to be proud of wars fought, won and lost. Unfortunately, their civil history is untold.

During the Stroessner dictatorship (1954-1989), a brutal military became synonymous with government. Recent legislation guarantees freedom of expression, but other human rights bills, such as torture, are excluded from judicial access.

According to the 1990 census, four and a half million people live in this predominantly agricultural country. You'll see rows of plastic-bag houses — families without land. It is a wrenching experience to pass them by. More than once, we couldn't. Our left-over food or surplus tomatoes found appreciative bellies. Agrarian reform seems to be eons away from effectiveness.

COUNTRY HIGHLIGHTS

The Chaco
Remoteness ensures adventure and wildlife equal to Brazil's Pantanal. The nearly extinct noble cowboy, *gauchos*, drive cattle over the roads.

Misiones
This southern region is named for the many Jesuits missions built around 1609.

Asunción

A mere 700,000 people inhabit the largest city, the capital.

The rivers Paraguai and Paraná

These mighty brown rivers are the lifeline between land and sea ports. They guarantee Paraguay sovereignty against her neighboring countries.

POINTS OF ENTRY

See chapters on Brazil, Bolivia, Argentina and Chile.

ON THE ROAD

Main arteries in the south and east are paved. Ruta 1 runs 370km south to Encarnación, via the historical department of Misiones. Ruta 2 passes east-west 320km through Coronel Oviedo to Ciudad del Este. Ruta 9, also known as the Trans-Chaco highway, runs between Asunción and Gral E Garay at the Bolivian border, via Filadelfia. The northern 239km is dirt, but the first 557km is paved from Asunción to Mariscal Estigarribia. Asphalt is being laid along Ruta 5, the east-west highway between Pozo Colorado (the juncture with Ruta 9) and Pedro Juan Caballero, on the Brazil border. Dirt roads are fairly good during the dry winter months, April through September.

Driving style

Paraguayan drivers are extremely impatient and seem to think that a honking horn will immediately unsnarl a traffic jam. Bus drivers are more homicidal than in other countries. Generally speaking, motorists obey traffic signals in cities.

Repairs

The Mercedes Benz capital of the world must surely be Asunción. In daily speech, the Mercedes is the folkloric symbol for corrupt power. Motorcyclists and bicyclists should have little problem finding necessary repairs for all makes. Labor is inexpensive although, in the absence of diagnostic equipment, mechanic's intuition procedes from the rule "if it runs, it ain't broken".

Our worst repair nightmare occurred with Diesa in Asunción (Volkswagen and Honda motorcycle). We entered for oil leaks and left with an enormous bill for unauthorized parts and labor. The engine leaked oil worse than ever. We protested the bill and labor by holding our own sit-down strike and quickly recovered a US$500 overcharge and corrective work.

Fuel
Ask for *super,* supposedly 93 octane and untainted by alcohol. The lower grade of gas contains 10-15% alcohol that can corrode your engine and ruin seals. It is known as *comun* or *alconafta.*

Cyclists
Ruta 2 and 7 between Ciudad del Este and Asunción have paved shoulders (*calzadas*), with bone-jangling, mini-speed bumps.

Maps
Shell Oil has published a long overdue set of maps for Paraguay. For US$7 get a detailed street map of Asunción, the country map produced by the Instituto Geográfico Militar and an excellent road map. Paraguay is one of the last countries where a compass is nearly as helpful as a hand-drawn map. Maps are no longer printed nor distributed by the *Touring and Automovile Club Paraguayo.* Bookstores in Plaza Uruguay, Asunción carry a more expensive assortment.

USEFUL INFORMATION
Public holidays
January 1 (New Year)
February 3 (Patron Saint Day)
March 1 (Heroes Day)
Good Friday and the previous Thursday
May 1 (Labor Day)
May 1415 (Corpus Christi)
June 12 (Chaco Armistice)
August 15 (founding of Asunción and Children's Day)
December 8 (Virgin of Caacupé)
December 25 (Christmas)

When to visit
Paraguay's winter is perhaps the best time to travel through this flat land. Cyclists will appreciate a mean temperature of 14° with mostly sunny and refreshing days. Winds predominantly blow out of the north and northeast which makes pedaling arduous. A sudden switch of wind from the south is a harbinger of cold. Dirt roads are dry and passable during this season.

The summer months, October through March, simmer with heat. The mean temperature hovers around 31°. There is little shade along the roads.

THE STORY OF TEA

The first thing you'll notice in Paraguay is *everyone* drinking. The ubiquitous cup contains the national drink, the *yierba-mate*, a tea of fresh or dried herbs steeped in hot or cold water and drunk through a metal straw with a sieve at one end, a *bombillo*. Cups are fashioned from either cow horn or a cork insulation covered by metal.

Significant social interaction surrounds the drinking of *mate*, with customary sharing of the same cup and straw. The cup should be held in the left hand. Add warm water (never boiling) to the herbs and allow the concoction to cool before adding more water. The herbs are now steeped and ready for any temperature of water that you choose. Never stir the herbs or they turn mushy. The tea herbs, *yierba*, are sold, packaged, in grocery stores.

A more adventurous approach is to customize your *mate* from the wares of street vendors. Merely pointing to a basket of roots and leaves will prompt vivid mimicry of maladies treated by each herb...menstrual cramps, sleeplessness or nervousness, stomach problems, lack of energy, overweight. Their effect can be benign, relaxing or send you ricocheting through your own mental space.

Money and banks

The unit of currency is the guaraní. It is fairly stable; US$1 = G1905 in 1994. More *cambios* than banks cash travelers checks but these are located in downtown Asunción. If stuck, go to a **Banco de Paraná** and beg the manager. Stores in border towns trade in all cash currencies so plan ahead and stock up on dollars.

Business hours

Most businesses open between 7am and punctually close at 12 noon. Stores re-open between 3pm and 3.30pm and close by 6.30pm. Many restaurants do not open until evening. The afternoon *siesta* hours are non-negotiable. Businesses close at 1pm Saturday and remain closed until Monday morning.

Language

Spanish is the first official language, followed by Guaraní. Most Paraguayans are conversant in both languages.

National parks

There seems to be internal confusion over the definition of a national park. The term is employed by private individuals and by military posts. In other words, not all parks are what they claim to be. In true national parks, camping is free and park rangers are dedicated to wildlife conservation and human education. The park service asked us to publish their list of official sites.

Defensores del Chaco	Soon to become, perhaps, the world's largest international park with expansions in Paraguay and in Bolivia.
Tte Enciso	In Boqueron.
Tinfunqué	In Pte Hayes.
Cerro Corá	In Amambay.
Serranía San Luis	In Concepción.
Ypacaraí	In Central.
Ybytyruzú	In Guaira.
Ybycuí	In Paraguari.
Caaguazú	In Caazazapa.
Lago Ypoá	In Ñeembucu.
San Rafael	In Itapua.
Ñacunday	In Alto Parana.

Security

Presently, remote camping is safe, however, *avoid witnessing any illegal activity!* No-one will hazard a definition of "illegal" (of course, ignorance keeps them alive), but warnings should be respected. In the Chaco and northeast, inform locals, park rangers or military where you're camping and your range of exploration.

THE NORTHEAST

The northeast quadrant abuts Brazil and is very much like a dry Pantanal.

Pedro Juan Caballero

This town borders Ponto Porá, Brazil by an invisible line through the center of the two towns. See *Chapter Nine, Brazil.*

Useful information

Borders cease attendance during lunch hours and at 5.30pm weekdays. They close on holidays and at 11am on Saturday, until re-opening Monday at 7am.

Brazil Consulate Look for the Brazil flag slightly north of the commercial shopping district on Rua Dr Francia.

Customs For clearance of a vehicle go to the modern-looking building at the south end of Rua Dr Francia.

Immigration This office moves periodically. Their latest address is Naciones Unidas 144, a small yellow building, a half block west of Rua Dr Francia.

Parque Nacional Cerro Corá

Thirty-two kilometers west of Pedro Juan Caballero and 60km east of Yby Yaú on paved Ruta 5, sprawls a park with howling jaguars. Cerro Corá was the site of Mariscal Francisco Lopez's death, which ended the war of the Triple Alliance (1864-1870). A military guard gives the monument around-the-clock protection. Dip into the Rio Aquidabán Nigüí for a chilling bath. Good drinking water can be found inside a marked rock. Lots of wildlife, hieroglyphics on nearby rock walls. Park rangers will guide you to see them. The administrative office is located near Km 180. Camping is free. No supplies.

Yby Yaú

A dusty crossroad town west-east on Ruta 5 and south-north on Ruta 3 to Coronel Oviedo, 301km to the south. The first 95km south to Santa Rosa are unpaved. The remaining 206km to Coronel Oviedo are asphalt. This used to be one of the main truck routes. Ruta 5 is paved to Concepción. There is a gas station, but few supplies. The most interesting aspect of Yby Yaú is its Guaraní name, roughly meaning "dirt eaters". It's not pronounced as you might think.

Concepción

The third largest city, last reported at 35,000 inhabitants, slouches along the east bank of the Rio Paraguai. Terrific old architecture punctuates the center of town, some of which has been renovated or maintained, and some of which is now the province of landless squatters. The central market swarms with ox-carts and three-horse carriages. It's always peaceful and nearly always quiet, except on weekend nights, when music emanates from nearly every quarter.

Boats   Tired of the road? Then hop a boat north to Brazil or south to Asunción. Negotiate directly with boat operators or go to one of the *agencias marítimas* located opposite the port office.

Places to stay

Picis Marina Club on river with expensive rooms and camping for US$2.30 per person, and may be free during off-season. A family of women are rebuilding the place, an abandoned electrical plant and dock.

The hotels **Victoria** and the **Francés** on Avda Franco are in the US$6 per person range; good with cycle parking.

Trans-Chaco Highway

Members of an Exodus overland expedition described the Trans-Chaco as the most memorable part of their South America journey. The driver laughingly added that it was helpful to have so many hands to push the truck through the sand. Regardless of how you traverse this wilderness, it should be a rewarding experience. Bird watchers and wildlife buffs will enjoy the teeming variety of critters.

Ruta 9 runs from Asunción to the border of Bolivia, 796km. During the dry season you can travel to or from Sucre, Bolivia in about 50 hours. Much of the way is paved; nevertheless, sections are still difficult enough to warrant Paraguay's claim that the Trans-Chaco road race is second only to the Paris-Dakkar rally. (The Trans-Chaco race is held annually around Sept 29. Race routes now stray into more arduous proving grounds than those found along Ruta 9.)

From Asunción, going north, stop at *Rio Negro* in the vicinity of Km 173 for good swimming, camping, fishing, modest hotels, restaurants and gas.

Pozo Colorado

This is a dusty intersection between Ruta 5 from Concepción, 146km to the east, and Ruta 9, 270km north of Asunción. There are two gas stations with restaurants, a military post and a tow truck operated by the Touring and Automobile Club Paraguayo.

Ruta 5 between Concepción and Pozo Colorado is nearly paved. Not much infrastructure, expansive, fenced *estancias*. Good bird watching.

North from Pozo Colorado to Estigarribia, via Filadelfia, is also paved.

Filadelfia If traveling north, lay in a good supply of food stuffs as the infrastructure becomes more basic. This delightful Mennonite community routinely captivates wandering travelers. Several small hotels in town. Ask around for camping.

Parque Nacional Tte Enciso Excellent park with camping is 141km north of Estigaaribia (approx five hours' drive from Asunción).

Continue north 62km on a good dirt road to the air force base at **Fortin Nueva Asunción**. For the ensuing 18km to **Fortin MR Long** (camp by river), watch for sand, loose dirt or deep mud, depending on the season, which can mire your vehicle. The worst sand bogs occur in the intervening 15km before **Geral E Garay**, on the border. You can camp and shower at the military base here. Get a Paraguay exit (or entry) stamp from the army.

If going on into Bolivia, bypass the two deserted military posts on the border: one Paraguayo and the other Boliviano. A passable bush track extends north from the border, 123km (four hours' drive during winter) into Boyuibe, Bolivia.

Asunción

This is the least populated capital city in the Americas. We enjoyed the novelty of a slow paced city. Grab a handful of brochures from the tourist office and set off on a walking tour of museums, cathedrals, cultural centers, artisan shops and parks. Colonial landmarks house McDonalds and Pizza Huts. It won't take long before new friends hail you in the streets like old buddies.

Getting there

From the north, you'll enter Asunción via the Trans-Chaco highway which passes the entrance to the **Jardín Botánico**, a campground, zoo and social center of town. To reach points south and east, traverse the congested Eusebio Ayala. Plans are to broaden this avenue and construction will undoubtedly add to existing problems.

Places to stay

Jardín Botánico at the end of Avda Artigas, along the Rio Paraguai is primo. Camping fees are US$1.10 per vehicle or tent, plus US$0.25 per person per day, 220 electricity, city water. Warm and cold showers in clean, but unattractive facilities. Alejandro has managed the fence-encircled, municipal oasis for nine years.

The surrounding park is tranquil Monday through Saturday, in spite of a so-called zoo (animal prison), the **Museo de Historia Natural** and the **Museo Indigenista**. Ironically, the very poor Maca indians, who were resettled to the perimeters of this park in 1985, are not revered in life. On Sundays, when everything else is closed, the park fills with families, sporting events, drinking bouts and musicians (second park entrance on Avda Trinidad). The park is serviced day and night by hundreds of metropolitan buses (US$0.43), 20 minutes to city center.

Reportedly, **Restaurant Westfalia** allows camping on their grounds. We couldn't find it.

Among hotels in the lower-middle price range look for the **Sahara**, Olivia 920 near Montevideo, pool and parking, frequented by overland companies. Cheaper is **Hotel Ñandutí**, Presidente Franco 555 and **Hotel Plaza** on Plaza Uruguay. **Residencial Rufi**, Cerro Corá and Antequera, has hot water, big rooms, and can accommodate bicycles.

Places to eat

The **Lido Bar**, centrally located on Palma and Chile opposite the Panteon de los Heroes, is extremely popular with locals from all walks of life, who can't figure out why it has not yet been invaded with foreigners. Maybe it's because of the Woolworth-style bar and stool decor. Prices are cheap, food terrific. They're famous for a cheesy *sopa de pescado*.

Also excellent, popular and inexpensive is **Panemac Pizzaria** at the corner of Chile and General Diaz. Slightly more expensive and better known is the restaurant **Asunción** at Estrella and 14 de Mayo.

Make a sweet tooth happy and visit a **La Molina** sweetshop and restaurant with locations throughout the city. Excellent, good value.

There are many fine expensive restaurants which you will have no trouble finding. Recommended, not for the food (overpriced and indifferent), but for an excellent stage show featuring local music and dance, is **La Jardín de Cerveza**.

Useful addresses
Boats   Up river to Corumbá, Brazil, or down river to Buenos Aires, Argentina, go to **Flota Mercante del Estado**, 686 Estrella or **Cruceros**, 14 de Mayo 150 at corner with Benjamin Constant. These agencies handle most bookings. Customs and immigration available at the port located on **El Paraguayo Independiente**.

Camping supplies   Try **Perfecta**, Estrella 488. It's a frightening place, owing to heavy trade in weapons, but they do carry many hard to find camping items. Also try **Nueva Americana**, a department store on the corner of Independencia Nacional and Mariscal Estigarribia.

Consulates:
   Argentina, España and Peru, processes visa within two hours, another office located in Encarnación.
   Bolivia, Eligio Ayala 2022 and Gral Brugez;
   Brazil, in Banco do Brasil near Plaza de los Heroes.
   Peru, Avda Mcal Lopez 648;
   Uruguay, Gral Santos 219 and De La Residenta;
   Venezuela, Mcal Estigarribia 1032 and Estados Unidos.

Markets   **Mercado 4** sprawls many blocks to both sides of Avda Pettirossi, beginning more or less at the crossroads of Avda Peru. You'll find a good selection of nearly anything, for prices higher than charged at more touristy places.

Upscale grocery stores are well stocked along Avda España and also along Ayala.

Post office   **Correo Central**, faces Alberdi at the corner of El Paraguayo Independiente, directly in front of the Palacio Legislativo. Postal rates are reasonable, the stamps are enormous and will cover ⅔ of a postcard, service is pretty good and helpful. Air schedules and package fares are posted.

Propane   **Corona Gas** on Avda Artigas, along the way to the botanical gardens, can refill most propane tanks.

Telephones   **ANTELCO** at Alberdi and Diaz offers two wall phones with push button DDI, credit card connections to North America and to many European countries.

The Touring and Automovile Club Paraguayo   Next to corner gas station on 25 de Mayo Y Brasil.

Tourist office   on Palma between 14 de Mayo and Alberdi. City maps and brochures are available in different languages.

Excursions

A myriad of handicraft centers extend east from Asunción along Ruta 2 toward Ciudad del Este. Some of these are:

Luque best prices for silver jewelry, harps and guitars; **Aregua**, 21km, for ceramic pottery (just what every cyclist needs); **Itagua-Nandutí**, 30km, for fancy, handwoven blankets and hammocks, finely stitched tablecloths; and **Caaguazu**, 178km, for wood products.

The southern Ruta 1 takes you 370km to Encarnación, on the border with Posadas, Argentina, and passes through **Carepegua**, 84km, known for cotton and wool blankets and hammocks. Beyond Carepequa lies the center of early Jesuit settlements.

SOUTHERN PARAGUAY

If headed to or from Brazil, you can choose among three routes. The most direct is Ruta 2 from Asunción to Ciudad del Este, 330km. Within Paraguay, this offers the most diversity and best infrastructure.

Ruta 1, via Encarnación in the south, wends through quiet, farming villages. Between Encarnación and Ciudad del Este, the countryside is pastoral. We enjoyed the quiet time, yet other travelers report it as "barren of stimulation". Some of the 17th-century Jesuit settlements can be encountered on this route, such as **Trinidad**.

History buffs recommend crossing into Posadas, Argentina at Encarnación and then striking the parallel route northeast to Argentina's Puerto Iguazu, 297km. This route has been described as beautiful and more interesting than any in Paraguay. The border crossing will certainly be more sedate here than in Ciudad del Este. The only drawback is Argentina is twice as expensive as Paraguay but you might find it is worth it..

A popular southerly circuit from Asunción allows you to combine a flavor of the two Paraguayan routes. From Ruta 1, turn north at Paraguari, 63km south of Asunción, and traverse a range of mountains to join up with Ruta 2 at Eusebio Ayala, 72km east of Asunción. The road is paved.

Continuing south on Ruta 1, beyond Paraguari, camp free at **Parque Nacional de Ybycui**, Atachoy. About 5km south of **Ita Km 37**, is **Camping El Bosque** with bathrooms and showers. At **Yaguaron**, the **Club Paraguay Park Village** offers camping on the north end of town.

Another 17km goes to the town of **Ybycui**. Turn north on to a paved road that stops 25km later in the national park. It is delightfully serene off-season and weekdays (up to 2,000 visitors on weekends). Rudimentary supplies are available outside the park.

Trinidad
Ruins of Jesuit missions are scattered approx 28km north of Encarnación. They're worth browsing. Camping is reportedly possible. A popular site is in **Jesus**. Turn left on to the dirt road (slippery when wet) shortly before Trinidad.

Encarnación
Cross the border into Posadas, Argentina, or loop north to Ciudad del Este in Paraguay. Argentina is very expensive, so stock supplies in Encarnación. Border formalities are quite straightforward. A bridge demarcates the two countries. There is an Argentine consulate here.

East — west on Ruta 2
Eusebio Ayala
Detour off Ruta 2 to find European-owned restaurants, small hotels and supplies. Twenty-six kilometers north by a paved pleasant road is **Parque Nacional de Vapor Cue**. Military personnel told us that this is not really a national park. Shrug. They grudgingly allowed us to camp anyway. Seven steamships that sunk during the war of the Triple Alliance are on display alongside the military museum, a hotel outside the entrance. Good swimming in a narrow creek, referred to as a river.

Parque Nacional Guayaqui
At Km 160 on Ruta 2, a river wends among trees and grassy knolls. Camping and facilities are free and there are food kiosks for those too tired to cook. Break the journey between Asunción and Ciudad del Este with a picnic or swim. The only drawback is its close proximity to the busy highway.

Coronel Oviedo
This is a major truck/bus junction connecting to Yby Yaú in the north, Villarica in the south, and the capital 132km to the east. The population of 21,782 seems to have other ambitions, but hasn't yet decided what it wants to be.

Ciudad del Este
If every resident stopped to be counted, population is estimated at 83,000; it seems like many more. The main attraction is cheap

shopping. Prices are cheaper than in Brazil or Argentina. Downtown is a morass of plastic and cardboard packaging in the evening, after the stores and kiosks have closed. Good values for travelers are dollars, food, alcoholic drinks, ice and fuel. Stock up if leaving Paraguay; likewise in neighboring countries, defer necessary purchases until arriving here. Ciudad del Este is the only city in the three frontiers where you can exchange money on weekends. Money changers hang out at the Puente de Amistad.

Getting there
The border between Brazil and Ciudad del Este is the Puente de Amistad. You can't miss it, it's the thing that looks alive with army ants. Look closer and you'll see they're shoppers crossing with their purchases on their backs. Customs and immigration isn't marked but it is the only building *on* the road. It's open twentyfour hours as is Brazil's customs and immigration, on the other side of the bridge.

Borders between Paraguay, Brazil and Argentina are open for visitors. You can go as far as Iguazu Falls in Argentina, spend the night and return to Paraguay.

Camping
Overland groups sometimes use the parking lot (and toilets) at **Itaipú dam** for overnight camping. Allegedly, this is the largest dam in the world. Tours and a film are available and said to be better than on the Brazil side. To arrive, follow the signs for Paraná Country Club.

Another alternative is at the lakeside boat club in **Hermandarius**, US$1 per person. To get there from Ciudad del Este, look for signs at a roundabout to Hermandarius, then follow signs north to the hydrofoil.

PRECOLUMBIAN STONE FIGURES
Left: Mayan figure at Copan, Honduras (PA)
Right: San Agustín, Colombia (HB)

THE PERUVIAN COASTAL DESERT
Above: The oasis of Huacachina (PA)
Below: Reed fishing boats, Huanchaco (PA)

THE INCA WORLD
Machu Picchu, Peru (HB)

THE ANDES AND THE JUNGLE
Above: Alpacas graze near Auzangate, Peru (HB)
Below: Rio Negro, Brazil (PA)

Chapter Fourteen

Peru

The Incas and Spanish were late-comers in a long history of civilizations whose legacies can still be viewed/marveled in their sophisticated ceramics, textiles and numerous archeological cities. In recent decades, terrorist groups strangled Peru, and thieves preyed on tourists and locals alike. Travelers hopped over Peru to Bolivia, and residents fled, until 1994 when the army arrested leaders of the *Sendero Luminoso*, *Túpac Amaru*, and cracked down on crime. A post-siege era of relief emerged with "The Big Sigh", and travelers are again flocking to Peru in record numbers.

Now the people are more optimistic and caring than ever and Peru has been restored to deservedly high rankings for security and adventure.

COUNTRY HIGHLIGHTS
Machu Picchu
Hiram Bingham rediscovered the "Lost city of the Incas" in 1911. Its name is now internationally known, and the setting of these ruins is without comparison.

Cuzco
The city with the longest continuous habitation in the Americas is stylishly spelled Qosqo, the Quechua name meaning "Navel of the Earth". Massive carved blocks of stone tower over narrow cobblestone streets, Quechua Indians, llamas and travelers in the city, aptly called the Kathmandu of the Americas.

Lake Titicaca
Reed islands of the Uro Indians dot what looks like an inland sea; the world's highest navigable lake.

Coastal desert

The sheer number of archeological sites is staggering and, in the desert air, their preservation has been remarkable. Some of the well-known sites are Chan Chan, Nazca, Sipan and the Moche pyramids — worth a visit.

Cordillera Blanca

Some of Peru's highest mountains are northwest of Lima. Mountain climbing and trekking are tops in this national park. Dramatic and challenging.

The Amazon

Iquitos, Peru's Amazon capital, cannot be reached by land. Accessible by sturdy vehicle or bicycle is Puerto Maldonado and the nearby reserve of Tambopata — a must for birders and wildlife enthusiasts. Before traveling this road, read *Inca Kola* by Matthew Parris (*see Further Reading, page 236*).

POINTS OF ENTRY

From Bolivia

The only feasible land border skirts Lake Titicaca between Copacabana and Puno. Standard border procedures are carried out in Kasani, Bolivia and Desaguadero, Peru.

From Ecuador

Tensions run high all along the border. There are two crossing points: Aguas Verdes/Huaquillas and La Tina/Macará. Neither are charming at the best of times. Officials are corrupt and will do and say anything to make your day miserable. Office doors were slammed shut in our faces, we were threatened with arrest and vehicle confiscation, all because we refused to pay for extraordinary services. At Aguas Verdes the road is narrow and extremely congested by vendors. Do not pass Peru's unmarked Control de Vehiculos, one building south of the Aduana and Friendship Bridge that spans a narrow canal.

From Chile

Between Arica and Tacna on the Pan-Am. Peru's side requires several hours of waiting in different lines. We were sent to the wrong line twice before I got impatient and demanded that the boss personally escorted us. My outburst shocked them (and me too), but it solved the problem.

ON THE ROAD

Roads are fairly decent. The Pan-Am is all paved and not heavily traveled except near Lima. Roads leading to the *altiplano* generally are not paved. Do not forget to tune your engine for altitude. Water is a scarce resource in the desert south of Lima.

Maps and guides

All the maps we've seen are outdated. Truck drivers provided us with the best road information, at times even sketching new routes. The Touring Y Automovil Club del Peru sells a road map and short route guides within regions, *Hoja de Ruta*.

USEFUL INFORMATION

Public holidays

January 1 (New Year)
Thursday and Friday before Easter
May 1 (Labor Day)
June 29 (Saints Peter and Paul)
July 28 and 29 (Independence Days)
August 30 (Santa Rosa de Lima)
October 8 (Battle of Angamos)
November 1 (All Saints)
December 8 (Immaculate Conception)
December 25 (Christmas)

When to visit

Beaches are best between December and April when they are hot and days are clear. From May through November cloudy mist shrouds the coastline, and Lima can be particularly dismal and cold. The mountains and jungle are hot during the day and cold at night (make that freezing, in the mountains) from April to October. And then begins the rainy season, November through April.

Money and banks

The newest currency, *nueva sol* is fairly stable and inflation is under control, at last. *Cambios* change travelers checks and are in tourist centers, eg: Cuzco, Huarez, Lima and in major cities with proximity to borders. **Banco de Crédito** changes travelers checks.

Personal security

Now that guerrilla activity has subsided and Peru is once again pretty safe, normal traffic flow has resumed on all roads. Further good

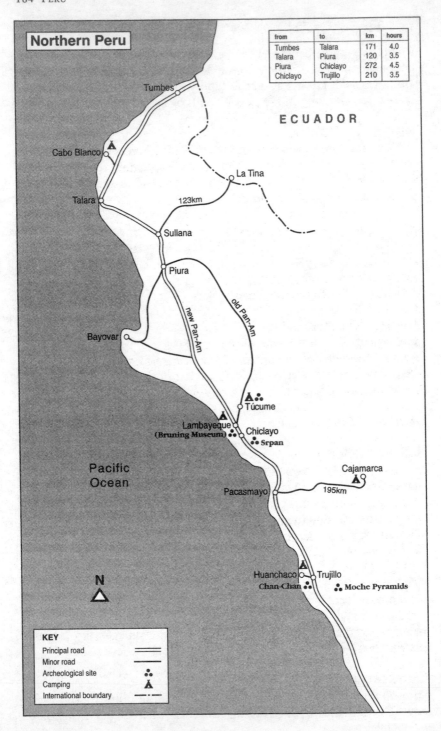

Northern Peru

from	to	km	hours
Tumbes	Talara	171	4.0
Talara	Piura	120	3.5
Piura	Chiclayo	272	4.5
Chiclayo	Trujillo	210	3.5

Tumbes

ECUADOR

Cabo Blanco

La Tina

Talara

123km

Sullana

Piura

new Pan-Am

old Pan-Am

Bayovar

Túcume

Lambayeque
(Bruning Museum)

Chiclayo

Srpan

Cajamarca

Pacasmayo

195km

Pacific
Ocean

Huanchaco

Trujillo

Chan-Chan

Moche Pyramids

N

KEY

Principal road	
Minor road	
Archeological site	
Camping	
International boundary	

news, crime has actually decreased! Robbery is not as frequent as before. Free camping is relatively safe within standard precautions. Of course, don't become lax with too many Pisco Sours and, as in Bolivia, keep your distance from drunks.

THE NORTHERN COAST

Fanfar
Moche ruins litter an extensive area several kilometers north of the turn off to Cajamarca. The Pan-Am bisects the site.

Tecume
A few kilometers east of Tecume begin two very extensive archeological sites. The mud-brick pyramids are massive and appear better preserved than at Chan-Chan. Thor Hyerdahl and Norwegian archeological teams are excavating the eastern sector. We had a blast roaming the area and imagining its prior majesty. Camping is permitted in the small area outside the museum.

Brüning Museum
Don't pass through Lambayeque without stopping to see this excellent museum of Moche and Mochica artifacts. It might be one of the best presented museums on the continent. It also houses the Sipán collection, when this is not on tour.

Sipán
West of Chiclayo, spectacular 2,000-year-old tombs are being uncovered in a very modest looking pyramid-like mound. *El Señor de Sipán* was found ensconced under a fabled gold funerary mask and breast plate, surrounded by artefacts and bones of loved ones (including the loyal dog). Two larger mounds have not been touched. Other than a reconstruction of the tomb in the bottom of a pit, not much has been conserved.

From Trujillo to Huanchaco
Plan several days here in order to see famed Chan Chán and the Moche pyramids of the sun and moon and then soak your tired feet at the beach. We recommend going directly to Huanchaco beach and making it your base for excursions. Turn off the Pan-Am into Trujillo and go directly west to reach Huanchaco.

Archeological sites
Crumbling mud brick pyramids are being restored, slightly south and west of Trujillo (look for small sign near Km 555, approx 1km south

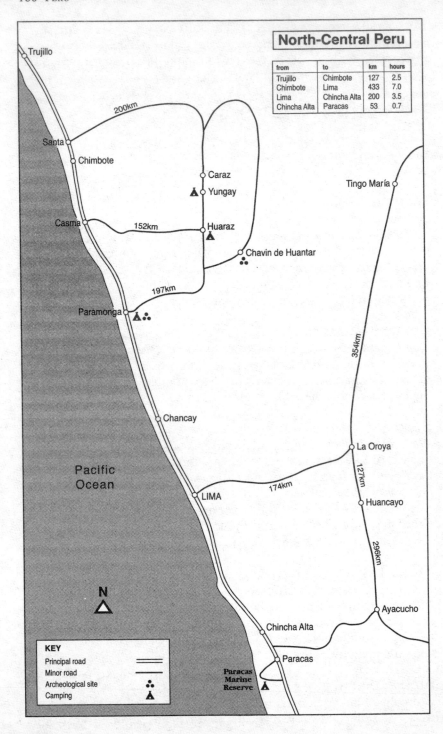

North-Central Peru

from	to	km	hours
Trujillo	Chimbote	127	2.5
Chimbote	Lima	433	7.0
Lima	Chincha Alta	200	3.5
Chincha Alta	Paracas	53	0.7

Trujillo

200km

Santa

Chimbote

Caraz

Yungay

Tingo María

Casma

152km

Huaraz

Chavin de Huantar

197km

Paramonga

354km

Chancay

La Oroya

Pacific
Ocean

174km

127km

LIMA

Huancayo

296km

N

Ayacucho

Chincha Alta

KEY

Principal road

Minor road

Archeological site

Camping

Paracas
Marine
Reserve

Paracas

of Moche bridge). The pyramids of the sun and moon, **Las Huacas del Sol y Luna** face each other like sister and brother. Like the Maya pyramids in Central America, these were built during successive periods of habitation. Eleven such layers have been identified in the sun temple. The restored friezes are more natural-looking than at Chan Chán.

Chan Chán is on the way to Huanchaco. It must have been a vast city, but nearly all that remain are 28 square kilometers of yellow brick foundations. For a view of Chan Chán's past splendor, go to the park office where nearby ceremonial centers have been conserved. Dolphin and fish motifs seem to leap out of the stucco, reminiscent of Santorini, Greece. You can roam alone but a guide will bring it all to life. If Chan Chán doesn't impress you with the transience of life, power and glory, nothing will.

Before Chan Chán, but on the way out of Trujillo to Huanchaco, you'll pass the **Casinelli** gas station squeezed into a fork in the road (take the left fork). Stop here, now or later. In the basement is a splendid museum! It's small, but the "curator" spins delightful stories illustrated with the ceramic pots. There are oddities, such as an alleged mummy of an adolescent girl with spina bifida shrunken to seven inches, and a locked cabinet of erotic art. From the Casinelli gas station, take the left fork to a roundabout where you'll continue straight to a second fork; bear left for Huanchaco.

The beach town of Huanchaco is the big hang out. Despite a constant parade of vacationers, townees and travelers, it has not yet reached resort status. Surfers ride waves alongside papyrus-reed fishing boats, *caballitos* — amputated versions of those at Titicaca. (They have an amazingly short life span: between 30 and 90 days.) Supplies are hard to find, myriad seafood restaurants close after the popular afternoon food feast, and discos open late.

Places to stay

Hostal Bracamonte, Los Olivios 503, near entrance to town and opposite the beach, rents comfortable bungalows and rooms in a garden setting. They allowed us to camp for US$4 with full use of pool, hot water showers, etc.

Nearby guesthouses rent rooms cheaper and also allow camping, for the same amount.

Pan-Am to Lima

Between Trujillo and Lima, the Pan-Am climbs and descends through valleys that are barren except for green ribbons of farmland at their base. Produce is supplied to surrounding towns as in the pre-Inca days. You'll see more Mochica ruins en route and pleasant oceanside villages to spend the night: Tortuga (Km 391 north of

Casma) and Albufera de Medio Luna between Barranca and Huacho. Residents are welcoming people back after being nearly shut down by guerrillas.

There is an obligatory police check point 43km north of Lima at Puente Piedra and another at a toll booth 45km south. Both places are consistently notorious for bribe demands. If hassled, wait for the undercover tourist police who monitor these spots in an effort to curb corruption.

Lima roads are well marked from the north but from the south, road signs are inadequate.

Cordillera Blanca An alternative route to Lima goes between the spectacular Cordillera Blanca and Negra. A well-marked dirt road juts west, slightly north of Chimbote at Km 207, follows the valley floor between the two mountain chains and rejoins the Pan-Am above Lima at Paramonga.

Huaraz

A mini Cuzco, without the architectural history, exuding a similar, lively flavor. Three times entire towns and valleys have been completely buried by earthquakes and avalanches. The snow covered mountain spires and deep canyons are truly worth your effort.

Hikers and climbers should acclimatize before setting out. Check with the **Casa de Guías** for trail maps, equipment and weather conditions. The canyon roads into the **Huascarán National Park** can be treacherous in bad weather. Motorists and hikers should seek and heed local advice.

Places to stay

Our favorite is **Hotel de Turistas de Monterrey** with thermal baths and heated public swimming pool, although it can be quite pricey. Highly recommended is **Edwards Inn**, Calle Bolognesi 121.

Lima

The capital of Peru is either very, very good or lousy. Lima has cleaned up its act in recent years; crime is down and nightlife is again picking up. As elsewhere in Peru, optimism beams from nearly every face. Travelers will soon discover reasons to spend time here besides that of necessity.

Buses and *colectivos* link the many distinctive sections of this sprawling city. It appears chaotic upon arrival by road but once you've settled, some sort of sense emerges from the apparent muddle. The airport is on the north end, which is unexciting; further south and west is the noisy, hardcore city and historic buildings.

South of the city center and historic buildings are the exclusive neighborhoods of Miraflores, on the ocean, and San Isidro. Either area provides a comfortable base for excursions.

Places to stay

Find a safe parking lot in popular Miraflores and you can choose from a wide range of accommodation. Recommended for comfort and security are:

Albergue Juvenil Internacional   Av Casimiro Ullao 324, Miraflores.
Hotel Esperanza   Calle Esperanza 350, Miraflores.

Useful addresses

Good grocery stores, consulates, clinics, repairs and museums are all here. Pick up a copy of the free *Peru Guide* for complete information and timely events.

Central post office   *Lista de Correos* at Jiron Junín, next to Plaza de Armas, Lima.
South American Explorers Club   Av Republica de Portugal 146, Breña, in Central Lima. The clubhouse maintains an extensive library and files of members trip notes. Non-members welcome for short visits to exchange info. Guidebooks, maps and used camping gear are sold.
Touring y Automovil Club de Peru   Av Cesar Vellejo 699, Lince.
Tourist office   *Infotur* at Calle Belen 1066, La Unión, central Lima and a kiosk in Miraflores.

THE SOUTHERN COAST

There is plenty to see and do here with short detours off the Pan-Am. Again, this is desert country. Dire shortages of water south of Nazca, with increasing distances between supply towns, promotes this liquid to top priority in the daily life of self-propelled travelers. Stock as much as you can carry, as frequently as possible. The road is excellent but deep canyons in the south will try the endurance of motorists and cyclists.

Paracas

The Pan-Am is fairly flat and fast for the 240km from Lima to Paracas and the nearby marine reserve. Some call the offshore sanctuary a poor person's Galapagos. We cannot confirm the comparison. As "poor people", we've never been to the Galapagos but have seen the astounding variety of seabirds and seals in the Paracas Marine Park and Ballestas. (Semi-annually, 1,000 workers descend on the islands to scrape *guano* from the cliffs and catacombs

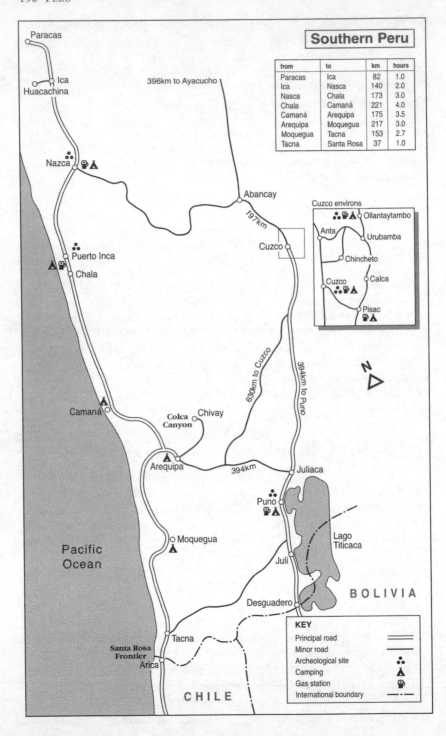

Southern Peru

from	to	km	hours
Paracas	Ica	82	1.0
Ica	Nasca	140	2.0
Nasca	Chala	173	3.0
Chala	Camaná	221	4.0
Camaná	Arequipa	175	3.5
Arequipa	Moquegua	217	3.0
Moquegua	Tacna	153	2.7
Tacna	Santa Rosa	37	1.0

KEY

Principal road	
Minor road	
Archeological site	
Camping	
Gas station	
International boundary	

of arches, caves and coves.) The mysterious *Candelabra* petroglyph that points to Nazca, is best viewed by water, en route to the reserve.

There is a plethora of hotels in Pisco. Alternatively, go one kilometer south of the dock and stay in the expensive **Hotel Paracas** on the bay. Camping is allowed outside. Good rough camping on the peninsula.

Boats

Boats can be hired from Pisco or 13km south at the Paracas docks. Aggressive competition for passengers among boat operators can be disarming but rarely results in discounts. Most expensive are the sleek motor boats. We held out and boarded a slow boat (US$10 per person and three hours each way) with a group of retirees from Paracas and enjoyed their serenades and snacks as much as the sights. The only bad turn came when they demanded that we stand and sing for them.

Ica

A scant 60km south takes you to Ica with a very good regional museum featuring Paracas textiles. There is a good vegetable market in the center of town.

Huacachina Detour from the Pan-Am at the last roundabout in Ica and follow signs to Huacachina for an amazing sight. A small brown lake is set among eucalyptus, palms, flowering trees, and white sand-dunes. These aren't ordinary sand-dunes. They are enormous! Rent a sand board from one of the food kiosks for a wild ride. You'll probably only do it once, unless you are really fit, because it's quite a climb to the top. There are hotels, municipal showers, and camping is permitted.

Nazca

Stop at the free observation tower at Km 421 (30km north of town) and/or an observation hill another 2km further, for a view of the Nazca lines. You can only see about five of these giant desert drawings from these two points, but it's worthwhile if you don't take the plane flight.

Planes The airfield is several kilometers south of town. Aero Condor charges US$47, for the 40-minute overflight. This is the only way to see the largest of the geometric shapes which are simply amazing. It is money well spent. Warning: many people get air sick in the small planes.

Places to stay
Camp opposite the airfield. Excellent grassy location among trees in front of the restaurant, hotel and swimming pool. Aero Condor owns it so they don't charge with flights, US$1 without. The same company owns **Hotel Algeria** in town that's popular with backpackers. We found ice in the ice-cream shops.

Puerto Inca
This is said to be the seaport that supplied ancient Cuzco with fresh shrimps and other seafood. The site is extensive, privately owned and shows signs of intensive looting. Scraps of human hair and cloth blow in the wind and piles of disjointed bleached bones are disturbing to see. Nevertheless, the number of structures and roadways is testimony to the productive endeavors of the Incas.

You can reach a series of secluded beaches by following the old Inca trails over rocky promontories. The central cove is excellent for swimming. Camping: US$1.50 per person includes showers and toilets (water brought daily from Chala), or pay US$10 for a hotel room. The restaurant is rather expensive so bring supplies from Chala.

The entrance to Puerto Inca is 140km south of Nazca and 5km north of Chala. Look for dirt track at Km 604, turn east for another 5km.

Arequipa
This is a fabulous colonial city with good eats, lively late nights and well-stocked markets. Antique shops are like mini-museums and, indeed, are housed in ancient buildings. The cathedral and buildings around the Plaza de Armas were restored after several devastating earthquakes. The central plaza is the focal point for sunset activities. Several universities inject a certain youthful vigor to non-stop cultural programs held throughout the city. Peaceful reflection is never better than in the gardens of **Santa Catalina Convent** where locals still come to petition the nuns for forgiveness. Popular excursions from Arequipa go to famous Colca Canyon, supposedly the world's deepest, and to active Volcán Misti (5,822m).

Getting there
From Puerto Inca and Chala, you're looking at 580km of deep valleys. The Pan-Am hugs coastal cliffs with spectacular views of blue ocean before turning inland at Camaná. Camp on the beach in La Punta to break the trip. There isn't much but barren mountains, condors and shifting sand-dunes until Repartición, about an hour outside of Arequipa.

From Tacna The Pan-Am from Tacna is even more desolate and has canyons deeper than on the north side of Arequipa. Without making big detours to the coast, you'll meet two obligatory *aduana* stops and three tiny towns with only meager food and water supplies.

From Cuzco A tolerable dirt road descends sharply from the *altiplano*. At Sicuani 133km south of Cuzco, turn west from the paved road to Yauri. There are towns and fuel en route. The final 47km into Arequipa are paved. The 521km route between Cuzco and Arequipa takes from 10 to 18 hours by motorized vehicle. Trucks and buses travel at night, so if unsure, wait and follow their headlights.

Places to stay
Backpacker hotels radiate outward from the Plaza de Armas. Further out, but within easy walking of the Plaza, is a plethora of good local hotels. Parking lots are scarce.

Hotel Jerusalén Calle Jerusalén 601; always popular and centrally located without parking.

Hostal Las Mercedes This gracious 1930 house stands by the river, on Vallecito at the end of Consuelo (no street number); tel: 21 36 01. It is convenient to the plaza, with good secure parking. Camping is permitted but the spacious rooms are terrific, US$30 double. We paid a small amount to camp and shower.

Hotel de Turistas Plazuela Bolivar, Urb Selva Alegre; tel: 22 99 33, with parking, but further from the action.

THE *ALTIPLANO*

A nearly flat plain sweeps along the horizon at the average altitude of 3,000m. Beginning around Cuzco, it extends south beyond Puno into western Bolivia and northern Chile. The beauty is strikingly stark. Snowy peaks jut skyward from the floor of the *altiplano*, where pastoral Indians graze flocks of llamas and alpacas, and Lake Titicaca glimmers like a jewel.

Cuzco
The longest continuously inhabited city in the Americas reverberates with history. Huge stone-block walls, chisled by the ancient Incas, nestle among the red-tiled roofs of contemporary Cuzco, the jumping-off point for excursions into the Sacred Valley of the Incas.

Nearly everything wanted by a traveler to Cuzco can be found in the proximity of the Plaza de Armas . . . even long lost friends. On Av de Sol you'll find the telephone company (ENTEL), post office and state tourist information office.

Local historical sites such as Sacsayhuaman, Ollantaytambo, Pisac, museums and monasteries charge admission. Invest in a US$10 ticket book, *Boleto Turistico*, sold at the tourist office and at any of the entrance gates; it is valid for ten days. Not to be missed is nearby Machu Picchu, but you'll have to stow your vehicle as there is no road.

Getting there

See the sections on *Arequipa* and *Puno*.

From Nazca A dirt road runs to Abancay and from there to Cuzco. This route fell into disuse when the *Sendero Luminoso* were in their heyday. It is now safe, but most traffic still goes through Arequipa. All roads can be treacheous during rainy periods.

Places to stay

From the northwest corner of the Plaza de Armas, Plateros runs two blocks before being renamed Saphi and along here are quite a few reasonably priced hostels and secure parking garages. Park in Saphi No 674 or in No 644 for US$1 per night. Hundreds of small hotels can be found along this and other streets that radiate from the plaza.

Hotel Cauhide At the end of Saphi; US$20 double.
Hostal Familiar Saphi 661; US$10-15 double.
Savoy Av del Sol 954 (opposite end of town from Plaza); US$90 double.

Excursions

Cuzco isn't so much a destination as it is a base camp for excursions, although many a traveler has found contentment within the close environs. Day walks in any direction will take you past any number of Inca ruins. Maps from the tourist office indicate the best-known and larger sites. Discovering your own *tambos* and baths is even more thrilling.

By road 30km from Cuzco is **Pisac** with a very colorful Sunday market. Climb to the archaeological park; a fortified hill overlooking the town also offers spectacular views of the Vilcanota river and Urubamba Valley.

Further along the valley, you should begin to feel the vibrations emanating from **Ollantaytambo**. Nearly intact concentric corrals; erect, massive block-walls abandoned suddenly by the Incas in mid-construction, and impressive terraces, contribute to its recent designation as a "high-energy center". Ollantaytambo is the new starting point for the Inca Trail and the train to Machu Picchu.

Naturalists are drawn to **Manu National Park** or the more

accessible **Tambopata** reserve near Puerto Maldonado. Jungle outfitters in Cuzco can put together excursions utilizing truck, mountain bike and canoe.

By rail Machu Picchu, the lost city of the Incas, is an impressive sight in the high Andes. You'll have to hike in or take a train. Two daily local trains depart from the **San Pedro** station near the Cuzco market and terminate in Quillabamba before turning around. Most tourists use the plusher *auto-wagon* departing from the **Wanchay** station at the end of Av de Sol, US$65 all inclusive. Departures also from Ollantaytambo.

Puno

The city is trying to attract travelers with festivals and improved security, and they're succeeding. Now they need to improve the weather and food and to heat the hotels. Before scooting off to Copacabana on the Bolivian side of Lake Titicaca, spend a day or two here taking in local sights.

Getting there

From Cuzco A fairly straight road parallels the railroad tracks along the *altiplano* between Cusco and Puno, 400km. It is more or less paved as far as **Sicuani** where camping is permitted at the Hotel Turistas. The road becomes rougher thereafter.

From Bolivia A paved road runs 150km from Desaguadero to Puno, skirting Lake Titicaca for much of the way.

Places to stay

Don Miguel Av La Torre, near the center and on the main road through town. It's a bit more expensive than other hotels, but everything works and parking is available alongside.

Hotel Uros One block from the railroad station, cheaper and less reliable amenities. Park across the street.

Lake Titicaca

The blues and greens of the world's highest navigable lake are striking under a bowl-shaped sky. Not too long ago, papyrus reed boats plied these waters, supplying the floating islands of the Uro Indians with fresh reeds, food and lake fish.

An interesting excursion (now by motor boat, US$12 per person) can be made to some of these islands. Amantani and Taquila are substantial to bear the weight of tourism, the floating (sinking) reed Uro islands cannot. They are the perfect examples of destructive tourism and, from that point of view, they shouldn't be missed nor walked upon.

We once found ourselves on a boat with eco-tourists, supposed anthropologists from a renowned museum, who quickly turned us into confirmed eco-cynics. The experience taught us the need to include respect for human life alongside any other ecological commitments.

Sillustani These cone-shaped funeral towers captivate the imagination as much as the site. Sunset is magnificent and spiritually rewarding. Sky colors are reflected in the bordering lakes. To get there, leave Puno toward Juliaca and take the sign posted road. It's not far.

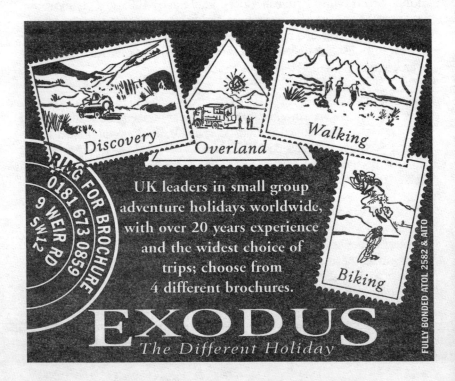

Chapter Fifteen

Uruguay

The rhythm of the country is set to two seasons and, in their way, they describe the meaning of life. "The Season", *la temporada*, begins December 15 and ends February. Summer tourists strain the infrastructure along the scenic coast beyond capacity. Argentineans compose the majority of these tourists whose tastes, and apparently ample pockets are catered to. Prices double, even triple.

During "Not The Season", which is the rest of the year, prices are slashed, entire towns board up, disappear or hibernate. You can travel all day without seeing another person. Punta del Este, a chic resort city, has only 6,000 year-round residents but, during "The Season", more than a quarter of a million tourists crowd the narrow spit of land.

COUNTRY HIGHLIGHTS

Much of Uruguay is rural and flat. Nearly 70% of the land is devoted to cattle and sheep, another 15% produces agricultural products. Half of Uruguay's three million citizens live in and around the capital, Montevideo.

Punta del Este
A world-class vacation city attracts world-class purses.

Parque Nacional de Santa Teresa
Spacious and ecologically diverse, this is the most user-friendly and best maintained park in South America.

POINTS OF ENTRY

If dots were placed on a map to mark each possible point of entry, Uruguay would look like a perforated cut-out. The following are the most frequently used border posts.

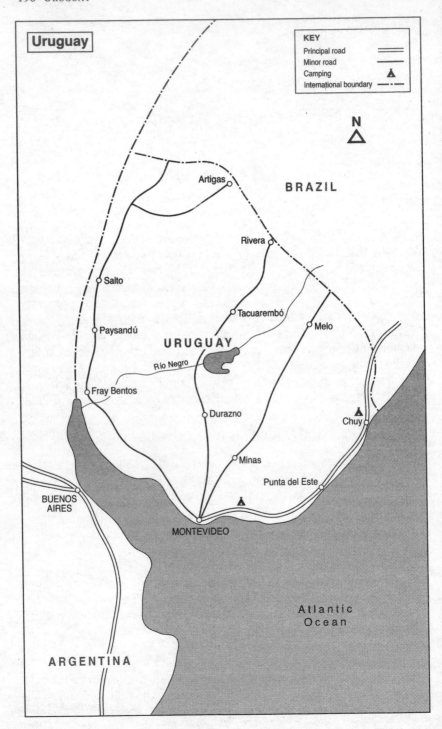

From Brazil

Entry points are Bella Union, Artigas, Santana Livramento, Aceguá, Rio Branco, and the two Chuys. The easiest is reportedly between Chui, Brasil and Chuy, Uruguay.

From Argentina

There are two land borders with Argentina, more specifically toll bridges, spanning the Rio Paraná. These are at Fray Bentos and, 122km further north, at Paysandú.

By ferry

Numerous ferries shuttle the Rio de la Plata between Buenos Aires and Colonia, Uruguay. Highly recommended is **Jet Ferry**. Roundtrip fare for a vehicle, port fees, and two passengers runs around US$170. Crossing time is 45 minutes in modern surroundings. **Buque Ferry** takes three hours in order to accommodate onboard gambling casinos. A third, and more luxurious, ferry service operates between Buenos Aires and Montevideo.

ON THE ROAD

The worse part of getting around Uruguay is mismarked roads. No road signs (often true) would be better than ones indicating the wrong direction. Ask and reconfirm by asking someone else.

Police use radar. You don't need to slow at each police station as in Brazil. Secondary roads are not paved. Bridges are very narrow, so approach with caution.

Gas stations are hard to find in the northern and western sectors.

Repairs are readily available by inventive mechanics, true craftsmen, who keep great old cars of museum quality plying the roads. Imported parts are very expensive. There isn't much available in the way of sophisticated motorcycle or bicycle parts.

Seasons

Cyclists and motorists should be aware of strong winter winds (June to late November) that sweep up from Argentina's pampas. If you're peddeling north, the wind should be no problem; southbound, it'll hold you nearly in place.

Maps

Locally produced maps look like placemats for a dinner table. A good map of Uruguay is hard to find, unless you go to Montevideo first. **Automovil Club de Uruguay**, Av. Libertador General

Lavalleja 1532, Montevideo. Esso gas stations sometimes stock and sell useable maps. They aren't very accurate and are hard to read.

USEFUL INFORMATION
Public holidays
January 1 (New Year)
January 6 (Ephiphany)
The week before Easter
May 1 (Labor Day)
May 18 (Battle of Las Piedras)
June 18 (Artigas' Birthday)
Juy 18 (Constitution Day)
August 25 (Independence Day)
November 2 (All Soul's Day)
December 8 (Immaculate Conception)
December 25 (Christmas Day)

Camping
Uruguay offers at least 67 organized campgrounds throughout the country. Nearly every municipality has camping facilities. The *Ministerio del Turismo* publishes a comprehensive brochure and map to the sites. Many, nearly most, have swimming pools, tennis courts, football fields, playgrounds, barbecue pits, 220 electrical outlets, mini-markets, restaurants, laundromats, even car rental offices, ice plants and propane gas refilling stations; rental cabins, small trailers and tents. During The Season expect to pay US$10-15 for two people with your own tent or vehicle, cabins average US$30-60 for four. Off season expect to find most campgrounds closed or, at best, functioning without amenities.

Off-season, showers are extremely difficult to arrange. Neither restaurants nor gas stations offer this service.

Fourteen youth hostels are scattered throughout, but they also close. For a listing contact: Asociacion de Alberguistas del Uruguay, Pablo de María 1583, Montevideo; tel: (02)404245. An informative guide is a weekly newspaper aimed to backpackers, Guia de Turismo Juvenil y Tiempo Libre.

Money
The Uruguay peso is pegged to the American dollar and is fairly stable. Old money circulates which necessitates subtracting three zeros from the end of each bill. 1994 exchange rate US$1=5.45 pesos.

Banks and casas de cambio not only discount the exchange rate for dollars but charge US$1 for each travelers check and add a 1%

commission on total. Nevertheless, all currencies are traded, making Uruguay a good place to stock up on dollars before heading into Argentina or Brazil.

Uruguay is quite expensive year round.

THE NORTH
Chuy

A smallish border town near the Atlantic Ocean, faces its Brazilian twin, Chui. It is more a truck stop than a tourist haven. Lots of import stores on Uruguay side. Unless desperate for a particular item, prices are no bargain. Fill up with gas on the Brazil side, groceries are somewhat cheaper there, too, but more expensive than further north. This is the only place with provisions for a while in any direction.

Useful addresses

Brazil Consulate   Fernandez 147.

Immigration   Customs and immigrations are housed together on Ruta 9, the main road, approximately 1.5km from town. Continue straight on this road through Chui and you'll hit Brazilian customs and immigration (Policia Federal).

Barra del Chuy

10km to the east of Chuy is this Atlantic coastal town with camping, cabins and supplies.

Parque Nacional de Santa Teresa

This is one of the most harmonious parks in South America. Hillsides are forested with native trees, majestic Royal Palms fringe park roads and the surf of the Atlantic Ocean laps sandy beaches.

Laguna Negra   Across the road from the park, this deep dark lake offers freshwater swimming and more camping.

We visited in September yet couldn't imagine this park so crowded that you couldn't find a comfortable camp site during The Season. There is lots to see and do beginning with the reconstructed fort of Santa Teresa built by Portuguese in 1752 and later snatched by the Spanish, bird aviaries, small zoos, children's playgrounds, barbecue pits, surfing, bathrooms with cold showers and potable water.

Cabo Polonio

Situated on the coast and surrounded by sheep and cattle ranches, Cabo Polonio becomes a ghost town off-season. It's very small at any time of the year. Attractions are the beaches and boat trips to the islands of Castillos and Wolf where you can see colonies of sea lions. There is a youth hostel (closes off season) here and camping. Along Ruta 10 you can also camp alongside river *balnearios*.

La Paloma

An attractive town of about 5,000 set among trees. It is a popular resort town, but more laid back and not as ritzy as other places, such as Punta del Este. Not much to do except to relax. There is a casino on the main street, Av Solari. Two municipal camping grounds close when Not The Season. Both **Parque Andresito** in the center and **Los Delfines**, approx 2km from the center on Ruta 15, rent cabins however, US$30 in low season and US$64 during The Season. We camped free alongside the lighthouse. The tourist information office in the center of town is very helpful.

THE SOUTH

Punta del Este and Maldonado

Punta del Este is a ritzy concrete resort, Maldonado is the adjoining inland city surrounded by Argentina's wealthy summer palaces. Residential neighborhoods carry such whimsical names as Beverly Hills, California Park and Florida Park. The opulent houses range from marvelous to institutional. Worth a gawk.

The main attraction of Punta del Este is status. Argentineans come here to be seen. During The Season more than 250,000 status seekers spill from highrise condos and luxurious homes; off-season maybe 6,000 are left to maintain a slower pace of life. Everything is very expensive. Off-season prices are no bargain: a movie will set you back US$8, a cup of espresso US$4, a souvenir sweatshirt (inscribed "New York") US$79, and a modest dinner for two, US$110.

Popular beaches are scattered along the bay side of Punta del Este. Rougher water on the north side is reflected in its name, Playa Brava. A well-appointed yacht club, on the bay side, is nice for wandering and dreaming (public restrooms).

Places to stay

Camping is not permitted on the beaches. All campgrounds are located on the mainland. Frequent bus service connects all municipal points of interest. We're listing only campgrounds which, as noted, also rent trailers, tents and cabins. Prices and amenities are in the same range as noted (*see Camping, page 200*). From north to south:

La Barra In El Placer, along the river banks, approx three blocks west of Ruta 10 and south of the rollercoaster bridge (great fun to cross).

Punta Ballena   South of Punta del Este. Turn off the coastal road at Km 128 on to a well marked, dirt road and follow 2km. Not on the ocean, nor in the town by same name, but attractive, shady, full-amenities. (Note: women, watch the leach who runs the laundry). Also, **Cardenal Azul** at Km 117. It is further from the action, but with ocean frontage and a relaxed, albeit posh, village atmosphere.

Useful addresses

American Express   Turisport, Edificio Torre Verona, Av Gorlero and El Corral (Gorlero is principal road). Better yet is an **American Express Bank**, Av Gorlero and La Galerna. No charge for travelers checks.

Tourist office   Computerized information, as well as real people, answer questions. Located in the bus terminal on Av Gorlero and Calle 32.

Montevideo

Nearly half of the nation's population enlivens the bustling capital. We bypassed it, due to its expense, but the following is a compilation of other travelers' reports.

Things to do

Gastronomic delights are the menu of the day at Mercado del Puerto, an old, wharf-side market rejuvenated by small restaurants and wandering musicians. Ask for wine *medio y medio*, potent and delicious.

For a scenic view of the city go to Casa Municipal and ride the glass elevator to the top.

If taking a hotel room, always ask first to see it. Lobbies are very grand but rooms are reportedly shabby. Check to make sure you have hot water.

Colonia

A quaint port town with colonial architecture that is worth a day or a few hours before taking the ferry to Buenos Aires. The pace is more relaxed than in larger cities.

Fray Bentos

The town of Fray Bentos is 14km south of the Friendship Bridge that adjoins Uruguay to Argentina. Detour if you need to buy provisions, because there is nothing between Fray Bentos and Gualeguaychú, 34km beyond the Argentinean border. At the border, in Uruguay, is a seasonal restaurant and *cambio* (closes early). Exchange rates are favorable in Uruguay.

Customs and immigration for both Uruguay and Argentina are housed together in Uruguay alongside of the toll bridge (US$4).

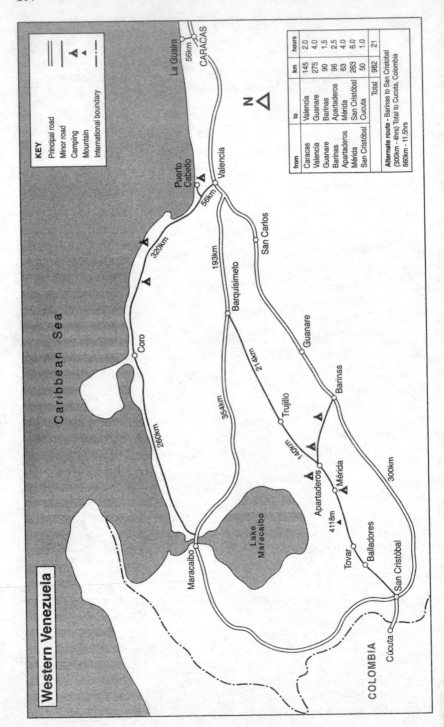

Western Venezuela

KEY

≡≡ Principal road
― Minor road
▲ Camping
▲ Mountain
·–·– International boundary

from	to	km	hours
Caracas	Valencia	145	2.0
Valencia	Guanare	275	4.0
Guanare	Barinas	90	1.5
Barinas	Apartaderos	96	2.5
Apartaderos	Mérida	63	4.0
Mérida	San Cristóbal	263	6.0
San Cristóbal	Cucuta	50	1.0
	Total	982	21

Alternate route - Barinas to San Cristóbal (300km - 4hrs) Total to Cucuta, Colombia 860km - 11.5hrs

Chapter Sixteen

Venezuela

Travelers to Venezuela are never ambivalent to this Caribbean nation, they either love it or hate it. We love it for the spirit of the people, who are a bit anarchic (perhaps justifiably so), and for the natural beauty. Rich oil fields, while generating pollution, have spared the land from agricultural rape, the kind of deforestation so evident in other countries. Venezuela is home to 30,000 species of flowering plants, 10,000 ferns, 6,000 different trees, 1,500 orchids, 1,300 birds and 20.5 million people.

Snow-covered mountain peaks stud the western edge and the central *cordillera* gently enfolds Caracas. Elsewhere Venezuela is flat. Almost half the country is rainforest or savannah, and in the southeast, dramatic mesas stretch skyward. The Amazonian region includes the Orinoco River.

COUNTRY HIGHLIGHTS

Mérida
Scenic mountain hamlets, untouched forests and terrific hiking make this one of the most beautiful Andean regions.

Mochima National Park
Coastal get-away islands are surrounded by crystal blue water, shimmering white sand beaches and stupendous diving reefs.

Paria Peninsula
This little visited spit of land cradles small fishing villages and offers glimpses of life uncomplicated by development.

Canaima National Park
Primeval silence inundates the expansive table-top mesa known as the Gran Sabana. Waterfalls abound, among them Angel Falls.

POINTS OF ENTRY

From Colombia

Cross through the mountains at Cúcuta, or by the lowland route at
Maicao, west of Maracaibo. See page 000, *San Antonia de Tachira,*
and page 000, *Maica.*

From Brazil

Enter (or leave) at Santa Elena de Uairen, see page 000, *Santa Elena.*
Note: There is no land entry point with neighboring Guyana.

By sea

Isla Margarita is the smallest port, and has only irregular
international service. A ferry connects the island to the mainland
(*see page 216, Puerto La Cruz*).

La Guaira is a major commercial port located near the main
international airport, a 30-minute drive north of Caracas.

Puerto Cabello is three hours' drive from Caracas and seven hours
from Maracaibo. Presently, Puerto Cabello is smaller and safer, and
port offices are more accessible than at La Guaira. Shipping fares are
the same here as in Caracas. If flying or air freighting a vehicle,
compare air fares to Maracaibo and to Caracas.

Border formalities

You will need a customs house agent who handles "personal
belongings". This is a special legal category that exempts foreigners
from normal taxes and required permits to enter and exit the country
with personal property. There are two reliable brokers.

HL Boulton, Maritime Customs Agents   Located in Puerto Cabello at
Calle Comercio, Norte No 38; tel: (042) 616853, 617377; fax: (042)
617684, in La Guaira they're on Av Soublette, Edificio Boulton; tel: (031)
25155; fax: (031) 25657.
Continental Custom Brokers   In La Guiara, Av Soublette, Edificio Las
Américas, Local PB-2; tel: (031) 24981; fax: 29835. Offices in Puerto Cabello.

The *Libreta de Pasos por Aduana* is not required but it certainly
makes life easier both within the country and at borders. Since many
other countries do require it and Venezuela is the only place that
allows its purchase by foreigners, buy one here.

Touring y Automóvil Club de Venezuela   Offices in San Cristóbal; tel:
(076) 434156. In Maracaibo; tel: (061) 81 858. In Caracas, Torre Phelps,
Piso 15, Plaza Venezuela; tel:(02) 7819743; fax:(02) 7819787. Look for the
blue neon sign, **Phelps**, on top of a tall building.

Visas

Consulates abroad insist that visas are not needed. This is patently untrue unless arriving by air. Visas are required of *everyone* entering by land. They are granted at the nearest consulate to the border. Apply at least 24 hours in advance. Provide one passport photo, a letter from your home bank (a photocopy of credit cards or travelers checks will do), an application form, and US$30.

Holders of tourist cards *cannot* cross the border into Cúcuta, Colombia, for a day of sightseeing or shopping and re-enter Venezuela. If you do so, you'll have to apply for a visa before allowed re-entry.

Do not accept the 72-hour, in-transit visa which costs the same as a multi-entry visa. It cannot be extended or changed inside the country.

Tourist cards are given to anyone arriving by air.

In Panama contact the consulate, Torre BCO Union, Piso 5, Av Samuel Lewis; tel: 642524, between the hours of 9am and 12 noon. In Colombia you can try Bogotá, Bucaramanga, Barranquilla and Rio Hacha. In northern Brazil contact the consulate in Manaus or in Boa Vista.

ON THE ROAD

A fine system of *autopistas* bypass cities and scenic sights. Traffic moves briskly on these superhighways. Toll tickets arc not always available so you might have to tell the cashier where you got on. Tolls are the cheapest in the Americas. Secondary roads are narrow and congested within cities; outside cities, they are peaceful.

During rainy season (late April until September), dirt roads flood. Areas most adversely affected by flooding are the *llanos*, Apure and Barinas states, and the backroads of the Gran Sabana.

Commercial tour groups are now required to hire a guide when passing through Bolivar state, from Ciudad Bolivar to Santa Elena at the Brazil border. A recommended contact: Dirección Turismo, Edf Bolivar, Av Bolivar, Quinta Yayita; tel: 22362; fax: 24525.

Driving style

Vehicular anarchy is the rule so be an alert, defensive driver. Heavy drinking and fast driving are leading causes of a very high, nationwide mortality rate. In the event of a fatal accident, responsibility falls on whomsoever is most inebriated.

Special planning is warranted in Caracas where roadways choke with traffic jams from early morning (5am) until early evening (8pm). Watch out for careless drivers on cellular phones.

Fuel
The cheapest fuel, anywhere, is sold in Venezuela, US$0.10 per liter. Allegedly, all gas is unleaded and is sold by octane: 95, 93, 91, 89, or 87. A gas station in Venezuela is called a *bomba*. Many close during the siesta hours.

Cyclists
Wide, paved shoulders provide cyclists with some buffer from the fast paced traffic on *autopistas*. Bicycles are supposedly prohibited, but not rigidly banned.

Maps
The best road map is produced by the oil company Lagoven. They're sold in their gas stations, but are hard to come by. Corpoven maps are easier to obtain and adequate, although difficult to read. A series of regional maps seem to be fainter copies of the Corpoven map.

USEFUL INFORMATION
Public holidays
January 1 (New Year)
Thursday and Good Friday preceding Easter
April 19 (Declaration of Independence Day)
May 1 (Labor Day)
June 24 (Carabobo Day – St. John's feast)
July 5 (Independence day)
July 24 (Liberator's Day)
October 12 (Columbus day)
December 25 (Christmas)

When to visit
Year round, temperatures vary little from 26°C, except in the Andean mountains surrounding Mérida. The rainy season begins in late April and continues through October.

Camping
Venezuelans love to camp, so much so that guidebooks refer to the "Venezuelan style". Any two trees from which to swing a *hamaca* will do. Organized campgrounds go against the grain of these free-wheeling people. *Club campestres* are private country clubs in cities. In rural areas, a *club campestre* is usually a restaurant, with maybe a few rental rooms, and an area where camping is permitted.

Money and banks

The Venezuelan currency is the bolivar, which is designated as Bs (pronounced "bees"). The official exchange rate is adhered to, but there is now a black market. If you are lucky enough to exchange immediately after one of the frequent devaluations, the country is cheap; otherwise it can be expensive. Spend all your bolivars before leaving the country as it is very difficult to officially reconvert. *Casas de cambio* outside the country usually pay a higher rate of exchange than inside. In 1995, an exchange limit was imposed restricting transactions to US$200 per day, per person.

Stock up on bolivars whenever you can find them. Outside of Caracas it is difficult to find places to exchange.

Banco Consolidado   Changes American Express checks but will not advance cash on credit cards.

Banco Unión   Their ATMs reportedly accept Visa.

National park system

Venezuela has set aside 15% of its country's surface in 39 parks and 17 natural monuments. Canaima National Park in the eastern Amazon region is the largest in Venezuela and the sixth largest in the world with 30,000 square km, approximately the size of Belgium. Mochima is a beautiful coastal park. Parks on the western border with Colombia are conduits for drug traffickers and are dangerous. The national park office INPARQUES is located in Caracas (see *Caracas*). Camp by permit only.

Ecology

In spite of rich natural resources, history, and diverse climatic zones, carelessness is destroying the natural beauty of Venezuela. The coastal region is densely dotted with oil refineries, ports and industrial plants that dump chemicals and other pollutants. Quite a few beaches (seven in Isla Margarita alone) are closed to swimming, due to contamination. Unfortunately, warning signs are not posted. Logging continues to reduce the dense jungle of the Amazon to scrub brush. Perhaps most insidious is consumer waste. Plastic bags, cans and bottles litter miles of beach and back roads, completely ruining otherwise spectacular views. Please bag garbage and keep it until you find a garbage disposal service.

WEST OF CARACAS

West of Caracas, all routes bend inland until Puerto Cabello on the coast. From there, a highway runs along the shore for about 200km.

Take the smaller, secondary routes to avoid the boring *autopistas*.
Cities between Caracas and Puerto Cabello tend to be industrial, hot
and congested. Poke around in them if you feel inclined. In **Cagua**,
30 minutes west of Maracay, you'll find the best deals for wicker
furniture and red clay pottery.

Puerto Cabello

The second largest port of Venezuela is located west of the inlet in a
naturally protected harbor. The city of nearly 90,000 is neatly divided
into a colonial old town (1731) and a new section. The old town
surrounds the port. Buildings are being restored to their former
charm as an increasing commitment to tourism.

A broad, attractive *malecón* follows the waterfront at the north end
of town. Here, the evening entertainment commences with the arrival
of artists, craftspersons, and vendors. Something is almost always
going on. A strand of restaurants are housed in buildings of fanciful
architectural design. A produce market meets daily on Calle Plaza
behind the restaurants.

Places to stay

Near the port:

Hotel Paris Av Anzoátequi (one block south of San José church which
faces Plaza Bolivar), basic, bath, fans, clean, safe, no parking.

Hotel Universal Calle Plaza 9-75, by the produce market, basic, air
conditioning, bath, and secure parking inside the complex.

Many fine, but higher priced hotels are available further from the
port district.

Hotel Bahía and **Hotel Suit Caribe** jacuzzi, parking.

Miramar Outside of town, at the junction of the Pan-Am and Este 1;
rocky beachfront, secure parking. Cheaper than in town.

Camping The beach west of the *malecon* is unsafe and polluted. *Palma
Sola* 25km west of Puerto Cabello is a 16km strip of sandy beaches, palm
trees, and seafood restaurants. It begins around **Morón** and is accessed
along its length by the Pan-Am. Alternatively go to Patanemo.

Useful addresses

Tourist information is gladly given at the library. The *biblioteca* is
located on the small plaza opposite the Port Captain's office and
next to Banco Venezuela. The tourism office on Plaza Bolivar is
rarely open.

Banco Consolidado Plaza Bandera, Calle Plaza.

Customs house brokers They fill the port district. A good starting place
is Calle Comercial.

Patanemo

Take the road east toward the naval base and continue through **Quizandal** (good restaurants, rental showers and small *lanches* to Isla Larga, US$3 per person, with nude sunbathing but little shade; no facilities). Past Quizandal, the road climbs, narrows and becomes twisty (could be tight for an RV). At the road's end is lovely little **Patanemo**.

The pace of life here is slow, with swimming, leisurely walks in the hills, and bathing in a nearby waterfall. Camp free on the coconut tree-lined, soft sand beach. There are a few cheap eateries but no facilities. Supplies in town are limited except for beer and ice. Vegetables and bread are sold out of private homes. Weekends are crowded, noisy times but most people leave by sunset.

Places to stay

La Churuata at the entrance to town, with small pool, restaurants, camping possible.

Morrocoy National Park

Popular with travelers is this offshore preserve of small islands. It is a terrific habitat for snorkeling, skindiving, waterskiing (jet skis), and birdwatching. It becomes very crowded and littered on weekends and holidays.

From Puerto Cabello follow the Pan-Am through Morón north to **Tucacas**. Thereafter, you go by foot. Wear footwear appropriate for wading. From Coro, at the entrance to Peninsula de Paraguaná, Morrocoy is 200km to the south.

Places to stay

Tucacas is expensive and grubby. A more pleasant option is to stay out of town. **Mi Bohio** is 20km south of Tucacas and provides room and campers with showers, toilets and a sandy swimming beach.

Coro

The area surrounding **Coro** comprises the Venezuelan desert, with golden sand-dunes, cactus, the flowering *cuji* tree and small adobe homesteads. Craftspeople specialize in furniture fashioned from the dried cactus. The population in the city exceeds 150,000. The dunes on the immediate outskirts aren't safe for casual strollers. In the very core of the modern city are shady plazas and restored colonial buildings that date to its founding in 1527. Some streets are blocked to all but pedestrian traffic and bicycles. Art museums, shops and cozy café bars offset the surrounding nouveau-cement structures.

There is nowhere to change money between Maracaibo and Puerto

Cabello. If you find yourself short, go to **Supermercado Hong Kong**. They accept US dollars, but not travelers checks.

Places to stay

We couldn't find much for camping in or near the city. Diehards will have to hustle up a spot on private property or pick a public lot, like the bus station. Within the city there are only a few hotels with enclosed parking and adequate truck clearance. **Hotel Independencía**, Calle Independencía, is very basic, with fans and private baths.

Maracaibo

Venezuela's second largest city, pop 1.5 million, and largest oil field, *Lago de Maracaibo*, are bundled into one flat and sprawling vista. While residents are proud of their rich cultural heritage, visitors rarely find much to enamor them. This is the last city before the Colombian border at Maicao. For entering travelers, Maracaibo might be a necessary stop.

Useful addresses

American Express   Turisol, Av 4 Bella Vista con Calle 67, Cecilio Acosta. Near the bank.
Banco Consolidado Av Bella Vista con Calle 67, Plaza del Indio Mora or the airport. Convert your money because there are few other places between here and Caracas or the border.
Colombia Consulate   San Martin at Av 3Y, 70-16 near Av 4, Bella Vista. Morning hours only.
Touring and Automóvil Club de Venezuela   Edificio El Lago, Local 1-A, Calle 77 (before 5 de Julio) No. 11-53.

Between Maracaibo and Maicao

Drive time between Maracaibo and Maicao averages two hours over flat lagoons and bridges. The indigenous *Guajira* people have built stilt houses over the swampy lagoons. Long-time victims of discrimination, their poverty is not self-made. If you want to learn more about the Guajiras, follow the road to El Mojan and then to Sinamaica. Boats tour the stilt-town for US$10 per person.

Maicao

A border town that's not very attractive, but procedures to exit Venezuela and enter Colombia are straightforward. This has been a notorious smugglers' gateway. Take precautions. Camp east of town, get up early and cross the border early. Vehicles can reach Santa Marta, Colombia, the same day.

CARACAS

The valley capital rests at a cool 900m elevation. Four million inhabitants jamb the center and their houses spew up and over the surrounding mountains. The smog is breathtaking on some days.

Caraqueños say of their city that everything is both possible and impossible. It is vibrant and cosmopolitan, museums and zoological parks are excellent, nightlife rivals Rio de Janeiro. Traffic is impossible.

Getting there

Three autopistas lead into and out of the valley of Caracas and they are almost always congested. Leave plenty of time to get to where you're going.

Highway Este 1 enters Caracas from the south, through Los Teques, from the direction of Maracay and Valencia. Autopista Este 9 communicates with the eastern cities of Guarenas and Barcelona. Connecting metropolitan Caracas with coastal Maiquetia and La Guaira is a 28km *autopista* which climbs to 1,040 meters, and passes through several tunnels. Pay toll entering Caracas; free to exit.

Many years ago we found a fourth way and it remains our favorite backdoor route into and out of western Caracas. Pick up Ruta 4 that diverts alongside Colinas de Vista Alegre and Bella Vista. Follow signs to El Junco, El Junquito, **Colonia Tovar** or La Victoria. Near Caracas the road is lined with junked auto yards; afterwards it is a spectacular, bamboo-arced, ridge road. Free roadside camping sites are available all along the two-lane road to the alpine village of Colonia Tovar. Continue west 35km on Ruta 4 through Colonia Tovar and the road climbs higher before descending steeply with tight switchbacks into the industrial city of La Victoria. From La Victoria, pick up the Autopista Este 1 toward Caracas or west toward Maracay.

Getting around Caracas

The metro system is a marvel. Today it is as pleasant, clean and efficient as the day it opened in 1983. The metro runs frequent, fast service between 5.30am and 11pm. The underground serves the city mainly east to west with connecting surface *metrobuses*. Route maps are posted at all the stations and in each cabin. It is wise to purchase round-trip tickets, *ida y vuelta*, as lines are long at rush hours.

Por puestos or microbuses run similar routes through the city for about US$0.50. *Taxi libres* do not pick up other passengers. Set the fare in advance, expect to pay US$2 per person for relatively short distances.

A delightful pedestrian walkway was created by blocking traffic on Avenida Libertador between Plaza Venezuela and Sabana Grande.

Trees, shopping, hotels, street vendors, and cafés make this a pleasant area to browse or to watch Caraqueños stroll. Another pedestrian area is in the historical district of El Silencio where you'll find small plazas, cathedrals, museums, government buildings and strolling musicians.

Places to stay
Find a guarded parking lot, leave your vehicle and look for nearby lodging. Utilize the public transport system while in the city.

Hotel Canaima Esquina de Abanico, Carmelitas, convenient to Metro, post office; secure parking; tel: 5611366 or 5611352.
Hotel Sudamerica Two blocks away from the Canaima; parking.
Limón Bellas Artes, Calle Este 10, No 228.

Useful addresses
American Express Turisol, second floor, C-2, Local 53F-07 of the CCCT shopping complex in Chuao; tel: (02) 9591011.
Brazil Embassy Located in Altamira, Barrio La Castellana, Av Mohendano, Banco Barinas, Piso 6; tel: 2614481. Visa hours 8.30am-12.30pm, same day issue, no fee.
Camping equipment The best stocked is **Proveedura Scout**, Plaza Lincoln (behind Maxy's and next to Palmar Chinese restaurant), Av Leonardo DaVinci, Colinas de Bello Monte, Caracas; tel: 7523179, 7513879.
Casa de cambio Change money at **ITAL**, Av Urdaneta, near main post office.
Colombian Embassy Guaicaipuro Sector Chacaito, Urb El Roasal; tel: 951 3631. Open 8-11.30am, Mon-Fri. Same day issue, US$10.
National park headquarters *Instituto Nacional de Parques* is located at the entrance to Parque de Este between Avenidas Miranda and Romulo Gallego in Se Bucan. Temporary camping permits for national parks are supposedly obligatory, but free. You may obtain them here or at regional offices (always closed).
Post office The main office for general delivery is located in the heart of Caracas: Correo Central, Norte 4, Carmelitas.

Excursions
Colonia Tovar
Follow Ruta 4 toward Colonia Tovar (*see Getting there, page 213*). Three kilometers east of Colonia Tovar dip down to the north coast and to small, quiet beach towns of **Puerto La Cruz** and **Puerto Maya**.
   Colonia Tovar, elevation 1990m, 16,000 population, was founded in 1843 by German settlers who manifest their influence with neat

white chalets and German sausages; strawberries and cream are a local specialty.

La Victoria
Continue west on Ruta 4 from Colonia Tovar toward industrial **La Victoria**. Four kilometers north of La Victoria is a shady, riverside *club campestre* with camping.

Yare
A half hour south of Caracas is the town of **Yare** where, each year, exactly 40 days after Easter, the townspeople celebrate Christ's refusal to be tempted by the devil. Colorful devil masks and street dances mark the occasion.

EAST OF CARACAS

Ruta 9 goes inland until Puerto Piritu in the east where it begins to flirt with the coastline. Once you get past the environs of Caracas, it is a five-hour drive to Barcelona. From there, it is possible to poke along rutted, but more scenic, secondary roads.

The second route runs along the coast, beginning at the port of La Guiara and running east via Higuerote and El Guapo to connect with Ruta 9 west of Clarines. A section of the road is unfinished, but it is passable. These beaches are popular on weekends since they are closest to Caracas. Around La Guaira, the water is polluted and the road congested.

If stuck in La Guaira, stay in **Macuto**, a modest seaside resort town with good bathing. Camping is very iffy so duck into a hotel.

Further on is **Higuerote** whose sandy beach is dominated by large tourist complexes. It is peaceful during off-season, but nevertheless expensive.

Good camping beaches lie between **Boca de Uchire** and **El Hatillo**. The towns are small and supplies limited. To reach this area, take the road east from El Guapo or turn north at the town of Clarines on Ruta 9.

Puerto Piritu
A coastal resort town, 16km northeast of Clarines, Puerto Piritu grew from a tiny fishing village. Off-season, it's quiet and easy to get around. Several tall vacation condominiums dot the otherwise low skyscape. The beachfront is a tree-lined, cement walkway with numerous restaurants. At the end of Calle Bolivar, the main street, is the public bathing complex, **Balneario Casacoima de Puerto Piritu**. At the eastern end of the beach a military post takes up much

of the beachfront until the road swings back to join the main highway,
Ruta 9.

Camping

Within Puerto Piritu, pull on to the beach immediately east of the
Balneario or go 1km further east. Near the end of the *malecón* is a
small, recessed parking area alongside the restaurant **La Churuata
del Espignon,** where the owner allows campers to use his facilities.
A watchman is on duty throughout the night. The *parrillas* and
seafood are tasty and reasonably priced, so give him your business if
you enjoy his hospitality.

Supplies

Fish A market meets on the beach west of the *balneario*.
Fruteria Puerto Piritu On the same road; stocks vegetables and fruit.
Panadarias Good bread, coffee, and pastry on Calle Bolivar, the main
road through town.

Puerto la Cruz and Costa Azul

Good beaches, a ferry to Margarita, tranquil offshore islands,
commerce and a sturdy infrastructure attract visitors and new
residents. The population approaches 300,000. Upmarket shopping
and restaurants pander to a burgeoning tourist trade. The *Paseo
Colon* skirts the treelined waterfront of *Bahía de Pozuelos*. It is a
well lit, pleasant and safe area for strolling in the evening.

Getting there

Puerto La Cruz sprawls across a traffic juncture stemming west to
east along Ruta 9 and south through El Tigre to Ciudad Bolivar. The
latter is the fastest, most direct route south to the Gran Sabana and
Brazil border. A four-lane highway, west of Puerto la Cruz, takes you
12km to the larger city of Barcelona, the capital of Anzoátegui state.
Salt flats between the two cities stymie their merger.

Ninety kilometers to the east takes you to Cumaná. In between are
what many describe as the most spectacular beaches in Venezuela.
Stock up on camping supplies here.

Isla Margarita

This resort-ish island is a popular destination, not only because it is
a duty-free shopping zone. It is serviced frequently throughout the
day by ferry. The terminal is on the west end of *Paseo Colon*. One-
way fares are US$4 first class, US$3 tourist class, cars US$8, jeeps
US$9, and motorcycles US$6.

Picnic islands

Small boats take passengers to the nearby islands or mainland beaches. Go to the east end of the *malecón* on *Paseo Colon*, to the parking lot adjacent to the restaurant **El Rancho** and the marina. Service begins at 8.30am and ends with pickup at 4.30pm. Boat operators are very helpful. Ask to see a copy of their map for the islands and beaches to which they offer service. The fares increase with the distance you travel from their homeport.

Mainland beaches are accessible by road and islands further to the east of Puerto la Cruz (eg: Mochima National Park) are serviced cheaper by other water taxis. From Puerto la Cruz, take the water taxi to the islands of **Playa Puinare**, **Playa El Saco**, or **El Faro** for US$3 per person, round trip. Safe parking in private lots near the waterfront; recommended is on Calle Bolivar, across from the service station.

Useful addresses

Casa de cambio   On *Paseo Colon* next to Hotel Riviera.
Dive shops   Technisub adjacent to the marina, or **Lolo's**.
Tourist office   In a well-marked kiosk on the *malecon*, is closed 12.30-2.30pm.

Costa Azul

A series of popular, blue water beaches give the name "blue" to this coastal stretch. Road signs clearly mark beaches and adjacent islands serviced by water taxi.

The first cove east of Puerto la Cruz is **Pamatecualito**, no camping, but water taxis service local beaches. They charge US$3.50 per person (US$4.25 per person for groups of "foreigners"). Boats go to Conoma, Conamita, Ña Cleta, or popular Isla de Plata.

The next beach east, **Valle Seco**, is narrow and small. Houses of fishermen and a vacation campground for the army make up most of the town. Further up Ruta 9 is the town of Arapo (no beach access). Don't confuse it with Isla Arapo.

Continue a few kilometers to **Playa Arapito** (20km from Puerto la Cruz) with palm trees, broad sandy beaches, two restaurants, bathrooms and showers, and large parking lot. Cost per vehicle is US$0.50 to enter and US$1 to camp. For shade and direct beach access go to the west side of the restaurants. Thieves reportedly work this area.

Safer and much smaller (75m long) is the cove, **Playa Vallecito**, also with palms, good restaurant, bathroom and outdoor shower (ask for the water to be turned on). Boat service to Isla Arapito and La

Piscina is good value. Good snorkeling habitats are right off the beach. Camping fee is US$1. About 4km further is **Playa Colorada**, famed for a red sand beach and oyster vendors. Restaurants and large parking lot block vehicular beach access. Recommended for camping.

Immediately across the road, two tiny stores sell basic supplies; ice at the *licorería* 200m east on Ruta 9.

Mochima National Park

The turn-off to **Mochima** is 21km east of Santa Fe. A 5km descent takes you past postcard views of blue water, red sand, sloping green mountains and islands. This is the eastern end of Mochima National Park. The attractive town by the same name lies at the foot of a mountain. This is a popular anchorage for cruising sailboats. Beach front is limited, by a cement *malecón* that extends west from the boat docks, at *Plaza de Tres Héroes*. Many homes rent rooms. An unnamed scuba center is located in a white house facing the *malecón*.

Boats leave all day to the islands with pickup at 4pm. To camp officially on any of the islands, you need permission from the national parks office (INPARQUES) in Caracas (the local office is closed). No-one asks to see a permit, anyway. Islands serviced from Mochima are Taguaruma, Gabarra, Las Maritas, Asovechima, Playa Blanca (boatmen recommend this one for beauty), Manare, Canoa, Cautaro, and Cautarito, with roundtrip fares ranging from US$6-10.

Highway 9 continues 12km east, to Cumaná, past vendors selling chili peppers in vinegar, rag dolls, and fruits. Buy a sack of the fruit called *meray*, to cure stomach ulcers.

Cumaná

Nearly every coastal city claims to be the site of the first colonial settlement in South America and so does Cumaná. It was founded in 1521 and now boasts more than 172,000 people who derive their living from commercial fishing.

Getting there

The road to the south passes through Maturín 299km and continues another 199km to Ciudad Guayana, the gateway city to the Gran Sabana. To the west of Cumaná lies the beaches of Costa Azul and to the east is the beautiful Paria Peninsula.

The city peters out along the **Golfo de Cariaco**. Six km east from the center of town, on the coastal route, is **Playa Guiriamar** and 1km further is **Playa Quetepe** with public parking, white sand beach and restaurant. The west end of the beach is lovely with picturesque shade trees, and would make fine camping, except it is absolutely filthy. Go 1km further to **Playa Tocuchare**, a small fishing community similar to coastal enclaves of yore. For a distance of 15km along the gulf, before and after **Mariguitar** (a resort with expensive camping), you'll find roadside picnic areas overlooking the water. East, past Cariaco, and you enter the Paria Peninsula. Roadside vendors display woven furniture, baskets and *petate* mats that make attractive floor coverings.

Ferries
A car and passenger ferry departs from the dock on the east end of town. Fares from Cumaná to Margarita Island are slightly cheaper than from Puerto la Cruz. Adult fare one way US$2.50, and US$5 for a car.

Ferries also run to **Araya** on the tip of the Araya Peninsula — which can also be reached by road via Cariaco 78km. The peninsular road runs 95km across the famous salt flats that played such an instrumental role in the Spanish claim to South America in 1625.

Camping
Camping is difficult in Cumaná due to its size. Your best possibilities are on the west end of the public beach, Los Uveros, where there are several busy restaurants with ample parking and shade. The eastern side of the city offers more opportunity, (*see Getting there, page 218*).

Supplies and repairs
Practically everything is available in Cumaná. Every make of vehicle can be serviced. Many bicycle repair shops offer basic repairs. **DiGas**, propane fill-up, on west end of town on the road to Carúpano.

PARIA PENINSULA
This lovely peninsula has escaped the stress of tourism, and it is still possible to find small fishing villages and friendly people. The peninsula juts eastward 160km, to the town of **Güiria**, with boat service to Trinidad and to the national park that covers the entire north end of the peninsula.

The first town in the Paria Peninsula, heading toward Carúpano, is **Saucedo**. Take the left fork, midway through town, to arrive at the beach, behind the cemetery. No facilities; very basic food supplies in the small stores. It reminded me of a town where old ladies gossip and their disapproval keeps everyone in line.

Guaraguao has a long sandy beach, no shade. It is fairly isolated due to a long, deep strip of small, uninhabited fishing *fincas*. Few supplies. Continuing east on Ruta 9, you'll come to the beach **Cayo**

Azul, and a kilometer further, the town of **Guaca**, which is famous for pickled clams and smoke-dried herring.

Many dirt roads turn off to various beaches which are interesting to explore but offer little opportunity for free camping. The best beaches are further east, beyond Carúpano.

This large, modern city hosts a famous Carnaval celebration when it is packed with hedonists. If going onto the Paria Peninsula, the road loops here and a decision must be made. The southerly route follows the lowlands to El Pilar where the northerly, hillier road connects. Ruta 9 runs east, another 160km, to Güiria. Fuel is readily available along the southern route. Fill your tank if choosing the northern Atlantic rim. Stock up on basic food items in Carúpano as they get more expensive further on.

RECIPE FOR VENEZUELAN CHIPI-CHIPI SOUP

Chipi-chipi is the name for the small, clam-like shellfish burrowing on many beaches within the tidal zone. In Florida they are called periwinkles. The shells are tinted purple, red, and shades of yellow. The biggest ones are found in knee-deep water.

For this recipe you'll need a mound of *chipi-chipi*. The Venezuelan style of harvesting them is to stand in the water and twist from the waist down — a variant of the *salsa*. When you find a curved shell beneath your toes, dig it out. Small *chipi-chipi* suffice, but bigger ones are more succulent.

Rinse several times in clear sea water, allowing the *chipi-chipi* time to expurgate any sand. Bring a pot of regular water to boil and add your mound of *chipi-chipi*. The broth tastes marvelous. It can also be thickened to toss with pasta.

Following the Atlantic coast, the northern loop, you'll next come to El Morro de Puerto Santo and the lovely town of **Río Caribe**. It is a small but flourishing fishing village. Once the chief port for cacao export, it is now attracting a cosmopolitan population. A hotel with parking is adjacent to the *malecón*. Supplies are available so stock up. Good camping along the Atlantic can be found 2km west of Río Caribe at *Playa Iguana* with restaurant, facilities, and watchman.

From Río Caribe the road twines inland through bamboo jungle and rugged hills. It's a spectacular drive and refreshingly cool after the heat of the coastal zone. You'll pass small communities where red cacao beans dry along the roadside. The most stunning of the villages is the **Comunidad de San Francisco de Chacaracua**, which has festooned itself in a myriad of colors in geometric designs, using the walls and grill work as its canvas. Every other year, the townspeople repaint their handiwork. Basic food supplies and liquor are sold here. Ice can be bought from people's freezers.

Five minutes' drive east takes you to the cut-off (well marked) to two major beaches and a number of minor coves. This entire beach area is being developed by Corpomedina who plan a 360-room Club Med, with an ecologically progressive bent. The road splits with the right fork taking you to **Playa Medina**, while the left fork takes you 10km to **Playa Puipuy**. Playa Medina is neatly manicured with natural flora, a coco palm beach, expensive restaurants and hotel rooms. Campers should follow the right fork to Puipuy, the designated campground for the complex. No entrance fee. This is another lovely beach, with umbrella-sized *palapas*, coco palms and sea grapes. Facilities, garbage pick-up and a restaurant are in place. Wander to the fishing village of Puipui to see what supplies you can find... fresh fish (or a dish of iguana) and fishermen's sea tales. Return to the main road to access the next beach, Congua.

The turn-off to **Congua** is an unmarked road in the small town of Santa Isabel de Carezo, which looks like a crossroad. The road straight through town will lead south to Río Seco (from Río Caribe 55km). If turning toward the beaches, you'll find that sections of the dirt road are really rough. Go 15km through jungle mountains, with fern covered streams, until you see a road to your left that is a nearly vertical descent. Congua lies at the bottom. It is a very small fishing village, with maybe 20 houses and a lovely beach. Camping is recommended for cyclists. Vehicles will have a hard time with the soft sand. No road runs parallel to the beach.

San Juan de las Galdonas is reached by continuing east 12.8km beyond the cut off to Congua, on a rough road that follows the ridge. The fishing village of San Juan wraps around a crescent-shaped cove on the west side and continues east around a rocky point to the Atlantic. A high tide claims much of the protected, western beach. On the east beach, near the soccer field, camping is great, but you'll have to put up with wind and sea spray.

There are two hotels in town on the main street, almost adjacent to the plaza and police station and above the beach used by the fishermen. **Las Tres Carabelas** is owned by a Spaniard, Javier de Pinedo, who offers ten lovely appointed rooms at US$10, excellent meals, and superb views of the ocean and town from his promontory. Across the street is **Hotel San Juan** with a good restaurant, and rooms, but no view. A public shower is located at the end of the only paved ramp to the beach, midway through town. Gas, from barrels, can be purchased from the unmarked building on the east end of the cove.

Walk to those coves without road access, or hire a boat to take you. US$16 per person to Unare or Playa Negro; see Oscar or Alfredo Velasquez where the fishing boats congregate.

Return to the main road and back-track 17km to the main highway at Santa Isabel or continue east along the mountain ridge. There is one more road that descends to Playa Tortuga between Guacuco and Guarataro. At the turn-off to Guacuco, the right-hand road goes to Río Seco (not indicated on maps). Sections were once paved but not any more. You'll need high clearance.

At **Río Seco**, you'll again pick up the main highway that runs west to El Pilar and Carúpano or east to Güiria. Fuel is readily available along this stretch.

Highway 9 runs alongside deep mangrove swamps that impede access to the Orinoco Delta and development. **Irapa** at Km 117 is a good-sized town that, like other places, claims Papillon washed on to their shores after his escape from Devil's Island. The beach is strung with coconut palms and lush vegetation. Camping is possible but residents warn of thieves. Papillon's ghost...?

Excellent camping is found about a half hour away. Pass through Campo Santa Claro, with a park office for Paria, and through the town of San Antonio. One kilometer before Yoco is the turn off to Playa Dorada, Punta de Piedra (9km) and the town of Soro (8km). A split in the road and a rocky point separate the two beach areas.

Soro town (population 800) lies approx 1km inland from its fishing beach, which runs into mangroves on the west end. *Cabaña de Tío Macuro* serves beer and fresh seafood. You can sling a *hamaca* here or at the *palapa* next door. Ask for Martin. The house at the curve belongs to the *Brujo* and *Bruja*. They purge evil influences and sell a remedy for wrinkles and other skin problems. Fishermen will take you by boat from here to Pedernales on the opposite shore of the Orinoco delta.

Punta de Piedra is much smaller, with maybe 20 houses and a broad, long, sandy beach studded with *palapa* shelters and one spacious salon/restaurant for gala occasions. The shelters are owned by Marcos Brito who charges nothing for camping (his is the last house on the right before the beach). **Playa Dorada** is separated from Punta de Piedra by a rocky spit of land. A hotel and restaurant supposedly operate here but we could never find it open.

A half-hour drive to the east takes you to **Güiria**, the end of the road. It is a growing port for international fishing boats and traders. Locals advise against camping anywhere other than the beaches furthest east from town. Playa Dorada is an overpriced restaurant and hotel with a filthy beach. La Salina is a better bet. The remainder of the peninsula is the Paria National Park and **Macuro** at the tip. Arrange boat transport with the independents who hang out at the north end of the port. Daily boats depart at 10am and return at 5am. The trip is three hours.

To Trinidad

Windward Lines Ltd operates a scheduled passenger/cargo ship with departures every Wednesday and 15th day at 11pm to St Lucia (US$159 per person), Barbados (US$149 per person), St Vincent (US$138 per person), and Trinidad (US$40-US$60 per person), plus US$18 departure tax. Cargo rates are high at US$50 per cubic meter.

THE WAY SOUTH

Two major arteries connect the coast with the region of Angel Falls and La Gran Sabana. The fastest route runs south from Barcelona through El Tigre to Ciudad Bolívar. The second is picked up from Cumaná (clearly marked signs). Also possible is south from Carúpano, through Maturín to Ciudad Guayana. This road is not clearly marked, but it is the most interesting as it takes you near the **Cueva del Guácharo** (the cave of the nocturnal oil birds), outside the town of Caripe.

To find the latter road, look for a sharp turn south, behind a gas station at Muelle de Cariaco (on the road between Carúpano and Cumaná). A few meters beyond the turn-off is a sign for Santa Rosa. After 45 minutes of slow driving into hill country, you'll pass a small dam, and 1km beyond the road splits. Take the left fork to Caripe (the right fork goes to Santa Rosa). Caripe is a twisty, attractive valley strung with coffee and vegetable farms. Immediately before the town of Caripe (hotels, restaurants and supplies), turn right at the signpost, *Las Cuevas...*, and travel 12km through hilly, tropical vegetation.

Park admission, US$4, includes a guide through 1.5km of caverns and the museum to see the nocturnal Guácharo bird. The most spectacular show occurs after dusk and before dawn when the caves are closed. Ten thousand birds rally each other with clicking sounds emitted at 7,300 cycles a second. Near the entrance to the cave, sound reverberates like a raucous sustained applause in a stadium. Ask permission to camp alongside the small park area and Ranger Herman Lopez will awake you at 4am for a private viewing of the birds.

Three kilometers west of the cave is the small town named for the birds with restaurants and supplies. Take the turning toward Maturín and you'll find bountiful fruit and vegetable stands before descending into the plains.

Cyclists note: The road from Maturín south to Ciudad Guayana is flat land. Heat rolls over it and there is very scant shade or water.

Ciudad Guyana

The gateway to the impressive Canaima National Park is through Ciudad Guayana, the umbrella name for a planned city of one million

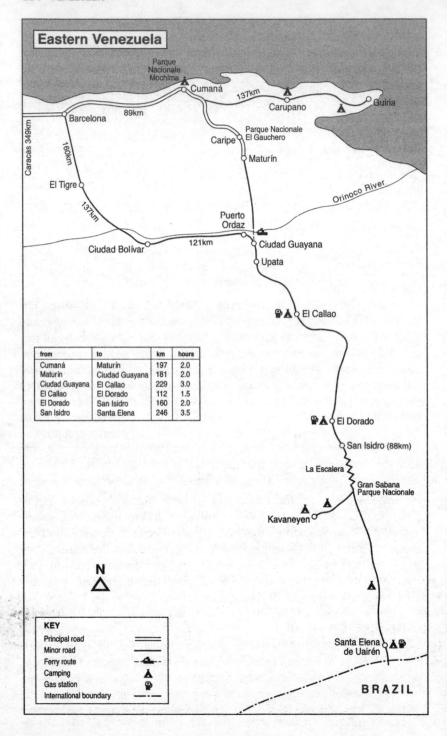

Eastern Venezuela

Parque Nacionale Mochima

Cumaná

137km

Carupano

Guiria

89km

Barcelona

Caracas 349km

160km

Parque Nacionale El Gauchero

Caripe

Maturín

El Tigre

Orinoco River

137km

Puerto Ordaz

Ciudad Guayana

121km

Ciudad Bolívar

Upata

El Callao

from	to	km	hours
Cumaná	Maturín	197	2.0
Maturín	Ciudad Guayana	181	2.0
Ciudad Guayana	El Callao	229	3.0
El Callao	El Dorado	112	1.5
El Dorado	San Isidro	160	2.0
San Isidro	Santa Elena	246	3.5

El Dorado

San Isidro (88km)

La Escalera

Gran Sabana Parque Nacionale

Kavaneyen

N

Santa Elena de Uairén

KEY

Principal road	
Minor road	
Ferry route	
Camping	
Gas station	
International boundary	

BRAZIL

inhabitants that encompasses four sections. Be aware that the highways through town are not always marked, and sometimes incorrectly marked. We won't pretend to give you coherent directions as we've managed to get lost on ten separate visits.

Excellent roads merge from every direction. A bridge spans the Orinoco river at Ciudad Bolívar 105km to the west. Directly north of Ciudad Guyana a rickety passenger/car ferry traverses the river between Los Barrancos on the north shore and the south shore town of San Felix, US$1 for a car and passenger. Some 199km north is ugly Maturín. Ruta 10 south is four-lane to Upata where pavement narrows to Santa Elena de Uairén. Hordes of rudimentary campgrounds, *club campestres* and no-tell motels line the road south.

Excursions

Refresh yourself in the ion charged air of cascades. In the city are **Cachamay** where the Orinoco and Caroní rivers blend their colored water and **La Llovinza**. Each is bordered by botanical parks.

Angel Falls Angel Falls is the world's highest waterfall at 979m. Air service is available at the airport in adjacent Puerto Ordaz or from Ciudad Bolívar. June through November are the clearest months for viewing this awesome spectacle. A costly hotel near the Canaima lagoon requires reservations. Day trips run about US$130 with lunch and time to play in the lower falls. Contact area travel agents. Helicopters can be hired at Km 32 and Km 76 on Ruta 10, midway to the Gran Sabana.

Ciudad Bolívar has a recommended hotel, *Hotel Florida*, Av Tachira y Mario Bricenol, near the airport. Safe parking. Camping sometimes permitted on grounds.

Tucupita Totally off the beaten track is the marshy Orinoco delta. Take the marked turn-off near Temblador, 87km north of Ciudad Guyana. A paved, narrow causeway runs between water, stilt houses and palm trees. It is always humid and, during the rainy season, the road is subject to flooding. Boat excursions can be arranged into the delta for birdwatching and to visit the Indians. Excellent, natural-fiber *hamacas* are made and sold here.

Supplies

Buy a spare gas tank as they're scarce further on. Fuel is available all along the route to Santa Elena, but you will need the extra fuel if you are planning to roam far afield. Stock up on mosquito repellant as well. Abundant and cheaper provisions are available in Upata, El Callao, El Dorado and in Km 88. (In El Callao we bought real butter that we hadn't found elsewhere.)

Further south

Upata The four-lane highway narrows to two at this point, 56km south of Ciudad Guayana, but it continues in good condition and with wide shoulders. Hotel D *Andrea* on Plaza Miranda has safe parking. *Club campestres* and auto dealers are abundant.

El Callao Worth visiting is this small town with Trinidadian ancestry. A one-way bridge crosses the Río Yuruari. In recent years, large mining corporations have routed the individual prospector. Gold and gem stores are still prevalent, but gone are the gold-weighing scales from the food markets.

Tumeremo All grades of fuel can be found at the Corpoven station and, behind, is an ice plant.

El Dorado Kilometer 0. For some unknown reason, the turn-off is so marked and the road is measured in either direction from this point. El Dorado lies 7km west of Ruta 10, 76km south of Tumeremo and 278km south of Ciudad Guayana. It is an excellent place to break. Its fame arises from an island prison where Papillon was incarcerated in 1945, and from the hopes of gold miners. These days, it is settling down from its former wild-west life style. The shady park in front of the church is serene for strolling families; restaurants and discos lend a quasi-cosmopolitan flavor. Good free camping on the road leading into town at the restaurant *El Rincón del Llanero*.

Slightly south of town, 7.5km, at the Río Cuyuni bridge is an obligatory police check point where everyone must sign in.

Kilometer 88 Now named San Isidro to distinguish the tacky sprawl of market stalls from those of nearby **Las Claritas** at Km 85. This used to be the end of the road, the last chance to fuel up before crossing the Gran Sabana. Fuel is available 88km to the south, at Kamoiran, 176km, and at Santa Elena, 228km. Top off your tanks, anyway. Take on water, ice and food provisions.

Camping is not possible. The few D category *campamentos* prefer to rent their cabins.

The Gran Sabana

The 1,300m climb to the Gran Sabana begins at Piedra de la Virgen, Km 108. The road is known as *la escalera*, the stairway, because it used to be an arduous ascent. Years ago we winched a jeep to the top, a dirty day-long job. Road engineers have since tamed it with smooth blacktop.

Unmarked from the north is a 40m, fern-fringed waterfall, Salto Danta Km 119. Climb higher and suddenly emerge to an expansive savannah, a mesa top, where the only sound is that of the wind and butterflies. Km 137 is a roadside park and monument to the road engineers, *Monumento al Soldado*, with barbecue grills and camping permitted. At this point, the border at Santa Elena is 190km straight ahead. Just a few kilometers south is the headquarters for **Canaima National Park**. On the west side of the road is a campground maintained by a tour company. Ask permission to camp.

Several waterfalls and tiny towns are adjacent to the main highway, but if you want to explore, a good sidetrip is to **Kavanayen**, 70km west of the mainroad. As in surrounding villages, the people of Kavanayen are Pemón Indians. A Franciscan mission watches over their flock. Camping is permitted outside the mission where rooms can be rented. In case of emergency, contact the mission which has a radio and can arrange air evacuation. More than a few hikers have fallen from a *tepuy* when trying to reach Angel Falls by foot. A small grocery store has basic food supplies. On the road to Kavanayen, sideroads can be taken to remote waterfalls. Very high clearance is needed and, when wet, these tracts may be impassable.

A Corpoven station is located at the rapids of **Kamoiran**, Km 176 on main road. One kilometer west you'll find a small store, restaurant, church and the neat, stone houses of **San Rafael**. Another small village at Km 197.

Kama-Meru Falls at Km 197 has an overpriced restaurant and bungalows for rent US$8-16. Camping is free but pay a small fee to use the toilets. A camping area has been established at Km 236 alongside the **Río Araya** falls. It is peaceful, but exposed.

Salto de Yuruani, Km 247, is difficult to reach by vehicle, but worth the effort. Hunt and choose your trail carefully as it is deeply rutted clay and boulder strewn. The entrance is unmarked yet easy to identify. Nearby Pemón village of **San Francisco de Yuruaní** has supplies and a parks office. Several tourist complexes with gift shops, huts and camping at Km 272 and Km 303, Santa Teresa. The famous river of jasper, **Quebrada de Jaspe**, is reached by a trail from the main road at Km 273 (no parking space). Excellent views of the massive *tepuis* Roraima and Kukenam to the east. Soon after, the descent begins to Santa Elena and the border.

Santa Elena de Uairén

This town of 8,000 people is pleasant, small and quiet with just a hint of moving upscale with veggie and pizza restaurants. Hotels range in price and accommodation. Shops in town will change money at low rates, also check with travelers. Stock up on food, ice and fuel.

The immigration office, DIEX, is on the hill opposite the bus station located at the big fork in the road. They close for lunch. Motorists will be referred to the *Guardia Nacional*, near the center of town, for permission to export a vehicle. This is not necessary unless your vehicle is licensed in Venezuela or if you don't have a *libreta*. Expect two hours of waiting and running between offices in Santa Elena and customs located at the border, 15km further south. When the typical runaround began, we went directly to the border where I lied to customs. I told them that we had been cleared for exit and waved two inches of accumulated documents and the *libreta*.

Roll forward ten meters and you're in Brazil where entry and exit procedures are smooth and courteous. Your vehicle will be sprayed for bugs and then you'll be directed across the road to the plain-clothed, Federal Police who are in charge of customs and immigration. Make sure you have a Brazil visa, if required, or you'll be sent back to Santa Elena where there is a consular official.

Reverse this procedure if entering Venezuela. A visa is required of *everyone* entering by land. You will be sent back to Boa Vista in Brazil if you do not have one. Overland groups headed north will be required to hire a guide in Santa Elena.

THE ANDEAN REGION

Simply because it has not been deforested, the Venezuelan Andean extension remains lovely. Valleys fill with wafting clouds and spires of snowy peaks scrape the sky at 4,700m. Fern-enclosed waterfalls and pools invite the traveler for a refreshing dunk. San Cristóbal and Mérida are the only large cities to contend with.

Getting there

From Caracas there are two main routes. The speedy, lowland route goes through Barinas then ascends to San Cristóbal, 55 mountainous kilometers from the Colombia border. Highland routes weave from Valera through Timotes to Mérida and from Valera to Arapuey then southeast along the western side of the sierras to San Cristóbal. The latter route by-passes Mérida. Sections of that road are little-traveled *autopista*. Smaller roads wend through tiny agricultural towns and arresting valleys. Many cute hotels permit camping.

Mérida

A cool climate and beauty make this one of the most talked about cities in Venezuela. Until recently, it was an inspirational locale to discuss art, nature and life over an *espresso* coffee. The university atmosphere jived peacefully with the countryside. Today, it is all there, but harder to find beneath the pressure of new hotels and the traffic-congested main strip. As always, nature still calls and this is a fine place to take a break.

Snow-capped Pico Bolivar, 5,007m, towers over the surrounding mountains of the Sierra Nevada National Park. A hiking/camping permit must be obtained from INPARQUES office in Mérida before tackling any of the summits. Several expeditionary agencies operate out of Mérida who outfit climbers and put together horseback or bicycle trips. The world's highest and longest *teléferico* will supposedly resume cablecar operation in 1996, after a cable broke in 1991, killing several workers.

Places to stay

Modern hotels with safe parking line the main strip. Budget travelers should follow signs to the *teleférico*. Within a radius of four blocks north and Plaza Bolivar you'll find E-F category hotels with enclosed parking: **Posada Marianella**, **Posada de las Heroinas**, **Posada Turística el Viejo Tejado**, **Montecarlo**, Av 7 between Calle 24 and 25.

Hotels and restaurants with camping dot the length of road north of Mérida until **Mucuchies**, the highest town in Venezuela and home to the cutest puppies that you'll ever see. We checked many of the camping/hotel/restaurants and found them to be reasonably priced and willing to provide hot showers to campers. Options to the south of Mérida are fewer.

Useful addresses

Banco Consolidado, Centro Comercial Viaducto, opposite the north bridge. *Casas de cambio* in center and at shops which exchange dollars for the current, fixed exchange rate.

Colombian Consulate at Av Las Américas, CC Mamayeya, fifth floor.

Guamanchi outfitters for mountain climbing located near the *teleférico*, Av 8 con Calles 24 8-39; tel: (074) 522080.

Tourism offices at corner of Av Próceres and Av Universidad, and at the base of the *teleférico*.

San Cristóbal

The first city encountered in Venezuela, coming from the border, is the capital of Tachira state, a major commercial hub circled by *autopistas*. There isn't much tourism appeal and most travelers merely pass through it. Stay alert to road signs when approaching from any direction.

Useful addresses
Banco Consolidado 5a Av, Edf Torre Este.
Touring y Automóvil Club de Venezuela, Edf Olga, Local C, Av Libertador. Note: Colombian consulates are located in Mérida and in San Antonia, not here.

San Antonio
This is an unattractive border town facing Cúcuta. Colombian border formalities are executed in a group of buildings on the north side of the bridge. Venezuelan formalities are confusing. A customs/immigration post has been established on the outskirts of San Antonia, on the San Cristóbal road. We were directed there but quietly moved on while they strip-searched a bus load of passengers coming from Colombia.

DIEX office, immigration, is in the center of San Antonia. The building is unmarked and hard to find without asking, Carrera 9 and Calle 4. We had our *libreta* stamped at the bridge.

Places to stay
We can't really recommend San Antonio as a place to stay. Friendly people live there and, I suppose, it has its enjoyable aspects. More desirable options include crossing into Cúcuta or soaking in the thermal baths of **Ureña**, 13km north of San Antonio, in Venezuela.

Chapter Seventeen

The Guianas

The Guianas consist of Guyana, Suriname and French Guyane. These countries are not included since it is extremely difficult to enter or exit by road from or to other parts of Latin America.

It is possible to enter Lethem, Guyana from Brazil, but to reach the coast from there is a true adventure. The time of year to attempt it is crucial. A 4WD vehicle, time and patience are necessary. Of course, a bike can be flown into Georgetown, or a motorcycle loaded on to a Caribbean steamer. There is no vehicle ferry between Guyana and Suriname. And, from French Guyane it is impossible to cross into Brazil with a vehicle. All transport is by motorized canoe.

If planning to visit the Guianas, carefully check visa requirements well in advance. We've tried, numerous times over ten years, to contact consulates in Washington DC and in Venezuela. No answer.

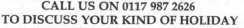

Appendix

Glossary of Road Terms

The majority of road signs depict international symbol signs which are easy to understand. The other signs employ words and phrases that may not be as familiar to non-Spanish speakers.

Alcabala	(Ven) A police check point located at the entrance to each town
Alto	Stop
Arenamiento	(Peru) An area of shifting sand
Automóvil	A car
Baches	(Chile) Potholes, uneven pavement
Bencina	(Chile) Fuel
Bermas	(Chile) Road shoulder
Bomba	A pump; a gasoline station
Borracharia	(Brazil) Not a place to get drunk, but to take bad tires. Sometimes includes multi-purpose workshops
Calzadas	(Paraguay) Road shoulders
Camion	Truck
Carona	(Brazil) To hitchhike. Officially prohibited on major roads.
Casa rodante	Literally a house on wheels but it refers to just about any vehicle that you live inside
Chave	(Brazil) A key
Cola	(Ven) To hitch a ride, also a tail
Columpios	(Mex) Wavy, roller coaster road surface. Only saw it once in southern Mexico but loved the word as much as the sensation
Concede el paso	Yield right of way

Concede las luces	Switch high beam to low when approached by a car coming from the opposite direction.
Cubierto	The covering of a tire, or the tire itself when referring to a tube tire; also refers to a blanket, or in a restaurant bread put on your table for which you'll be charged extra.
Cuidado	Slow down, proceed with caution
Cuota	(Mex) Toll road
Curva Peligrosa	Dangerous curve. Such warnings are usually posted after the worst is past
Depressão	(Brazil) A lethal depression bisecting the road. They can be as deep as a ditch and are rarely marked
Desinflanado	Disinflated, as in a tire without air
Derrumbes	Falling rocks or rock slides
Despacio	Slow
Desvia	Detour and good luck
Desvio	(Brazil) Same as above. Accompanied by the challenge of finding your way back to the road you were following
Direita	(Brazil) Right, eg: on the right side
Direito	(Brazil) Straight ahead
Eje	Axle
Escuela	School zone, slow down
Esquerda	(Brazil) Left, eg: a left-hand turn
Estacionamiento	Parking; parking lot
Estrada	(Brazil) A road
Fechado	(Brazil) Closed
Ferrocarril	Trains, railroad crossing
Frene con motor	Downshift to aid braking, indicating a steep rapid decline where brakes can go up in smoke
Galon	A liquid gallon
Garage	Parking lot or parking garage
Gasolinera	A refueling station
Gato	A car jack (also a cat)
Gomercá	Tire repair
Llanta	(Col) Tire
Lombada	(Brazil) A back-breaking speed bump

Neblina	Clouds, fog
No encandile	(Paraguay) This is a peculiar one. As near as I can figure out, it means don't use headlights/don't dazzle
Novo	(Brazil) New, and can also refer to unleaded fuel
Ondulacão	(Brazil) Same as a *lombada*, a mountainous speed bump
Pare	(Chile) Stop
Parquemento	Parking lot
Peaje	Toll booth
Peatones	Pedestrians, people crossing the road
Pedágio	(Brazil) A toll booth
Peligro	Danger, usually unspecified. Look for a broken bridge, collapsed road, rock slides, a blind curve... heavy UFO traffic, just about anything. Sometimes the signs are not removed after the problem is fixed, sometimes the problem is a permanent fixture. Don't assume, be careful
Peligro de Muerte	Threat of Death, a warning posted around military installations in Chile. Stopping alongside or entering a restricted area can result in severe penalties...
Pendientes	(Chile) Dips, undulations or slopes in road
Perigo	(Brazil) Danger
Pesaje	Truck weigh station (you don't have to stop)
Pneu	(Brazil) A tire. A frequent subject of conversation
Posto	(Brazil) A gas station
Puente Angosto	Narrow bridge, one vehicle at a time
Quebra Molas	(Brazil) Break your springs, if you don't ease over these speed bumps
Remolque	Tow truck
Repuesto	Repair or replacement parts sold
Ripio	Rock and gravel road
Rompemuelle	(Peru) Indicates a spring buster, a speed bump
Saida	(Brazil) Exit

Solo carril	One lane
Soronizador	(Brazil) A series of small speed bumps that jangle your teeth when you drive over them
Superficie Resbalosa	Slippery surface, high incidence of skidding autos
Taller	A workshop
Tope	(Mex) A speed bump
Troca de óleo	(Brazil) Oil change
Tumulo	A speed bump
Una vía	One way
Vado	A ford, a water crossing, a man-made depression for drainage or overflow from a river
Valeta	(Brazil) An open drainage ditch bisecting the road
Vulcanizador	Tire repair

FURTHER READING

South American Explorers. A quarterly journal published by The South American Explorers Club. Headquarters: 126 Indian Creek Rd, Ithaca, NY 14850, USA. Tel: 607 277 0488.

Practical guides

Bauman and Young; *Guide to Venezuela.* The definitive and hefty reference with 900 pages.

Bradt, Hilary; *Backpacking and Trekking in Peru and Bolivia.* Bradt Publications, 1995. Excellent and indispensable.

Box, Ben (ed); *Mexico and Central American Handbook.* Trade and Travel Handbooks.

Box, Ben (ed); *South American Handbook.* Trade and Travel Handbooks. The definitive resource for South America.

Bradbury, Alex; *Guide to Belize.* Bradt Publications.

Branch, Hilary Dunsterville; *Guide to Venezuela.* Bradt Publications.

Burford, Tim; *Backpacking in Central America.* Bradt Publications.

Conrad, Jim; *The Maya Road* (La Ruta Maya). Bradt Publications.

CTC Publiguias; *Turis Tel.* Centro Casillas, Santiago de Chile. Written in Spanish, these maps of Chile and guide books are sold for the entire country or by region, *Norte, Central, Sud* and *Camping Chile* which alone is sufficient.

Ellman, E. and E. Weisbroth; *Bicycling Mexico.* Hunter Publications.

Lougheed, Vivien; *Central America by Chickenbus.* Repository Press, Prince George, B.C., Canada, 3rd edition 1995. Accurate descriptions of small towns and cities, cultural perspectives and resources. This vivacious guide to Central America is highly recommended for all travelers to the region.

Mallan, Chicki; *Belize Handbook.* Moon Publications. This guidebook is so good that I can't keep it on my shelf.

Quatro Rodas; *Guia Brasil.* This Portuguese guide to Brazil is full of invaluable road information, repairs, city maps and mini-descriptions of scenic sites.

Sienko, Walter; *Latin America by Bike, a complete touring guide.* The Mountaineers. Offers valuable tips on weather.

Travel narratives and regional authors

Amado, Jorge; *Doña Flor and Her Two Husbands, Clove, Gabriela, Cinnamon*. Novels translated from Brazilian Portuguese into English that paint vivid pictures of *Macumba* ceremonies and Bahian life.

Bishop, Elizabeth; *North and South: A Cold Spring*, 1955. A collection of her poetry contrasting life in cold and hot climates. *Brazil*, 1962. A travel book translated from Portuguese.

Culberson, Ed; *Obsessions Die Hard*. Teakwood Press. 1991. Kissimmee, Florida. Ed was the first motorcyclist to cross the Gap.

Mathession, Peter; *At Play in the Fields of the Lord*

Parris, Matthew; *Inca Kola*. Weidenfeld & Nicolson, 1990/Phoenix 1993.

Jones, Tristan; *The Incredible Voyage*

Health

Wilson Howarth, Jane; *Healthy Travel: Bugs, Bites & Bowels*. Cadogan, 1995.

Maps

Healey, Kevin; **International Travel Map Productions**, PO Box 2290, Vancouver BC, V68 2WF. These include Central America (1:1,800,000), Yucatán Peninsula, Baja California, Mexico; Guatemala and El Salvador, Belize, and Costa Rica.

AAA publishes a Central America road map that is as good as any that you'll find for the region. In each capital city, inquire into the availability of maps produced by the Instituto Geográfico Militar (IGM). Show a passport at the office. Most of the time, they're out of stock.

MEASUREMENTS AND CONVERSIONS

To convert	Multiply by
Inches to centimetres	2.54
Centimetres to inches	0.3937
Feet to metres	0.3048
Metres to feet	3.281
Yards to metres	0.9144
Metres to yards	1.094
Miles to kilometres	1.609
Kilometres to miles	0.6214
Acres to hectares	0.4047
Hectares to acres	2.471
Imperial gallons to litres	4.546
Litres to imperial gallons	0.22
US gallons to litres	3.785
Litres to US gallons	0.264
Ounces to grams	28.35
Grams to ounces	0.03527
Pounds to grams	453.6
Grams to pounds	0.002205
Pounds to kilograms	0.4536
Kilograms to pounds	2.205
British tons to kilograms	1016.0
Kilograms to British tons	0.0009812
US tons to kilograms	907.0
Kilograms to US tons	0.000907

5 imperial gallons are equal to 6 US gallons.
A British ton is 2,240 lbs. A US ton is 2,000 lbs.

Temperature conversion table

The bold figures in the central columns can be read as either centigrade or fahrenheit.

Centigrade		Fahrenheit	Centigrade		Fahrenheit
—18	**0**	32	10	**50**	122
—15	**5**	41	13	**55**	131
—12	**10**	50	16	**60**	140
— 9	**15**	59	18	**65**	149
— 7	**20**	68	21	**70**	158
— 4	**25**	77	24	**75**	167
— 1	**30**	86	27	**80**	176
2	**35**	95	32	**90**	194
4	**40**	104	38	**100**	212
7	**45**	113	40	**104**	

OTHER BRADT GUIDES TO
CENTRAL AND SOUTH AMERICA

Backpacking in Central America Tim Burford
From day walks through the villages of the Guatemalan highlands to the 5-day crossing of the Darién Gap, featuring everything from volcanoes and river journeys to mountain trails. Particular focus on the region's wildlife.

Backpacking in Chile and Argentina (3rd edition 1994) Hilary Bradt and others
Spectacular mountain scenery, well-run national parks, excellent food and wine, good transportation and safe cities. A hiker's and traveller's paradise!

Backpacking and Trekking in Peru and Bolivia (6th edition 1994) Hilary Bradt
The classic guide for walkers and nature lovers, detailing hiking trails through some of the world's most magnificent mountains.

Climbing and Hiking in Ecuador (2nd edition 1994) Rob Rachowiecki and Betsy Wagenhauser
The definitive guide to the volcanoes, mountains and cloudforests of Ecuador, plus general travel information and chapters on rock climbing and mountain biking, by two former residents.

Guide to Belize Alex Bradbury
Central America's most popular destination for visitors with an interest in the natural world, written by a professional diver and biologist.

Guide to Cuba Stephen Fallon
Detailed history, lively and informative secions on Cuban culture and traditions, and essential travel information.
"Useful and much needed" *The Washington Times*

Guide to Venezuela (2nd edition 1996) Hilary Dunsterville Branch
Every place of interest to visitors to Venezuela, with an emphasis on the national parks and wild areas, but with plenty of city information.

South America Ski Guide Chris I Lizza
From Tierra del Fuego to the world's highest ski slope in Bolivia. Detailed descriptions of 35 ski areas with 25 original trail maps, ski history, travel advice and itineraries.

For a calalogue of these and other guides to unusual places, contact Bradt Publications, 41 Nortoft Road, Chalfont St Peter, Bucks SL9 0LA, England. Tel/fax: 01494 873478.

NOTES

INDEX